COACHING TENNIS SUCCESSFULLY

SECOND EDITION

UNITED STATES TENNIS ASSOCIATION

Human Kinetics

Library of Congress Cataloging-in-Publication Data

Coaching tennis successfully / United States Tennis Association.-- 2nd
ed.
        p cm.
Includes index.
   ISBN 0-7360-4829-4 (pbk.)
   1. Tennis--Coaching. I. United States Tennis Association.
   GV1002.9.C63U55   2004
   796.342'07'7--dc22

                                    2003018063

ISBN-10: 0-7360-4829-4
ISBN-13: 978-0-7360-4829-3

Managing Editor: Wendy McLaughlin; **Assistant Editor:** Kim Thoren; **Copyeditor:** Pat Connolly; **Proofreader:** Erin Cler; **Indexer** Betty Frizzéll; **Graphic Designer:** Nancy Rasmus; **Graphic Artist:** Francine Hamerski; **Art & Photo Manager:** Dan Wendt; **Cover Designer:** Keith Blomberg; **Photographer (cover):** ©United States Tennis Association; **Photographer (interior):** Human Kinetics, unless otherwise noted; **Illustrator:** Brian McElwain; **Printer:** Versa Press

Human Kinetics books are available at special discounts for bulk purchase. Special editions or book excerpts can also be created to specification. For details, contact the Special Sales Manager at Human Kinetics.

Printed in the United States of America   10 9 8 7 6 5 4 3 2

Human Kinetics
Web site: www.HumanKinetics.com

United States: Human Kinetics
P.O. Box 5076
Champaign, IL 61825-5076
800-747-4457
e-mail: humank@hkusa.com

Canada: Human Kinetics
475 Devonshire Road Unit 100
Windsor, ON N8Y 2L5
800-465-7301 (in Canada only)
e-mail: orders@hkcanada.com

Europe: Human Kinetics
107 Bradford Road
Stanningley
Leeds LS28 6AT, United Kingdom
+44 (0) 113 255 5665
e-mail: hk@hkeurope.com

Australia: Human Kinetics
57A Price Avenue
Lower Mitcham, South Australia 5062
08 8277 1555
e-mail: liaw@hkaustralia.com

New Zealand: Human Kinetics
Division of Sports Distributors NZ Ltd.
P.O. Box 300 226 Albany
North Shore City
Auckland
0064 9 448 1207
e-mail: info@humankinetics.co.nz

CONTENTS

Part IV Coaching Tactics

Part V Coaching Matches

ACKNOWLEDGMENTS

The USTA proudly acknowledges the contribution of the professional staff in player development (now referred to as high performance) and sport science for their guidance and expertise through the first edition of this book and revisions where appropriate in this edition. Specific staff members included Lew Brewer, Paul Roetert, Linda Jusiewicz, Lynne Rolley, Nick Saviano, Stan Smith, and Tom Gullikson. Also, thanks to Riki Schafer who assisted in editing the second edition.

We are particularly grateful to two highly respected and successful high school coaches who supplied much of the material for the first edition based on their years of experience: Mike Hoctor, now retired, was coach extraordinaire at Astronaut High School in Titusville, Florida, and inductee into the Florida Athletic Coaches Hall of Fame; and Becky Desmond, coach of both boys and girls at Downingtown, Pennsylvannia High School and was recipient of numerous awards, including the Educational Merit Award from the International Tennis Hall of Fame.

A special note of mention for Casey Sandor, coach of the girls varsity team at Staples High School in Westport, Connecticut. Coach Sandor's teams have won several league championships and captured the state championship in 2003 after several second-place finishes. I watched her carefully as she spun her magic in coaching high school girls for the three years when my daughter was a member of the team. Her insight into handling young ladies, inspiring them, and helping them become a cohesive team is reflected in this book.

Throughout my nearly 40 years of tennis coaching and teaching, scores of dedicated and successful coaches of high school teams have inspired and amazed me with their wisdom, dedication, and commitment to helping young people learn to love to play competitive tennis in a team setting. High school tennis has continued to gain popularity for both boys and girls since the early 1970s when participants totaled about 100,000. Today, over 300,000 players *every year* salute you for helping them enjoy tennis!

Ron Woods

INTRODUCTION

The United States Tennis Association proudly counts over 600,000 members, a significant number of whom are high school coaches, players on school teams, and parents of those players. This book is designed to help all involved in competitive school tennis enjoy the experience and to help players and coaches perform at their highest level.

The material presented here reflects the cutting edge of tennis coaching today as refined by the USTA national coaching staff along with our sport science experts. By combining USTA concepts with the practice experiences of highly successful coaches, the USTA has created a solid source for coaching high school and summer tennis leagues. If you coach a tennis team—be it Olympic, college, high school, or even USA Team Tennis for Youth—you'll find lots of helpful advice within these pages.

Part I sets the stage and lays the foundation for your coaching style and philosophy, offering advice on critical interpersonal communication skills and tackling the difficult issues of motivating your players. These are the fundamentals of coaching at any level of play.

Part II deals with planning for both the overall season and each practice in an organized, efficient way. Instruction from this section will save you time and effort that can be better spent doing what you really love—working with young people on the court.

The nuts and bolts of on-court coaching are presented in the third section. Tennis technique is presented in a simplified fashion with the suggestion that each player's game be customized rather than forced into one ideal form. Tennis skills are then developed through practical drills that are explained and displayed in diagram form.

Tennis tactics for both singles and doubles are the focus for the fourth section. Styles of play including examples of professional players who can serve as role models are presented along with strategies to counter various styles.

Finally, the concluding section will help you prepare players for match play, including tips on scouting opponents and conducting prematch practices. Your role as a coach during match play is also analyzed along with important advice for helping players deal with a win or a loss after a match.

All of us who have contributed our insights and experience in this book recognize the dedication of thousands of tennis coaches throughout the United States just like you who are eager to add to their coaching skills. We hope this book fills that need in part and we congratulate you on your quest to continue to learn from other coaches, and especially from your players.

CHAPTER 1 DEVELOPING A TENNIS COACHING PHILOSOPHY

After a few years of coaching, your coaching philosophy will be a lot easier for you to explain than it is when you are just starting out. If you are just starting out as a coach, then like most beginning coaches, you may think your approach to coaching is unique to you. More likely, your approach is borrowed from coaches you played for, observed, and admired.

Over the years, it will become clearer to you just what your objectives are for coaching and how you might plan to achieve them. Your coaching should depend on the age, skill level, and dedication of your athletes.

The easiest way to begin to identify your coaching philosophy is to list those things that you value in sport and the objectives you have for your players. For example, if you believe the team experience can be a terrific influence on young people, then you will emphasize certain attitudes and behavior that place the welfare of the team before that of individual players. Many coaches believe in extolling the virtue of striving for excellence through sports. While few would dispute the power of this goal, in some communities sports are treated more casually, and fun, social interaction, and good sporting behavior are valued more highly.

COACHING FOUNDATIONS

Development of a coaching foundation, such as learning, is an essential and continuous process. It begins the first day you decide to become a coach and ends only if you shut yourself off from new ideas and new experiences. No matter your previous playing or coaching experience, there is a lot to learn to ensure that your tennis program is the best it can be for every player who makes the team.

Strive to Learn

All successful coaches borrow bits and pieces of their coaching philosophy from other coaches. This includes learning about coaches from other sports and other levels of play. Once you eliminate the sport-specific Xs and Os, all coaches are really doing the same thing—teaching players skills to use throughout their lifetime as they compete in all areas of life. You should avoid, however, adopting certain coaching philosophies from coaches of other levels of play who may have different objectives in mind. If you admire a famous coach of professional athletes, you must be careful not to fall into the trap of letting that coach become your role model for working with high school kids. Professional sport has different values, and coaches of professional athletes may have coaching philosophies that are not appropriate for dealing with adolescent high school players. Adopting one of these philosophies is not fair to your players, and their response is likely to disappoint you.

You should seek out sources of material—videos, clinics, workshops, and conferences—that can strengthen your skills and knowledge. The United States Tennis Association, the Professional Tennis Registry, and the United States Professional Tennis Association all offer coaching workshops throughout the year. Generally these events are reasonably priced, and if you can glean two or three ideas from each event, your coaching skills will grow significantly over the years.

Your local state high school association may also offer workshops for tennis coaches. These workshops are a great opportunity to share ideas with your colleagues from other schools and from around the state. You'll find that other coaches of high school tennis have lots to share and are open to helping you become a better coach.

Find a Mentor

Although learning from books and videos is key, learning to apply the knowledge you gain is even more important, and this can best be accomplished with the help of a mentor. Coaching has a base of knowledge that emanates from sport science. It includes understanding biomechanics as the basis of technique and motor learning as the process for learning sport skills. It also includes knowledge of physiology for fitness training, nutrition for healthy diet, sport psychology for mental toughness, and sports medicine to prevent and treat injuries.

Once you feel comfortable with your understanding of the science of coaching, you must also acquire the skills to apply the

science. This is where the "art of coaching" comes in.

All successful coaches and teachers can tell you, usually at length, about their coaching mentors or role models. Sports at all levels are replete with coaches who have learned to install a West Coast offense, a pressing defense, or a team pride philosophy from their mentor. An experienced coach who is willing to mentor you can provide insight into how to apply the knowledge you have gained.

Find out who the best tennis coach is in your area and ask that coach for help. Visit a team practice, watch the coach teach on the court, and ask for time to share opinions and solutions. Asking for advice and guidance from those who have been successful can

Get advice and note examples but remember to coach your own way and be consistent, concise, and caring.

drastically reduce your learning curve. Don't overlook other coaches at your school; these coaches may be better tuned in to your players than outside coaches. If they have been successful in high school sports, you want to find out why and consider adopting some of their techniques.

Finally, a word of advice that all successful coaches have followed: Take what you can from books, workshops, and mentors and meld that information into a coaching style that fits you and your situation. Just as no two tennis players play the same way, no two coaches are the same, and good coaches develop their own system to fit the situation. Coach in a way that fits your outlook on life and your approach to sports. To do otherwise would be a mistake.

Build Partnerships With Staff and Tennis Professionals

Many high school coaches across the country are not members of the teaching faculty at the school. Some are teaching professionals while others may be tennis players or enthusiasts from the community. Still others may teach in another school building within the same school system or in a nearby community.

If you are outside the school faculty, get to know the administration, faculty, and staff that work with your players on a daily basis. Your tennis team is an extension of the school and its athletic program, so your coaching philosophy should be consistent with that of other school sports. You'll also have to learn the policies, procedures, and rules that have been established for athletes at the school.

Make an effort to get to know as many people as you can at the school. You should attend school functions and introduce yourself to coaches of other sports. Many high school kids play more than one sport, so coaches of other sports can be helpful. Other school staff may become important

when your players are struggling with other areas of their life, such as academics, social issues, or applying to college.

Reach out to the tennis teaching professionals in your community who have worked with your kids in the past (and who are perhaps continuing to coach them). These professionals are great resources for you and can help your players develop their tennis skills, especially outside of the high school season. Most states have established limits on the amount of time coaches can work with their potential or current players before the season, so you may have to rely on coaching from others to help players reach new levels of play.

Most tennis teaching professionals are certified by the United States Professional Tennis Association or the Professional Tennis Registry. They have demonstrated their competency to teach the sport and have passed a practical and written examination. Most teaching professionals constantly improve their skill and knowledge by attending continuing education courses, workshops, and conventions. There are more than 12,000 teaching pros in the United States.

Your job is different from that of the teaching professional. The time you spend with your team is limited, and in practices you will act as an organizer and facilitator, typically dealing with 12 to 20 players as a group. During your tennis season, your focus will be on helping players compete effectively by helping them become independent competitors on the court. Work on tennis technique, for the most part, is better left to the off-season without the pressure of match play. That's when you need the assistance of local teaching professionals to support the development of your players.

As a high school coach, your major tasks are to develop the "team atmosphere," to help players apply strategy and tactics in their matches, and to help them build their competitive skills both mentally and emotionally.

ESTABLISH COACHING VALUES

Your coaching values are a reflection of who you are, what you believe in, and what is important to you in life. Over the years, your values may change as the lessons of life influence you. Consider some statements from coaches about their approach to coaching:

• "There is no 'I' in *team*. The welfare of the team is paramount, and each player has to commit himself to team goals. Sometimes this means sacrificing what you would rather be doing to help the team be successful."

• "Every player has a right and an obligation to become the best player she can be. We respect the right of each individual to be herself, and we owe her the respect and support that we can provide."

• "Fun is the key to enjoying tennis. Our aim is to make practices, matches, trips, and being with each other fun. If it's not fun, it's not worth the effort."

• "Discipline is important to young players. The skills learned as a member of this team and the self-discipline required are lifelong skills that you'll remember long after your playing days."

• "The tradition of our tennis program is to 'strive for excellence.' We want kids who are dedicated to becoming the best they can be both on and off the tennis court."

You can readily see the differences in these statements made by successful coaches. Each statement may fit into a more developed coaching philosophy that points in a certain direction. Is your program going to be coach centered or athlete centered? Team or individual oriented? Focused on outcome (measuring success by wins and losses) or performance (asking each player to give her best effort)? You probably already have a pretty good idea what your philosophy is, but once it is established, you must share it with players and parents.

One popular coaching style is referred to as "cooperative." In this style, the coach and players work together to set team and individual goals, team policies and procedures, and standards of behavior. The players also accept responsibility for their individual

As you establish your own coaching values, remember, above all else, the key to enjoying tennis is having *fun!*

effort. The atmosphere that is established by this approach is that of a group working together toward mutually agreed upon goals. You have to be confident as a coach in your ability to influence and mold young players in directions they have agreed to pursue, even in the face of distractions, other priorities, and immature decision-making skills. The bonus at the end of the season is a terrific learning experience for everyone involved. Coaching never becomes boring or a chore since each team is different, and the rewards for a successful season of competition are so much sweeter because everyone had a part in it.

It's a great idea to start the season with a team meeting where you convey some of your coaching values to prospective players. If you can put these values in writing and ask players to share them with their parents, you've laid the groundwork early in the year. An excellent follow-up is to have a potluck dinner at one of the player's homes, perhaps the team captain, and share your values while the parents and players are all together. This is also the time to communicate school rules for athletes, the schedule for matches, and your expectations for support from both players and their families. Don't miss the opportunity to help parents understand the demands on their child's schedule, to encourage parents to have empathy in dealing with the stress of competition, and to assure parents of your support for the academic commitments of their kids. Give them some time for random questions and respond as best you can or promise to get back to them with an answer at the appropriate time.

Throughout the season, there may be other opportunities for parents and players to gather to prepare for an upcoming match. Other times it may be best to restrict these get-togethers to just players. Whatever works in your situation, you shouldn't overlook how this type of event can unleash the power of families supporting the tennis team.

At the season's end, you should plan some type of celebration to bring closure to the season. Make it lighthearted, recognize the contribution of every player and parent, and provide a big send-off for your graduating seniors. Some team votes for honors such as "biggest eater," "best team spirit," or "slowest second serve" can add some humor to the traditional votes for next year's captains and most valuable player.

Making Tennis Fun

The athletes of today still crave many of the same things athletes have always wanted: direction, discipline, an opportunity to play, and a chance to compete. Tennis can provide all of these things and more.

At the same time, tennis, like other sports, can burn out young players by forcing them into a highly structured, competitive program at an age when they are not ready to deal with it. You need to balance the competitive structure of a team with the opportunity for self-exploration, self-expression, and participation in an activity where players can make choices. It is up to the coach to set some guidelines and share a philosophy of coaching, but players need to have an active role in making day-to-day decisions. After all, tennis is a voluntary activity, and players deserve to have a voice in group decisions. In their quest to establish their sense of self-worth and identity, teenagers will embrace the opportunity to participate in setting team goals, policies, and procedures.

Young athletes choose to play sports because they are *fun!* Over and over again that simple word emerges at the top of their list of reasons for participating. It's up to you to figure out what "fun" is to your players and how you can create an atmosphere that promotes feelings of having a good time. Chapter 3 includes a more detailed discussion of some ways to foster feelings of fun on your team.

SET COACHING PHILOSOPHY STANDARDS

Coaching is never a static endeavor. The players you work with will change from year to year as will their talent level. The game of tennis also changes as a result of new technology, application of sport science to training, and through imitation of the top players in professional tennis.

In spite of these inevitable changes, you must establish a set of overriding coaching principles that you believe in. These tenets provide the roots of consistent and continued excellence for your players and your program. Here are some principles for you to consider:

- Focus on results, not excuses.
- Emphasize performance, rather than winning.
- Respect teammates and opponents.
- Establish priorities of family, schoolwork, and team.
- Expect steady, gradual improvement through smart practices and hard work.
- Have fun!

Give Results, Not Excuses

All sports, and tennis is no exception, can become a game of excuses: poor court conditions, the wind, a lucky opponent, bad line calls, or an "off" day. Players often grasp at excuses for their performance to protect their ego.

Your job as a coach is to ignore excuses and refocus on the things your team can control—physical condition, competitive attitude, management of mistakes, strategy and tactics, and a willingness to deal with adversity throughout a match. You should expect your players to give their maximum effort in each match regardless of the circumstances. If they do that, they can hold their head high and move on to the next challenge.

Winning Versus Development

Winning in high school sports is a relative term and can misdirect the effort of both coaches and players. An overemphasis on winning focuses on the outcome of matches rather than the performance of each player. The focus on winning that is so prevalent in our society is a self-defeating philosophy since half of the competitors will lose in every tennis match played. A much better approach is to redirect your team toward putting forth the *effort* to win.

When players and coaches believe "as long as we win, everything is okay," the team's development suffers. After a victory, errors are often undetected or dismissed. After a loss, every little detail of poor play is dissected and criticized. The result is that players develop a false sense of security after a win, and after a loss their confidence takes a dramatic nosedive. The beauty of playing competitive tennis on a team is that of the four possible outcomes of a match, most of them can be positive:

1. If the team wins, and the individual player wins, there is satisfaction in a job well done and an increase in confidence. This is the time for coaches to advise players on areas in which they can still improve performance through better focus, smarter shot selection, and attention to detail.

2. If the team wins, but an individual player loses, you can help that player by pointing out that she made a contribution to the group effort just by competing. While her ego may be a bit bruised, a losing player can be proud of the team victory. Chances are she will also be very receptive to advice from the coach in looking forward to practice and the next match.

3. If the team loses, but an individual player wins, you need to reinforce the positive performance by that player. She can take some consolation in the fact that she was successful against a team that obviously was a challenging test for the rest of the team. Point out the things she did well and encourage her teammates to raise their level of play to hers.

4. If the team loses, and every player loses as well, it is clear that your team has been outplayed on that day. Perhaps the other team had more talent, more experience, the benefit of a home crowd, or just competed at a higher

level. This is the time to salve the bruised egos of your players, express confidence in their capacity to improve their performance, and point out some general team errors that can be corrected.

The point of competition after all is to provide a testing ground for young athletes. It should not become an end in itself. Long-term development of your players as competitors and maturing young adults is a better overall view that is the hallmark of successful tennis programs over the years. The best way to achieve strong development over both the short and long term is to set goals (see chapter 3).

Respect Teammates and Opponents

The principle of respect for teammates and opponents should be established from your very first practice. Players must abide by a code that is consistent with the rules and traditions of tennis as well as those established by your school. Players should neither put down teammates or opponents nor brag about their own skills. In a sport like tennis, which is unique in that there are typically no officials to supervise play, respect for other players is essential in order to compete. Encourage and expect your players to focus their attention on playing hard, playing smart, and having fun.

Establish Priorities

Team goals and accomplishments are important, but you must also help young players recognize the more important priorities in their life. Assuming that most young people, with their family's help, have established some spiritual dimension in their life, the other priorities for high school athletes should be (1) family, (2) schoolwork, and (3) team.

• **Family.** Positive interaction with and support from their families is crucial to the success of most players. Parents have to make sacrifices to enable their kids to participate in high school sports, and they should be invited to be a part of the process. You can help parents adjust to a supportive role by distributing written information detailing the expectations for their child and your advice for their role as a parent of an athlete. Encourage them to support the team by their attendance at matches and their acceptance of team rules and standards of behavior.

• **Schoolwork.** Each player on your team should be expected to be a student first and an athlete second. Coaches need to accept the fact that tennis is an extracurricular activity that is second in importance to schoolwork. Stress the importance of performance in school to your players and help them budget their time so that they can be successful both on the court and in the classroom. Sports sometimes provide an easy excuse for a lack of attention to homework assignments and a lack of preparation for tests. Apply the same principles you espouse on the tennis court and help your players adopt them in their life as a student.

• **Team.** A team-first attitude can be summed up this way: dedication to the game and devotion to the team. Share these priorities with players and parents early in the season and reinforce them every day. You've chosen to coach a tennis team, not just a collection of individuals, and team-building activities should be interspersed throughout the experience. Take time to do things together off the tennis court and encourage teammates to bond under the leadership of your team captains, who can set the standard. Senior players can take underclassmen under their wings and smooth the way for their acceptance into the group.

Because tennis is often thought of as an individual sport and is played that way on the professional tour, many people struggle with the team concept. You need to set the standard by treating each player with respect regardless of position and by encouraging every player to share in the success or failure of the team. You should resist the temptation to allow one or two superstars to dominate the team yet provide an opportunity for special talents to develop.

Nothing compares with the camaraderie players share as teammates, working as a unit, knowing their team success depends on one another. And no amount of personal pride gained from an individual achievement or award can match the shared feeling of accomplishment that can result when the team's priorities come before any individual's.

SUMMARY

Here are the best ways to develop your own coaching philosophy and to allow your players to reach their full potential:

- Be eager to learn; stay current by reading, attending clinics, talking to fellow coaches, and seeking a mentor.

- Develop a sound coaching foundation that fits your personal beliefs, attitudes, and style.

- Make tennis fun for your players as they practice and compete.

- Be objective when you evaluate wins and losses; develop performance goals that encourage players to focus on a winning effort rather than the outcome of matches.

- Develop a coaching philosophy that promotes respect for teammates and opponents and focuses on a gradual improvement over time.

- Find ways to overcome obstacles rather than embracing excuses.

- Help your players understand the priorities of family, schoolwork, and team.

CHAPTER 2 COMMUNICATING YOUR APPROACH

What factors determine whether you will be successful as a coach? After reading chapter 1, you might be inclined to say, "The difference is a positive coaching philosophy." Others might say that previous tennis experience as a player and knowledge of the game are the key factors. But if these were the chief determinants, why do so many former star players fail as coaches?

If you've coached for some time, you understand the importance of effective communication with players. No matter what you know or how well you play the game, unless you can transfer that understanding to your players, success will elude you.

KEYS TO EFFECTIVE COMMUNICATION

Communicating effectively in a variety of situations will have a significant impact on your success as a coach. Situations that require skillful communicating include

- helping your players perform their best in important matches,
- dealing with aggressive parents who pressure you to move their child up in the team lineup,

- motivating players to work harder at improving a skill or their fitness level,
- consoling players after a difficult setback and encouraging them to put it behind them, and
- rallying support for your team from the school community.

In these situations and others you may encounter as a coach, it will be helpful to concentrate on the following seven keys to communicating effectively:

1. Be real.
2. Listen first.
3. Use a two-way street.
4. Be honest.
5. Be caring.
6. Set an example.
7. Be consistent.

Be Real

Just be who you are. Share this tip with your players, their parents, and the school community. Kids will learn a lot from adults like you if you let them. Use a style of communication that's natural and easy for you.

When having conversations with your players, you can share your life in a natural way by talking about your family and work. Your taste in music or movies reveals a side of you, too. Other topics may include volunteer work that you do or even banter about your own tennis game, which helps your players form a more complete picture of you as a person.

Listen First

Communication starts with listening to players and parents and being sensitive to their hopes, goals, and attitudes about competitive tennis and life in general. This will help you find out how to motivate players, because they will tell you if you take the time to listen.

Someone once asked, "Who learns the most in a conversation between a wise man and a fool?" Of course, the answer is the wise man. The point is that even though you're older, more mature, and typically more knowledgeable than your players, communication still needs to start with you listening to them first!

Sometimes coaches get caught up in overcoaching and directing every move for their players. This is especially true of older coaches who often believe it is important to teach young people everything they know and thereby prevent the mistakes they made themselves as young athletes. You should also avoid falling into the trap of listening to players by simply maintaining silence while they speak. The problem here is that the kids may not feel the understanding and empathy that you are experiencing, or you may misunderstand their real problem.

Active listening is a skill that helps you communicate your interest and understanding to your players. While they talk, you show attention and involvement in their ideas with your eyes, nods of understanding, and patience as they complete their thought. Then you respond with probing questions to be sure that you have grasped their meaning. Or you might reflect their comments back to them in your own words to check your receiving skills. A conversation might take the following form:

Player: I can't believe how bad I'm playing. My serve really stinks.

Coach: It's natural to be nervous the day before an important match. I'd be worried if you were too cocky.

Player: But what about my serve? I'm just not hitting it well.

Coach: Your motion is fine, but remember to relax and put more spin on your first serve. Maybe you're trying for too many aces.

Player: Yeah, I've got to remember to take my time when I get anxious.

Coach: Now you've hit on the key. Remember to breathe deeply, bounce the ball a few times, and then let it go. You've got a real weapon with your serve when you slow the whole process down.

The coach is showing empathy for the player, who is anxious about the match. The coach manages to gently suggest some corrective action while expressing faith in the player to deal with the situation.

Use a Two-Way Street

Good communication goes two ways. Athlete–coach interchange can be spoken, written on paper, or transmitted by body language. Your role is to let players know you are accessible and open to an exchange of thoughts, feelings, and frustrations. At the same time, let them know that you expect them to communicate with you. Whenever they feel uncertain about team policies or their status on the team, or confused about the direction of their tennis game, it is their responsibility to seek your counsel.

Consider the following situation that has been replayed numerous times:

Player: Coach, my family is going to Florida over our spring break for a family vacation, so I won't be able to attend practices during that time.

Coach: I'm surprised to hear this news, especially since spring break is

If you want to be a good coach, you have to listen and be listened to.

only a few days away. I wish you had talked this over with me earlier to explore some options.

Player: I intended to tell you earlier, but my parents delayed their plans and just told me yesterday that all the arrangements have been made.

Coach: Did you and your parents consider your commitment to the team and the schedule of practices that was announced before the season began?

Player: Yeah, we talked about it, but they didn't seem very concerned.

Coach: How do you feel about it?

Player: Well, a week in warm weather sounds great, but I'm afraid missing the practices might jeopardize my position on the team. I know you plan to have some of that time devoted to challenge matches.

Coach: Is there any chance you could reschedule your departure by a day or two, play a couple of challenge matches, and then join your family? I know family trips are important and your parents realize the opportunities for family getaways are few and far between as you and your sister get older. Why don't you talk to them, express how you feel, and see if a compromise can be considered?

Player: So . . . if I can rearrange my trip and join the team for a couple of practices, it's okay?

Coach: I'll do my best to work it out if you can get support from your folks. I'd like to help you out, but some compromise will certainly help your situation.

Player: Thanks, Coach. I'll let you know tomorrow.

The lesson here is for players and coaches to give each other adequate notice of circumstances that affect the planning of practices and matches. They can then gauge the importance of variations through candid talk, consider possible compromises, and set a clear plan of action. Remember, if family is to come first, a family vacation might very well take precedence over tennis practice. Of course, if families refuse to consider the welfare of the team, coaches may be left with little choice but to penalize players for missing announced team commitments.

Be Honest

It's all in the eyes. People can tell when you're being straight with them by body language and eye contact. Get in the habit of saying what you mean and what you believe and then standing by your word. Because most events in junior and school tennis require the players and coaches to act as their own officials, opportunities for dishonest behavior are plentiful. Let players know by what you say and what you do that you value honesty above all else and expect them to do the same.

When you speak directly to a player, make eye contact, especially if you're delivering bad news, such as a demotion in the lineup. Help the player deal with the news objectively and rationally while using your eyes to communicate your sensitivity to his disappointment. Help him out by rehearsing how each of you will convey the news to teammates, friends, and parents. If the only reason for the move is the consistently better performances of a teammate, point that out. Reassure the player that no changes are forever.

Care

Show players you care about them, not just their tennis. Adolescence is a tough time of life marked by struggles for independence, a search for identity, and a yearning for social acceptance and popularity. Players need to know you're in their corner, concerned about their schoolwork, glad to meet their friends, eager to know their parents, and willing to share a part of yourself with them.

Set an Example

Be the kind of person you'd like to have on your team. (This is not as easy as it sounds.) Tennis teams reflect the style and substance of their coaches. Some schools have a reputation for poor line calling, some for poor on-court manners, whereas other schools enjoy the highest respect from opponents. When a school team has a reputation for being poor sports over a period of years under the same coach (even though there are new players each year), this suggests that the coach is likely responsible. Be sure you're setting the right example and insist on high standards of conduct both on and off the tennis court.

In the heat of battle in a tightly contested match, a coach's behavior will have a powerful impact on players from both teams, the opposing coach, and spectators. Because tennis matches are typically not controlled by officials, it is your job as a coach to set the tone of the competition as friendly but competitive, to enforce the rules fairly for

both teams, and to handle disputes calmly and rationally. Coaches who lose control of their emotions can hardly expect their young athletes to do better. Coaches who use inappropriate language, profanity, or taunting are tacitly telling players it's okay for them to do the same. At the beginning of the season, you should tell your players the goals you have for yourself as a coach. Also tell the players that you expect them to help you achieve your goals just as they expect your help.

Be Consistent

Your credibility as a coach will result from communication and behavior that is consistent from one player to another and consistent from one time to the next. The kids at your school have a right to know what you expect of them on the tennis team and how they will be treated.

The secret to consistent coaching behavior is to have a sound coaching philosophy

Coaching Your Own Child

The key to coaching your own child is to separate your duties as a coach from your duties as a parent. On court you should treat your child as you do every other player on the team. Sometimes coaches make things tougher for their own child than for other players on the squad so that there is no appearance of favoritism. This is a mistake. Your child deserves the same treatment afforded every other player on the team.

At home, return to your role as a parent and leave tennis back at the courts. Don't discuss tennis-related matters at home unless your child initiates it. Never suggest after-hours practice to improve a faulty serve or ground stroke. Remember—if the rest of the squad doesn't have to listen to you suggest unwanted evening practice sessions, why should your child? Above all, let your child know that you accept her for who she is and that you don't expect more from her because you are the coach.

and principles to guide you in your decision making. Using your personal philosophy and coaching style as the guide for your interactions with players will produce a consistent pattern of behavior. The effect on your players will be a feeling of security and confidence in your coaching approach that is like a rudder in the sometimes rough seas of competitive sport.

If you act like every player on the squad is important to the success of the team, your players will follow your lead. You should also treat players the same after wins and losses. Other things that you should do consistently include letting players know that cheating will never be tolerated, expecting their full attention at practices and matches, and insisting that they compete as hard as they can in every match.

COMMUNICATING IN MATCHES

As coach of a team of players, you have the difficult task of trying to deal with each player in an individual way. Comments must be tailored to each player's style and personality. One of your primary goals should be to help your players become independent competitors who are able to handle any situation effectively. To foster independence, allow players to make their own decisions and to deal with the consequences, good or bad.

The challenges of competitive tennis require effective practice sessions to prepare for a match, adjustment to the opponent and the flow during the match, and an ability to evaluate and analyze the result after the match. What you say to your players before, during, and after matches is crucial to their development of independent analysis and adjustment skills for meeting the challenges of competition.

Before the Match

For some players, a sense of humor and a little horseplay may be the antidote to counteract prematch jitters, whereas others may react better to an objective review of the game plan. If suggestions or reminders are in order, make them brief and limit them to no more than three. A longer list of prematch hints will not be retained by the players and is only a reflection of your nervousness and anxiety. As a secure coach, you know that everything has been done to prepare the team during the practice sessions in the weeks before. Last-minute cramming for a match is no more effective than the all-night study vigil for a school exam.

Your final prematch remarks to each player and the team as a group should encourage them to have fun and enjoy the competitive challenge. By your manner and comments, you should exhibit a positive, supportive, and encouraging attitude no matter what the expected outcome of the match. Above all, you should convey your expectation that the players will do the best they possibly can for that day.

Here's a situation you may encounter:

Coach: Jamie, where have you been? Everyone else is out on the court warming up, and you're 15 minutes late.

Player: I was in the bathroom, Coach. I don't feel so well.

Coach: Do you feel sick? Or are you a bit nervous about the match? I know how much you want to play well against this team.

Player: I'm not sure . . . I just feel nauseated and a little weak.

Coach: Well, why don't you join the team and hit a few balls to see how you feel. Concentrate on just getting to every ball in your strike zone and you'll likely feel better. If not, let me know. I know this is a big day for you, but I know you'll do fine if you concentrate on your movement. Don't worry about the match. It will take care of itself if you move well.

Player: Okay, I'm ready to play.

It's clear this player is feeling the prematch pressure, and your job as a coach is to reassure him and offer some specific direction on what he can do to fight through it. Younger players are often victims of these feelings, and even experienced competitors become anxious before important matches. Reassurance and specific directions are the keys to diffusing the situation.

During the Match

At some levels, absolutely no coaching is allowed during matches. In many high school leagues, coaching is only allowed after a set is completed. In other settings, the changeovers to the other side of the court provide brief but frequent opportunities to coach during a match.

Even if coaching is allowed in a team setting, many players have experience in individual tournament play where coaching is not permitted. As a prudent coach, you should have a thorough discussion with each player about coaching during matches so that you can agree on the timing and amount of coaching to be expected. (These discussions should take place well before the match.) Some players respond well to coaching and like the support of an objective observer; others are distracted by it and perform better when left alone.

When things are going well in a match, little coaching is necessary other than well-chosen remarks of encouragement and reminders for the players to enjoy their good play. However, if trouble develops, you might find that a few key comments can help refocus a wandering mind. An error-prone player can benefit from suggestions to be more aware of balance and positioning, or to pay more attention to error margins. Players may also welcome suggestions for handling a particularly troublesome shot or opponent. In doubles matches, the team concept often provides an opportunity for coaching. When you notice that doubles partners are seeing things from different perspectives, you may be able to help them plan and agree on the tactical adjustments they need to make.

Make it clear by your body language and gestures that you are on the side of your players, and make suggestions in a nonthreatening, uncritical way. Obviously, most players are trying to do their best, and they will welcome a comment from a friend but will likely ignore a critic.

After the Match

Immediately following a match, your response should depend on the player and perhaps the outcome of the match. Some performers are ready to interact with a coach by the time they reach the sidelines; others need some time to be alone to work through the results of the struggle just ended. A pat on the back or an arm around the shoulder is likely to be the safest, most effective way for the coach to convey to the player that he is okay, win or lose. This is the time to rejoice in a good effort and reinforce things done well. It is not a time to point out errors or to ignore an athlete, regardless of the outcome.

Once all matches are completed, win or lose, your team should meet as a group. Many teams have adopted the practice of congratulating the opposing team with a cheer or lining up and shaking the hand of each opposing player. These practices provide an honorable ending to the match and teach your players to handle winning and losing with class.

At the conclusion of a match, your role as a coach is to behave naturally but with a sense of perspective. Let young people enjoy a good performance whether they won or lost, since that is the goal you've set as a team. Soothe feelings of disappointment after tough losses and point out any bright spots in their play. Give them reason to hope for better results in the future by making positive statements, and reassure them of your commitment to help them improve for future matches.

You should also remind the players of their next commitment—either the next match or practice—before they disperse. You will need to emphasize this since the players may be distracted by the results of the match.

COMMUNICATING OUTSIDE THE TEAM

Your success as a coach requires effective communication with people outside the small circle of your team. The most important group is the parents of your kids, since they can do so much to support their son or daughter in meeting the responsibilities of being part of the team. Parents need to understand and support the school and team policies for athletes. At the same time, you must be sensitive to the family life of each player and to the obligations, expectations, and conflicts that may arise.

Others who are not so closely connected to the team, such as the media, deserve professional courtesy and consideration. Remember that they have a job to do and that your enthusiastic cooperation will simplify their task. Most local media professionals will promote your program and your players and will help build pride in the community for the efforts of your team.

Parents

Because parents (or guardians) typically present as many communication challenges as players, you should make a special effort to share with them your expectations and your coaching philosophy. A good way to do this is through a preseason meeting.

Schedule the parents' meeting at the school and mail invitations about two weeks in advance. If a player's parents are living separately, be sure to invite both parents. In the invitation, include highlights of the topics you'll cover so that parents will be interested in attending. Try to include enough information so that the parents can readily see how their interest and role may affect the success of their child in the sport.

At the meeting, create a relaxed, pleasant, and friendly atmosphere (you may want to offer light refreshments at the end). Make sure that you start and end the meeting on time, have an agenda prepared, and allow ample time for questions from the audience.

You can prevent many misunderstandings by committing key policies and procedures to writing and sharing them with parents and players. It may be a good idea to ask both players and parents to sign certain documents and return them to you. This allows you to be sure they have read the contents and agree to follow the procedures described.

Here are some topics that you may want to include on the agenda:

- Motivational remarks and your coaching philosophy
- Goals for the season
- Team selection procedures
- Lineup selection criteria
- Practice policies and procedures
- Match procedure (including parent role)
- What parents can do at home to support player participation
- Relevant school policies
- The partnership among player, parent, and coach

Many parents of tournament players feel that their child gains nothing by attending a high school practice with less-skilled players. Your top singles players and their parents need some assurance that you are dedicated to helping them improve during the season. You should clearly outline the team attendance policy before the season begins, and then communicate with parents and players who may need individual adjustments.

Some coaches allow their top players to miss practice once or twice a week, or by arrangement, to play against better players or to receive a lesson from their teaching pro. If you agree to this compromise, it is reasonable to expect those players to return the favor by working with teammates on their games during subsequent team practices.

Help parents understand that their children can gain something from the experience of team play at the high school level that isn't available in individual tournament play. Working as a member of a team, where the team's goals take precedence over individual goals, can teach players lessons that will make them more productive as working adults.

Communicate to parents that the best thing they can do for their children is to accept them as they are, win or lose. Parents need to be supportive, not critical, of their children. If you see a parent's actions undermining your efforts to put the sport in proper perspective, talk to the parent immediately. Don't lecture parents on parenthood; just remind them that everyone involved with the team, from coach to player to parent, wants the same thing. Give parents a role that makes them feel as if they are contributing to the success of their child and the team. That role would be supporting their child's on-court effort (as well as the rest of the team) without being too critical.

At every level of youth sports, there are some parents who simply become too emotionally involved in the athletic accomplishments of their children. You may need to conduct some parent training in your orientation sessions before the season or deal with situations as they occur. The pushy, overinvolved parent needs to realize the consequences of pushing a child too hard or too far.

Here are a few ways to get the point across and set proper parameters for parents:

• Develop some rules for parents regarding their conduct at home and at matches, and hand out these rules during the preseason meeting. The rules can include such things as what to say to their children before and after matches, how to act during a match, when to let their children make their own decisions about extra practice sessions, and tips for empathetic listening when their kids just need to sound off.

• Organize a few skits with parents playing the roles of players and vice versa. These can be fun and humorous and still get the point across.

• Create some clear procedures for your players to follow at the end of a match. These procedures should include speaking with you first after the match. Win or lose, good perfor-

mance or bad, you need to help them assess their performance first. Parents who are too emotionally involved or upset at the end of a match are not equipped to offer the best advice, support, or perspective.

Faculty and Staff

The athletic director (AD) is the key person you will communicate with on the staff and needs to be fully informed of every issue concerning your team. If you can establish a good rapport with the AD, this will go a long way toward accomplishing the administrative and organizational tasks required to operate efficiently. The athletic director helps in scheduling, transportation, and budget allocation. Communication with your AD about your program's goals and direction will determine your program's success.

Most administrators dislike surprises and want to be informed early regarding operation difficulties, behavior problems, or sensitive issues. You should take the time to drop short notes or stop by the athletic director's office regularly for a chat. Better yet, invite the AD to come to a practice or a match so that you can compare notes.

Other members of the school faculty need your attention, too. Let them know that you value the education they provide to your team members. Ask them to keep you informed of any anticipated academic problems, and perhaps you can work together to head off danger.

Encourage players to invite their teachers to stop by matches and watch. This will promote the student–faculty relationship and may even generate new tennis enthusiasts on the faculty.

Many schools have a monitoring system to ensure that varsity athletes are making academic progress. Poor academic performance can result in a player's suspension from the team, so it makes good sense for you to keep on top of players' school performance. At certain critical times, tutoring or makeup tests may conflict with team practices, and you'll have to adjust to the policies of your school.

Team Supporters

Within the school family, everyone should be aware of the players on the team and the challenges the team faces throughout the season. You have to do some public relations work or enlist the aid of parents, a booster club, a team manager, or a team reporter. You can lobby for articles in the student newspaper, establish a team bulletin board to announce team news, and use the public address system to broadcast announcements about team achievements.

At home matches, consider having team supporters keep score, or ask them to keep simple statistics by charting the match. Try to make sure that comfortable seating is available for fans. Match score tenders should be on every court, and you should be sure that players put up the score when changing sides. You probably can't imagine attending a football or basketball game without a scoreboard, but tennis teams often fail to keep fans updated on the score and then complain about the poor turnout.

The Media

If you want good media coverage, you should find out what you can do to make the job easy for reporters and to make them look good. A preseason lunch with reporters is a good idea. It allows you to exchange plans for the season and establish the procedures for reporting during the season.

Most newspaper reporters have the impossible task of covering multiple sports and lots of team results every day. You should provide the results for each match in an easy-to-understand format, and add some "juicy" match highlights that convey the flavor of an exciting team win, a heroic individual effort, or a disappointing loss.

Your team manager should drop off the results as soon as possible after a match to avoid newspaper deadline problems. Telephoning or faxing results may work if time and travel distance are factors.

Coaches who whine about press coverage usually haven't taken the time to cultivate the media. Some coaches are notorious for only sharing news of great wins and ignoring or "forgetting to submit" news of poor performances. You've got to be fair, consistent, and open with the press if you expect the same from them. Encourage local reporters, including school paper reporters, to interview your players before and after matches. This sends a message that it is the players' team, not the coach's. It also gives players the experience of being interviewed, which can be very educational.

It's a good idea to prepare your players for press interviews by providing them with a checklist of dos and don'ts and by helping them practice fielding some difficult questions. In fact, you should probably join them in trying to answer some difficult questions. The following are a few tips you may want to remember and share with your players:

- Develop some stock answers that convey enthusiasm and a positive outlook, and emphasize these phrases with any reporter.

- Be alert for human interest stories or comments that can help a writer. For example, if a reporter asks about your interests, it's better to identify specific performers or types of music you enjoy than to just say, "I enjoy music." Talk about your family, friends, hobbies, and school interests to present a more well-rounded impression.

- Stick to upbeat, encouraging words about your team, school, and community. And remember that none of your comments are really "off the record," so be as open as you can and then simply close the interview.

- Be careful about slang, jargon, or coach-speak. Try to put your thoughts in simple, convenient phrases.

- Convey your humility after a good team performance and spread the credit around to the team, assistant coaches, parents, or other key people.

SUMMARY

Here are the keys to communicating effectively:

- Good communicators are honest and genuine in their approach and start by listening to others first.

- The process of communication is two-way, with both sides expressing, listening, and responding.

- Coaches have to accept and utilize their natural position as role models for young athletes. Actions speak louder than words.

- Communicating before, during, and after matches is critical. The impact of the moment is heightened by the competition, so these times demand a special approach to young athletes.

- The school family, including administrators, teachers, students, and parents, is crucial to team success. You have to spend time with each group to garner support and understanding.

- The media is a special challenge. Promote your team players and build a tradition of openness and cooperation that will help your kids become hometown heroes.

CHAPTER 3 MOTIVATING PLAYERS

One of the most frequent questions asked at coaching conferences and workshops is "Since kids these days are tough to handle, how do you get your players to listen to you?" This question is a telltale sign that a coach is unsure of how to motivate players.

Motivating competitive athletes is one of the crucial elements of successful coaching. It requires a keen understanding of young people and the pressures they face, particularly in the adolescent years. It also requires a firm grasp of the techniques and tactics that have proven successful over time.

A high level of motivation results in athletes who are committed, energetic, and driven toward success. Motivated players can endure frustration, practice for hours, survive pressure, and rebound from disappointing performances. The trick to producing and sustaining high levels of motivation is to know what motivates adolescents.

Motivation is the result of people trying to fulfill their needs, and for young athletes the most important psychological needs are self-identity, peer approval, recognition, and perceived success. If you understand these basic needs and how to help your players satisfy them, your players will be well motivated.

The final section of this chapter discusses how to develop mental toughness in your players. Excellent technical skills and a sound understanding of tennis strategies will only carry your players so far. Mental toughness is the final component your players need to succeed in the competitive arenas of practice and matches. As you will learn in this chapter, goal setting is closely tied to motivation. Your players should develop goals for technique, fitness, and mental toughness.

CHALLENGE FOR FUN

Everybody would probably agree that having fun is important in sports, but getting a handle on just what fun is may be difficult. When you spend some time with young athletes, you learn that they are looking for a challenge to test their skill. If the challenge is well matched to their skill and ability, sports are fun.

On the other hand, if the challenge is too great, kids get anxious. And a challenge that is too easy to achieve naturally produces boredom. You need to strike a balance between challenge and skill (see figure 3.1). Your role as the coach is to make sure tennis is fun by adjusting the challenges your players face so that they are pushed to improve but experience success along the way.

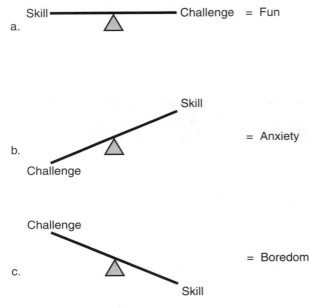

Figure 3.1 Challenge versus skill diagram.

Here are a few tips to make tennis fun:

• Treat each player as an individual and help her discover the needs she can satisfy by competing in tennis.

• Help every player set personal performance goals that ensure some success.

• Recognize player success through token awards, praise, and publicity.

• Make practices fun through frequent changes of activity, creative drills, and game simulations; let the players choose some activities.

• Make matches fun by encouraging your players, emphasizing personal improvement, and reducing pressure to win. Look for things you can reinforce after the match.

• Promote team spirit and let athletes enjoy the natural bonds that develop during a season's adventures. Help each player feel like a part of the team. Encourage players to spend some time together off the tennis court to reinforce the team bonding that many of them crave.

You can't simply treat all players the same and expect success. Instead, you must find out what motivates each player and use that information wisely. The most serious and intrinsically motivated athletes want to improve their skills and often use sports to discover their limits or to identify their strengths or weaknesses.

These players are often team leaders and can help influence team attitudes and behavior. You need to support their efforts, be sure their expectations are realistic (they may tend to be overly ambitious), and be wary of the possibility of them feeling self-induced pressure to perform.

A significant percentage of players are more extrinsically motivated and may participate on your team to be part of a group, to win approval of their peers, to be popular, or to receive trophies or awards. Once you realize what makes them tick, use that information effectively. Help these players achieve the recognition they crave, and also help them to experience the benefits of inner satisfaction and pride in personal success. Personal success can come through the development of goals and perseverance in working to achieve them.

Creative Coaching Solutions

On the tennis court, Scott always seemed to be indifferent to coaching suggestions. Although he was a talented player, he needed help with parts of his game. But no matter what was suggested, he seemed to ignore it. Finally the coach asked Scott to help him teach a particular skill to JV players on the team. As they taught the skill, Scott and the coach interacted as they had never done before. Scott shared suggestions as to how to best teach the skill to these players. He recognized that his opinion was respected, and from that day on he listened to coaching suggestions about his game. He didn't always agree, but he listened!

INDIVIDUAL GOALS

Perhaps nothing you do for your players will have a greater impact on their motivation than helping them learn to set effective and challenging, yet also realistic, goals. Goal setting is a critical lifetime skill that is worth spending significant time on so that your players master the process. Your players should write their goals down on paper, not just think about them.

In tennis it is important to set individual player goals first and then develop team goals as a group. This sequence will ensure that each player has clarified her individual goals, and you can then make sure that the team goals do not conflict with these personal goals. For example, players who want to improve their serves may set the goal of working on serving for 30 minutes at the end of every practice. If the team sets a team goal of running, movement, or fitness drills at the end of each day, there is a conflict. To keep motivation strong, it's best to try to accommodate the individual goals within the team goals.

Outcome Versus Performance Goals

Young athletes need to achieve success to increase their feelings of self-worth. Realistic, attainable goals help ensure the chance of success and directly affect motivation. You should help your players define success in terms of their own performances and successes rather than by comparing their performances to others.

The main difference between outcome and performance goals is the amount of control your players have in achieving them. Outcome goals are those over which players have little direct control, such as winning a league title or defeating a particular player. The problem with outcome goals is that players can work hard and prepare well for competition and still lose a match on a particular day. Or your players may set unrealistic goals that include victories over players with better skills. The team that adopts goals like these is setting itself up for trouble. Winning league, district, or state championships; compiling a specific number of wins; or winning every close match are examples of goals that set the stage for failure.

Players should focus on their own individual performance goals. It's a good idea to have your players divide their goals into four main categories: tennis technique, strategy

Professional players are great role models for young athletes.

and tactics, fitness, and mental toughness. These four categories define the major areas for possible improvement and help organize thinking and planning. Many players (and some coaches) will overlook setting goals in one of these categories, thus handicapping the chance for overall improvement. The following are good examples of measurable goals:

• **Technique goals** should address racket skills: "To hit 25 successful second serves, with good spin and depth, at the end of every practice."

• **Strategic or tactical goals** involve playing percentage tennis and choosing the right shot at the right time: "To reduce errors on passing shots by playing the first shot a little safer and allowing the net player to make an error."

• **Fitness goals** should be specific to individual weaknesses as shown by physical testing: "To increase the number of sit-ups and push-ups I can perform in one minute by 25 percent within the next six weeks."

• **Mental toughness goals** become increasingly important as the intensity of competition increases: "To maintain a strong, confident fighter image during matches even when things don't go my way."

As players think about their goals, you should help them further categorize the goals as long term, intermediate, short term, or goals that could be achieved now (see table 3.1 for some examples).

Long-Term Goals

Young players need to have long-term goals—these are their dreams. Encourage and support their dreams of someday playing professional tennis, earning a college scholarship, or defeating a former hero. But make sure your players don't get lost in their long-term goals. Although they should be encouraged to set long-term goals, you likely won't want to ask them to write these goals down and share them (unless they want to). As much as possible, keep the players in the present by focusing on their shorter-range goals that apply to the current year or the next two years.

Intermediate Goals

Intermediate goals are the stepping-stones to achieving long-term goals. Many of the goals in this category apply to tactical or mental skills or to team leadership. Progress in this area may be the hardest for each player to realistically measure. Generally expect intermediate goals to take six months to a year to accomplish. Being able to hit a dependable backhand passing shot with topspin could easily take a summer to learn and an entire season of play before a player "owns" the shot. Review intermediate goals at midseason and again at the end of the year. Praise your players during postmatch evaluations if they have made progress on an intermediate goal during match or ladder play.

Although the high school season typically extends only 8 to 14 weeks, you should help your players think in terms of a whole year in planning goals. Even if they play other sports, it's reasonable to expect some skill or fitness improvement during the off-season. Just a few weeks of concentrated work on a specific weakness can make a huge difference before the next season rolls around.

Short-Term Goals

Short-term goals are the daily training commitments your players must make if they expect to improve at a steady rate. These goals usually focus on mechanical changes in stroke production or strategy in match play (see table 3.1). Once again, you should insist that short-term goals are performance based, not outcome based. These goals should be reviewed weekly by each player. If a player appears to be losing focus on her short-term goals, step in and remind her of the priorities she has set for herself. All it should take to achieve these goals is discipline and hard work. The best time for you and the player to assess short-term goals is when you work one-on-one with the player. A simple yet powerful short-term goal for high school players is developing a specific game plan for each match they play, writing it down, and with your help evaluating its effectiveness after the match.

Now Goals

Now goals are used by every player every day at practice and should be personally evaluated at the end of each practice. At least half of the now goals should be worded in terms that make them easy to measure, such as 80 percent of ground strokes crosscourt or 100 percent effort and concentration during drills. Time management during practice will improve tremendously if you constantly remind players to work on their now goals during drills that apply (see table 3.1).

TEAM GOALS

Team goals should be set each season and should follow the same principles and patterns as each player's individual goals. This is the time to set standards of performance that put the mark of excellence on players at your school and help establish a tradition and sense of pride.

Table 3.1 Sample Goals

Intermediate	Short-term	Now
• Walk away from errors and compose myself before the next point. • Stop blaming situations I can't control when I'm under pressure, such as line calls and wind. • Improve my doubles play by encouraging my partner instead of blaming him when things aren't going our way. • Change my grip on the backhand and develop a topspin passing shot.	• Continue to work on changing my forehand grip to make it easier to slice approach shots. • Come in when midcourt balls allow me to rather than hanging at the baseline during crucial points. • Spend extra time on my backhand approach shot. • Hit with more wrist snap on my second serve to create more spin. • Prepare a specific game plan before each match I play and evaluate the plan after the match.	• I will give 100% concentration and effort during drills in practice. • I will not change the incoming ball's angle in drills from the baseline unless I can step inside the baseline. • During two-ball drills I'll hit 80% of my ground strokes crosscourt behind the service line. • During passing shot drills, I will hit all of my backhands with topspin so that the ball doesn't float as much as when I hit underspin. • During service placement drills I'll try to hit 90% of my second serves into all three placement areas with depth.

Discuss team goals at the annual preseason meeting. Let the players decide on the goals, with leadership from the seniors or team captains. Each year's team is a little different, and their goals will probably reflect some variations from past teams. Your main function in this process is simply to record the goals for the group, but when they're stuck, you can use a gentle guiding hand to help them with ideas. Team goals can be described in a preseason handout for every player to see.

You might suggest that players consider some overall team issues in these goals, such as respecting each other and opposing players, helping teammates practice their weaknesses, calling lines fairly, following team rules, and supporting teammates during matches. Team goals help to focus your efforts on the important issues and create a group effort to achieve. Your players can spur each other on to greater efforts and encourage a sense of unity. If you do a good job of setting team goals, the difficult situations that occur (and decisions that you have to make) during the season can be handled by a simple comparison to the team goals.

A frequent problem on tennis teams is individual needs conflicting with team goals. For example, most teams expect every player to attend team practices, especially on days prior to tough matches. A typical team goal might be 100 percent attendance at such practices. But what if your star player also has a high national ranking and a long-term relationship with a personal coach who is preparing him for summer tournament play? The coaching sessions with his personal coach may conflict with your team practices.

If you look at your team goals and see one that says "every player's personal development is important," then it may be clear that exceptions for a top player must be made to maintain that player's interest and motivation. Your team will benefit from having a talented and committed player who is there most of the time, and you will avoid making the player face the hard choice of an all-or-nothing commitment to the team.

Tennis teams are different from team sports like football or basketball in dealing with conflicts between individual and team goals. Most highly talented tennis players compete in USTA sanctioned tournaments year-round, and the high school season is just one component of their competitive year. Consequently, a player having a personal coach is quite normal, and you need to work together with that coach for the long-term welfare of the player.

RULE VIOLATIONS AND PUNISHMENTS

Rather than publish a list of team rules that emphasize negatives, use the team goals and individual goals as guidelines for both player achievement and behavior. If players are not making progress toward their goals, meet with them to discuss and refocus their priorities.

Because most adolescents are affected more by peer pressure than anything else, you should use such pressure in a positive way. Encourage your veteran players to bring the rookies along and to set the tone for team behavior. A few well-timed comments from an upperclassman will often whip the newcomers into line without any comment from the coach. Whether the issue is tardiness, on-court behavior, a casual attitude toward practice, or a lack of effort in fitness training, sanctions that come from teammates are a powerful influence on most players.

When players do violate school or team policies, you have to take some action. Here are a few suggestions to keep in mind:

- Separate infractions that are serious enough to inform parents and school officials from those that can be handled within the team.
- To be sure the issues are all clear, give players the opportunity to explain their behavior. Then ask them to suggest the appropriate action for their behavior.
- If a player's infraction violated the rights or affected the lives of other players on the team, have the affected players participate in the resolution of the problem.
- If you want young athletes to love exercise and to be proud of their fitness, *don't ever* use physical activity as punishment!

- For those who can't follow the rules, withhold privileges such as playing in matches or making road trips.

Sometimes, the punishment you choose results in unintended consequences. A typical response from coaches over the years has been to punish players with a physical task that is repugnant to the players. Running a long distance (e.g., five miles) for many tennis players is an unwelcome task. Excessive repetitions of sprints or push-ups, or longer practices when players are fatigued, have all been used as punishment by coaches. The problem is (1) the punishment may produce an overuse injury that causes the player to miss valuable practice time or even a match, or (2) your players will develop a mind-set that physical exertion is unpleasant and to be avoided. You are reinforcing what they already suspect—that hard physical work is no fun. The problem you create is that your team will not enthusiastically embrace physical training for strength, endurance, or speed. They will not see it as a positive tool to help them improve their performance.

The Right Punishment

Brian, a ninth-grade varsity player on the high school team, felt pressure to perform because of his success as a younger player in the community. During an early preseason match, Brian let out a vulgar outburst that couldn't be tolerated in a school setting. After a second warning, the coach defaulted Brian. The coach thought that it was important to send a message early in Brian's high school career so that the problem would not escalate. After that, every time Brian used foul language he was defaulted. The default was meant to motivate Brian and help him control his temper. Instead, the discipline gave him a cop-out. When the going got tough, Brian used foul language so that he would be defaulted and not have to face a loss. Another way to help Brian control his temper had to be found. What worked wonders was benching him for a match. The benching was a wake-up call to Brian and made him realize that if he wanted to play varsity tennis, controlling his emotions was important.

- Never withhold understanding and empathy for a youngster who makes a mistake. You've probably made a few errors in life, too.

- Keep internal team troubles within the group as much as possible. Public embarrassment and humiliation can devastate an adolescent athlete and will likely drive him from the sport.

- Rewards are a powerful influence on behavior. Giving positive feedback when you see players doing something right is a good first step. Better yet, strive to say something positive to your players every day, and watch their eyes light up.

- If you've done a good job in setting individual and team goals, you have a built-in reward system. Recognition for players who achieve their goals is a key; reinforce the effort and discipline they put forth to accomplish the goal.

- Use your public relations skills to recognize player achievements. Is there anyone who doesn't like to hear his name on the school loudspeaker, see his name in the newspaper, or notice a picture on a school bulletin board capturing a memorable moment?

MENTAL TOUGHNESS

Players and coaches often cling to the theory that mental toughness is genetic—that a player either has it or doesn't have it. But, in fact, mental toughness is every bit as learned as the strokes in a player's repertoire. Any player can develop the skills necessary to handle match pressure.

Tennis is more mental than most sports. The benefits of mental training can result in players reaching as high a level of performance as possible on any given day. This doesn't mean that players will be at the top of their game every day. What it means is that they have learned to maintain an inner calm no matter what is going on around them.

With self-confidence, they are not trying to prove anything to anybody and can remain focused in the present. These skills, which maximize a player's performance potential, can be learned.

To improve mental toughness, players must honestly assess how well they handle match pressure. All players bring insecurities to competitive sport. Relationships with parents, friends, and teammates, as well as previous match results, mold each player's personal outlook and self-confidence under pressure. Help your players improve their match play coping skills with a plan that can measure their progress.

Your program might include the following components:

1. Building self-confidence through goal setting

2. Accepting the challenge of competition

3. Managing mistakes and self-talk

4. Controlling the speed of play through rituals

5. Focusing attention

6. Being a good sport and making fair line calls

7. Using visualization techniques

Each of these components needs to become part of your regular practice routine. You need to map out the objectives for practice and include some that address mental toughness skills each day. Create a situation in practice that requires the use of mental skills, and then use that opportunity to help players adjust their attitude or learn new skills. Drills or games that simulate pressure are essential to use in practice to get players accustomed to dealing with it. To create pressure during practice, you can use the impact of an audience, unique scoring systems, or penalties for failure to successfully complete a task.

Build Self-Confidence

Self-confidence is the key to mental toughness. Without building self-esteem, no amount of positive thinking will work for the player under pressure. Your role as a coach is to let players know that you accept them and will support them regardless of the outcome of any match. They need to know that you are on their side when they step onto the court to compete.

During a match, some coaches make the mistake of vocalizing their displeasure with a competing player within earshot of other players who are watching. If the coach criticizes the player on the court, not only will this hurt the confidence of the competing player, but the other players will remember the coach's lack of support when they are on the court.

The most time-tested method for building self-confidence is to help players set specific, measurable goals and to give them the opportunity to succeed at reaching those goals. Each success increases their confidence, and they will be ready to tackle the next goal that may be even more challenging. Add up a string of goals achieved, and your tennis players will begin to believe that they really can do it.

Unfortunately, some players who lack self-confidence try to build their own confidence by behaving inappropriately, often to impress their peers. Players who become obnoxious during play or throw their rackets often have low self-esteem. Such acts are unacceptable and should be dealt with immediately. Take the player aside rather than embarrassing him in front of his peers. Praise his positive efforts, but tell him that his behavior will not be tolerated. Then you need to give him some alternative methods of dealing with his frustration during play. At the same time, you should try to bolster his general self-confidence.

Accept Challenges

Fear of losing is the single most counterproductive feeling a player encounters when a match is on the line. The competition, not the victory, has to be what your players love. You need to help them learn to "love the battle," and your response to their performances will reinforce their understanding of this. If you praise them and rejoice only when they win, they will learn that winning is all that matters.

A better lesson to teach them is that the only thing you will judge them on is their "effort" in a match. The beauty of this is that they are totally responsible for their effort. Teach them to act like confident competitors who move around the court with determination, good body posture, and good emotional control. If they do this and put forth their best effort, their odds of competing successfully become significantly better.

Steel Elbows and Lead Feet

Players react differently to pressure, but two common manifestations of nervousness or choking are the appearance of steel elbows and lead feet. Both conditions prevent players from reacting to the ball and usually happen at crucial points of a match. Your players must recognize the possibility of this happening to them, and you need to arm them with solutions to overcome these conditions. Here are some suggestions you can make to your players:

- Remind yourself to be light on your feet. Visualize playing tension free (light and quick) in practice.

- Between points, bounce on the balls of your feet in the ready position as a reminder to react quickly.

- Concentrate on important points of focus during play. Key in on your opponent's stroke so that you can react to the direction of the shot as early as possible.

- Try to complete your stroke preparation before the ball bounces on your side of the court.

- Remind yourself to stay down (and keep your head still) at the point of contact as you hit your stroke. Exaggerate the finish of the shot through the full range of motion.

These reminders for helping players reduce reaction time can be encapsulated in the following words: *react . . . bounce . . . hit*. Sometimes just repeating these three words will help a player reduce reaction time and escape the tense feeling of slowness that has overcome her during play.

If players set their goals exclusively on winning, they will soon learn that they don't control the play of their opponent, lucky bounces, net cords, the wind, or other external factors. If they set their goal to just "playing well," they may also be disappointed since all players have days where they do not play well. They may not play well due to luck, the opponent, the conditions, or their partner's play in doubles.

Seemingly lucky net cords, bad line calls, and inclement weather are not within a player's control. The effort exerted during a match is the only thing that can always be controlled by the player. Once you make your players realize that they hold the key to feeling good about themselves (the key is giving a good effort every time out), then win or lose, the match will be enjoyable and rewarding.

If players develop the attitude that they will keep trying no matter what occurs around them during a match, uncontrollable situations will not faze them. An opponent may hit a winner or dribble the ball over the net on a very important point, but your players will recognize these situations as beyond their control. Be sure to praise your players if they give an outstanding effort no matter what the score turns out to be.

Manage Mistakes

From the first day of practice, your players need to learn the appropriate response to their mistakes. You can teach them an invaluable lesson that first day by helping them understand that the tennis court is a "mistake center." This is a place where they can experiment with different shots, test those shots in different situations against various types of opponents, and measure their consistency in performance.

Sometimes it is helpful to distinguish between mistakes and errors. An error on the tennis court may be a lapse in judgment during which a player tries a shot that has little chance for success. For example, trying to hit a second serve flat and hard would be an error in judgment. On the other hand, aiming higher and applying more spin to a second serve but still missing it long would be a mistake, but not an error.

The difference between mistakes and errors is simply that if the player tried the right shot, but missed it, she should not be upset about that mistake. However, if the player chose a shot that was too risky and had a low percentage for success, then she really did make an error in judgment.

Talk Positively to Yourself

It seems that talking to yourself during play is an occupational hazard of tennis players. Most players either talk to themselves audibly or mentally during a match. Usually the self-talk centers on personal cues to improve stroke production or deal with an opponent's tactics. As long as the self-talk is positive and motivational, the player can only benefit. Problems occur, however, when the talk becomes self-deprecating.

Tennis is difficult enough when your only obstacle is your opponent. When a player becomes his own worst enemy by cutting himself down during play, it's like he's playing with a 30-pound anvil around his neck.

When a player starts beating himself up with negative self-talk on the court, you should try to give him some positives to combat this defeatist attitude. Here are some things you can tell a player in this situation:

- Be your own best friend rather than your worst enemy. Imagine if your doubles partner treated you the way you're treating yourself. You'd dump him as a partner!

- Restrict your self-talk to things that are stated in a positive way. "Hit the ball higher," "Nice and easy," "Finish the shot," and "Get there earlier" are examples of acceptable admonitions.

- Be able to laugh at yourself or the match situation. It is much easier to remain positive if you don't approach a match as a do-or-die ordeal.

- Don't feel sorry for yourself when everything is going against you. Accept the fact that your opponent is getting all the breaks as part of the challenge of competitive sports.

• Dig in and remember that you only have to be accountable for giving your best effort.

Control Speed of Play

Inexperienced competitors typically have lots of difficulty figuring out the optimal pace of play. That includes the time within a point, between points, between games, and between sets. The most common tendency for players who are feeling pressure is to rush everything.

During a point, players should be encouraged to keep the ball in play for several shots. It is helpful to enforce a rule in practice that every point must begin with the ball crossing the net successfully three times before the point is "on." This tactic gives players a chance to play themselves into a point, helps them resist the tendency to go for a winner too early, and, of course, it allows more opportunities for the opponent to make a mistake.

Between points, rituals are helpful in establishing the pace of play. As soon as the point ends, players should relax physically and direct their attention to the ground or to the strings of their racket. Next they should return to the baseline, take a deep breath, and plan their next point. When serving, bouncing the ball several times gives players time to focus their attention on the direction they plan to serve. When receiving serve, a few hop steps can increase their readiness to react and move.

Between games, players should take the full time allowed to relax, drink fluids, and plan their tactics for the next game. They shouldn't dwell on past games or points but instead focus attention on the present. Some leagues allow players to take a break if they split sets, and that time can be used to recover physically, relax, drink fluids, and talk to the coach. Your job as a coach is to help them focus on one or two tasks in the third set and to express your confidence that with effort they will be successful.

Focus Your Attention

Maintaining an inner calm when all around you is chaotic is easier said than done, espe-cially for teenagers. But this inner calm is the emotional state all tennis players are trying to achieve during match play. When a player is in this frame of mind, her game flows effortlessly and free. Unfortunately, achieving this state during competition requires mental discipline that most teenagers find much more difficult to master than hitting a forehand.

Tenseness and self-doubt are tough to over-come during a match that holds particular significance to a player. Excuses for poor play keep entering the player's mind and distract from the task at hand. When this happens, a player has to learn to blow the whistle on himself. Teach your players to dismiss this self-doubt by silently telling their mind to *stop* dwelling on the negative.

The question for many players is, What should they direct their attention to? There is no easy answer to this question, and you will need to help your players experiment with different objects of concentration to see what works best for them. If players are relatively inexperienced, they may need to remind themselves to get to the ball earlier, be on balance as they strike the ball, keep their head steady, or follow through. These technique cues can help players who do not have full control of their shots. Experienced players who can perform their skills with little conscious thought should focus on the tactics and the best shot to play based on the situation. These players will be better off concentrating on their shot selection than on technique issues. For all players, the less conscious thought the better. Too much thinking may produce a "paralysis by analysis." Match play is not the time to be trying new shots and novel strategies, or to be analyzing how you look to the crowd.

Common distractions to be avoided include spectators, weather conditions, lucky shots from the opponent, sounds from other courts, and the match score. When a player leaves the court knowing how other players on her team have fared during a match, it should be clear that she wasn't focused completely on her match.

The way to avoid these distractions is to teach players to keep their eyes on their own court at all times or on the strings of their racket. At first, this is not an easy thing to do. It all starts with the right practice habits, which you can set from the first day. In the final analysis, players should work to focus their attention on the tennis ball while blocking out all other distractions. The ball is inanimate, nonjudgmental, nonthreatening, and just begging to be caressed thoughtfully and purposefully.

Be a Good Sport and Make Fair Calls

A sad fact in today's sports world, even at the high school level, is that winning usually becomes the first priority of players and coaches. Fortunately, tennis doesn't come under the same public scrutiny as, say, football, basketball, and baseball. As a result, very few tennis coaches feel the pressure (unless it is self-induced) of having to win to maintain job security. Thus, tennis coaches can help each player in their program learn the most important lesson they can teach by making good sporting behavior their first coaching priority.

Good sporting behavior is a form of communication with your opponent during a competitive match. It's an aspect of mental toughness that must be applied in every competitive situation if a player is going to enjoy competition without looking for excuses. Teach your players to respect the effort of their opponents because it is this effort that allows your players to test themselves during match play. By being a good sport, you show respect for your opponent while maintaining your personal dignity. Once the match is completed, you can praise your player's effort regardless of the outcome. This all sounds so simple—what could possibly go wrong?

The values a player learns from his coach, parents, and teammates determine whether good sporting behavior during match play will be possible. Unfortunately, what coaches say and what they communicate to a player with their body language and casual remarks are not always consistent. If you, the coach, place winning above any other individual goal, the pressure you put on your players will make good sporting behavior impossible for them to achieve. Parents usually try to put winning

in the proper perspective. However, if a child keeps hearing about how much money has been spent on lessons, with very little gain on the team ladder, then pressure to win will again erode good sporting behavior. When you sense that parental pressure is a problem, take the parents aside and try to make them understand how they can best support their child's participation in tennis.

Peer approval is very important to today's teenagers. Coaches sometimes overlook the fact that all players need to be accepted by their teammates. If the players on your team judge their teammates by wins and losses, then the pressure to win will again make good sporting behavior impossible. Teach your players from day one to respect their teammates' efforts, as they would a doubles partner, because every member of the team is working toward the same goals. Positive support from teammates makes competing easier for everyone.

The role models from professional sports do not always help you to encourage good sporting behavior. Taunting, trash talk, and overboard celebration have become all too common in all sports, and your players are likely to see this behavior often on television. To counteract this trend, you might obtain some videotapes of tennis players who display model sporting behavior and spend some time viewing them as a team. In addition to watching the shot-making ability and match tactics, call attention to the mental toughness skills of the professional players and stop the action when you catch a player exhibiting good sporting behavior.

In high school tennis, players have the opportunity (unlike most other sports) to learn to accept the opponent as a partner in playing a match and to allow the other player to make line calls. Athletes from other sports are always amazed at this tradition and seem to envy the ability of the sport to allow such a custom. There will be times when you wish there was an umpire in the chair to overrule a line call by an opponent, but you need to embrace the chance to help your kids deal with tough situations.

Here are some tips you can give to your players for dealing with line calls:

• Assume from the beginning of the match that your opponent will call the lines fairly, and commit to doing the same. Don't be influenced by past experience with a particular team or player.

• At the first occurrence of what appears to be a questionable call, remind yourself to aim farther inside the lines to eliminate close calls as much as possible. You don't need to play the ball near the lines to win matches.

• Remember that your view of the ball is very likely to be less than accurate and may be influenced by your own hope that it landed in. Coaching hint: Have your players stand as a group on one baseline and position yourself at the sideline near the net. Hit a series of balls out of your hand and aim them near the baseline on the opposite side of the court from the players. As each ball lands, all your players should gesture thumbs up for a ball they thought was good, and thumbs down if it was out. Station a judge right on the baseline to rule on the correct call. You'll find that the players on the opposite baseline will make more errors than correct calls due to their distance and angle from the ball. The lesson should be clear—call the balls on your side and let your opponent handle the other side.

• If several calls appear to have been questionable, on the next close call, walk deliberately to the net and politely inquire whether your opponent was sure of the call. That should serve notice that you have some doubt, but you've done it in a respectful manner.

• As a last resort, call for assistance from your coach. Sometimes an appeal from both coaches to both players will calm the situation. If not, the coaches may agree to place a volunteer linesman on the court to overrule any obvious missed calls.

Use Visualization Techniques

Many players can use visualization to picture themselves hitting their strokes cor-rectly while maintaining a positive inner calm. To teach this skill, you must video-tape each of your players at some point and allow them to watch themselves hitting the ball well. This is different from using video to analyze their skills and suggest changes. In fact, some players have developed a prematch ritual that involves watching previous successful matches with a sound track of their favorite music to reinforce the positive images.

Other players, particularly young ones, may find success by visualizing other players hitting the ball. Again, video of great professional players can provide a strong mental image to copy. You need to acquire a good video library of positive role models and top match play. In addition to watching these during rainy day practice time, players should be able to check out certain videos for a few days to watch at home. If you are just getting your library started, ask for help from some of your players in taping matches during the Grand Slam tennis events.

Many excellent books are available on visualization and how it relates to mental toughness in sports, including *Mental Toughness Training for Sports: Achieving Athletic Excellence* (Loehr 1986), *Coaches Guide to Sport Psychology* (Martens 1987), and *Psyching for Sport* (Orlick 1986).

SUMMARY

The following tips will help you motivate your players on and off the court:

• Motivation of adolescent athletes requires an understanding of their needs, including self-identity, peer approval, recognition, and perceived success.

• To be successful, you need to know how to make tennis fun, which, according to 10,000 high school athletes, is a lot more important than winning.

• Goal setting provides the road map for your players for the season.

CHAPTER 4   BUILDING A TENNIS PROGRAM

High school coaches often ask what the keys are to building a successful tennis program. It's a simple question, but there is no simple answer. Every program has its unique set of circumstances. What works well at one high school will not necessarily work well in your school. However, there are certain fundamental principles and building blocks that are typical of successful programs.

Nothing is more crucial to the continual success of a program than the presence of a "feeder system" in town to get lots of kids playing tennis at least by middle school. Next, it's up to you to devise the best system for selecting the high school team from many aspiring players who show up at tryouts. You must also skillfully build support from your entire community, including students, parents, faculty, and townspeople.

Within the team, well-designed team policies, and the corresponding rules and consequences, are essential. Finally, you need to develop team spirit and pride in the program each year and carry over those feelings from year to year.

COMPONENTS OF A SUCCESSFUL PROGRAM

The players are the key ingredient to any good tennis program. But the talent on your squad will change from year to year, so you need some constants to make your program run smoothly. The components described in the following sections will help you achieve and maintain a solid program.

Feeder System

Over the years, the presence of an effective feeder system that introduces kids in your community to tennis early (and keeps them playing) is clearly the most important factor in building a tennis dynasty. The relatively short season and the rules that prohibit coaches from working with varsity teams during the off-season force coaches to rely on other programs to produce good players year after year. You can take an active role to ensure that your town has excellent recreational tennis programs for youngsters, and you can perhaps even direct or teach the program during the summer.

Many high school coaches become the leaders of summer recreational tennis programs. You can conduct these programs using the high school tennis courts or join with the parks and recreation department in your area. Programs for kids should introduce lots of young players to the game and give them a chance to play all summer. An added bonus is that you can often employ current varsity players as instructors for younger children. Your players then become role models for those they teach (while also earning a summer income).

One of the facts of life in tennis is that communities that are relatively affluent tend to consistently produce more good players. This isn't a secret, but simply the result of families in those communities being able to afford to expose kids to tennis at an early age. They can afford to send their kids to tennis camps, pay for weekly lessons with a tennis professional, and transport them to tournaments in

Varsity players make great instructors and mentors for younger teammates.

the summer. If you don't live in a community where this is the norm, the alternative is to build a local community tennis association. You can also work with the parks and recreation department to strengthen tennis offerings for all ages.

USA School Tennis, a program backed by the United States Tennis Association, is another good way to ensure an endless supply of tennis players. The USTA staff that covers your geographic area (referred to as a USTA section) administers a program in the schools to introduce kids to tennis. This program focuses on elementary and middle schools. It includes an offer from the USTA to provide free curriculum guides and in-service training to physical education and classroom teachers who agree to teach a tennis unit. The goal of the unit is to introduce kids to tennis skills and then encourage them to join an after-school program where they get to play. The USTA provides a limited number of rackets to schools at no cost, and you can also request to host a tennis assembly at your school to get the kids and teachers excited about the game.

Of course, just exposing thousands of kids to tennis doesn't develop players. The next crucial step is to encourage kids to sign up for USA Team Tennis, a USTA program for kids in three divisions: red (ages 6-12), white (ages 10-14), and blue (ages 13-18). Kids of all skill levels are welcome, and they are assigned to teams that practice and play for at least a six-week season. You may want to start a USA Team Tennis program at the elementary schools in your district. Don't let the lack of tennis courts set you back; thousands of kids are having fun playing after school on playgrounds or on parking lots using mini-nets and smaller courts. If weather is a factor, set up a team tennis program in the gym or all-purpose room using mini-nets and softer balls that bounce slower. Your USTA section staff can help you secure the equipment. They can also offer coaches training, coaches resources for practices, and guidelines for play. In some cases, they may even help defray the costs. You should also investigate the possibility of national, state, or local funding from other sources that support after-school programs.

If all of these plans sound like a lot for you to take on, you may want to consider forming a local community tennis association. Recruit a few parents, local leaders, tennis coaches, senior tennis players, league players, and others who love tennis. This group can lobby the town government or parks department to provide court use and hire instructors. The group can also organize fund-raising activities to make tennis affordable for every kid who is interested. Eventually, your high school team will include tennis players who grew up in the program, and these players can become assistant coaches and work with the next generation of players. Your job as the high school coach is not to do all the work yourself, but to recruit others to join with you to promote tennis in your town.

Whatever direction you decide to take, you should call the people at your USTA section for help. Their existence depends on people like you who want to encourage more people to play tennis more often. They'll talk with you, send you materials, and maybe send some skilled clinicians to your community to help boost whatever program you are promoting. Start now by logging on to www.USTA.com to identify your section and read about USA School Tennis, USA Team Tennis, and community tennis associations. All of this help is there, waiting for you to say, "We need this in our town!"

Support

No tennis program will ever succeed without the combined support of students, faculty members, and people in the community.

Student Support

Tennis is not usually viewed as a popular spectator sport in high school. However, as your program grows, students will express an interest if you make them aware of scheduled matches and results.

Use the morning announcements and school newspaper to keep students aware of tennis happenings. Emphasize team results

but don't overlook the individual accomplishments of specific players. A few kind words that mention kids by name during announcements or in the school paper are priceless.

Student attendance at matches can be encouraged in a variety of ways. First, make sure there is an optimal viewing area and comfortable seating with rest rooms nearby. Second, make sure that the individual match score is visible on every court and that the overall team match score is displayed prominently. One of the quirks of tennis is that often spectators don't know the score. What could be more boring than watching a contest without any idea who is ahead? If the expense of scoreboards is too much for one year, add one or two a year, or ask that perhaps they can be made by your school personnel.

Another good idea is to encourage students who are taking tennis in their physical education class to attend at least one match. It'll help them understand the game and swell your crowd too. Lots of school coaches support each other, and if tennis is a fall sport, you may want to exchange ideas with the cross country, soccer, or field hockey coach.

Faculty Support

Communicate constantly with your administrators to let them know what you are trying to accomplish. As long as your program's goals fit into the philosophical and educational framework of your school, you will have their total support. Once you have gained the support of the school administration, don't abuse it. If you ignore teaching duties during your tennis season, skip faculty meetings, or leave school early every day, you'll lose the respect of your fellow teachers and the principal. Such behavior makes it impossible for the administration to support you when you need them. Rather than putting yourself and your athletic program on a pedestal and expecting special treatment, strive to fit in with the flow of your school.

If your school has a booster club, you should attend its meetings. If it's a general

Wheelchair Tennis

You may not be aware of the fact that tennis is also played by thousands of players around the world who are wheelchair users. The official rules of tennis as defined by the International Tennis Federation (of which the United States is a member) provide for wheelchair play. These rules can be found in the ITF publication *Rules of Tennis* published each year by the USTA. Contact our publications department. Essentially, wheelchair rules allow the player in a chair two bounces of the ball before it must be returned, rather than one. The second bounce may land either inside or outside of the court boundaries. This rule applies whether players in wheelchairs are playing against other players in chairs or against able-bodied players who must play the ball on the first bounce or out of the air.

There have been a significant number of wheelchair tennis players who have competed successfully on their high school team and several who have gone on to play collegiate tennis. Just this year, a wheelchair player from Oakville High School in St. Louis, Missouri, received his varsity letter after compiling a win–loss record of 15-3 for his senior year.

Able-bodied players may be "psyched out" when they are first matched against a player in a wheelchair. Your coaching advice to them should be that they should play the ball and not the player. After a while, they will adjust to the fact that balls that have bounced twice will still be in play.

Coaching wheelchair players takes some special skills since they have limitations that require some adjustments in technique from that used by able-bodied players. You can expand your knowledge in this area by contacting the USTA to obtain coaching manuals or answers to common questions. They may also put you in contact with an experienced coach of wheelchair players who can speak with you one-on-one. The goal of the USTA is simply to provide the opportunity for all players to participate in the sport and to ensure that no obstacles are present to discourage prospective players who use wheelchairs.

With the proper support and guidance all people can enjoy the sport of tennis.

athletic support group, your presence will encourage their support of your program. If your school has specific booster groups for each sport, organize your players' parents and invite them to take on some of the fundraising responsibilities.

Community Support

As one of many athletic teams on your school's campus and in your city, your tennis team has to establish its niche in the community. Support from the community at large can go a long way toward increasing participation and providing you with the little extras needed to run a successful program. If you're just beginning to develop a tennis program, start building a base of support in the community now. Go to your local tennis courts or country club and see who the businesspeople are who play tennis. If you play, join the weekend round-robins and other local tennis events.

In developing a successful tennis program, your responsibilities extend far beyond just coaching on the court. You must promote your program in the community. You could begin each year by sending a copy of the schedule (and goals for the upcoming year) to each parent and booster who has contributed to your program in the past. Communication is the key to community support. Tennis may not be a high-profile sport in your school or community, but with promotional work on your part, your program can get its fair share of interest and financial support.

SELECTING THE TEAM

Every coach's goal should be to provide a quality experience for as many players as can be properly supervised on a squad. If you've developed a good feeder program for the earlier grades and have strong summer programs in your town, it's quite likely that more players will show up at the first team practice than you expected. This can be a two-edged sword. You may be faced with the challenges of too many players on a court, not enough assistant coaches, and the inability to provide responsible attention to such a large number of players. A good rule of thumb is to eventually trim your squad to a maximum of four players per court. This will ensure that your players have opportunities for singles play on some courts while other players drill with six players on a court.

Some coaches have been fortunate enough to create junior varsity (JV) teams led by assistant coaches who may be volunteers. You might find teachers, parents, part-time tennis teachers, or college students who would love to help out with a JV team. Court space problems can be solved by staggering practice times with the varsity or securing other courts in the community (e.g., at parks or at middle schools). If you can organize a junior varsity team, the emphasis should be on developing the players' fundamentals, exposing them to match play, and teaching them the basic strategies. The coaches you choose to provide this experience may need your help in accomplishing these goals. Periodically, the varsity players can also work individually with the JV players to give them the extra attention they will crave.

If you must cut players because of lack of court space, insufficient supervision, or school policies on squad size, you should use preseason round-robin play to establish a squad. Your goal is to select the best prospective players and give every player a fair chance within a short period of time.

At the beginning of each season, it probably makes sense for you to divide players into two groups: those who are returning and those who are new. Your time is best spent evaluating the new prospects (as soon as your state rules allow). Your returning players should practice against each other and, to some extent, help in the selection process.

Assessing the Talent

A high school coach's task is to do the best job possible with the players available. Once you have assessed the talent, you should formulate a coaching plan to enhance the current players' chances for success. Flexibility within this plan is absolutely essential. A willingness to adapt to the different players who come out for your team will enable you to maximize each player's skills. There are generally three kinds of players you'll encounter:

1. Skilled tournament players who will likely be your team leaders.
2. Good athletes from other sports who bring athleticism and a team-first attitude.
3. Program players (nonvarsity) who bring enthusiasm at practice and match support.

Your challenge is to blend these different groups of players into a cohesive unit in which each player contributes in his own way. How you involve each group in your program determines your chances for success.

If your team includes players with tournament experience, they will probably occupy the top slots in your lineup. Some high school coaches allow these tournament players to work exclusively with their teaching pros, interacting with the team only on the day of a match. This decision usually leads to poor team chemistry.

If the skill level of the tournament player is greater than your technical knowledge of the game, the best solution is to allow the player to work with her teaching pro during the week but also attend some high school practices. Players with tournament experience should work with other members of the squad during practice. The tournament players can share their experience and skills and thus give something back to the program rather than just take from it. Team unity will be enhanced, and no members of the team will be perceived as receiving special treatment from the coach.

Team members who also play other sports usually form the backbone of your program. The team-first attitude of these players can be contagious to the more individual-minded tournament players. A good coach will use these players' team

skills and enthusiasm during drills to strengthen the team's fiber.

The remainder of your squad will be made up of players who do not get to play regularly in matches. In some programs, these players are ignored; however, you may discover that if you give these players a meaningful role in achieving team goals, their contributions are immense. At some schools, nonplaying players chart matches, keep score in umpires' chairs, and run the desk during tournaments.

Every coach has a favorite style of play. College tennis coaches often recruit players who can serve and volley and play an all-court game. These coaches know that this style of play can yield the greatest success in collegiate singles and doubles.

As a high school coach, if you have a player who is a baseliner and is also effective with long rallies, you probably won't want to redevelop him into a serve-and-volleyer. The style that best fits a player mechanically, physically, and psychologically is what you should enhance. You may feel that every player should charge the net at the first opportunity, but if a player is not effective this way, you should help him develop a playing style that promotes his natural ability.

Round-Robin Play or Flight Play

Most experienced coaches stay away from individual single or double elimination tournaments for team tryouts. Too much is left to the luck of the draw. Instead, you should divide prospects into groups based on their previous tennis experience (which you can evaluate from a quick questionnaire) and their grade in school. Each group or "flight" should include 3 to 6 players.

Players should play matches against every player in their group for the initial placing. Players with the best record in each group should then compete against each other until you develop an overall team ladder for position.

The match play should be the equivalent of at least one set, although some variations may help save time. No-ad scoring makes play move faster. Many coaches are beginning to favor "short sets" that consist of playing two sets of four games each to win. If players split sets, they play a tiebreaker to determine the winner. This pattern is better than traditional sets or "pro sets" since a loss of one set doesn't put a player hopelessly behind.

Once tryouts are over, usually in a few days, the new players are placed in position on a team ladder with the holdover players. Players then have the opportunity to challenge players above them. The rules for challenging players on a team ladder must be carefully thought out and explained thoroughly to your players to prevent misunderstandings. Sample rules for a challenge ladder are shown in figure 4.1.

The number of players you decide to keep on the varsity team will vary depending on your state and conference rules, available courts, and school rules. High school teams across the country play many different formats. Typically, there are several singles positions and several doubles positions. Some states and conferences allow a player to play both singles and doubles, while others do not. For example, the rule in one state is 4 singles players and 3 doubles teams without player repeating. This means at least 10 players are required for a team match. Of course, you would need to have substitutes, so a full varsity squad might include 14 to 20 players.

Choosing Doubles Specialists

Using the rules for team play previously mentioned, you can see that more than half the players in a varsity match will be doubles only players. You should keep this in mind during tryouts. If the players play some doubles rather than all singles during tryouts, this can also help solve court space problems. Look for doubles players who have a steady, consistent serve, like to play at the net, return serve well, and enjoy working together with a teammate. Both the skills and the personality required in a doubles player are often different from a singles player, so don't overlook your need for both types of competitors. More discussion on doubles teams can be found in chapter 12.

The Challenge Ladder Process

To maintain order in the challenge process, ladder rules are necessary and may sometimes need interpretation from the coach (see figure 4.1). These rules allow challenges to occur throughout the period before dual match play begins. After match play begins, and the lineup is set, a player must beat a starting varsity member in two consecutive challenge matches to take her spot at varsity practice. This allows players to improve their status on the team during the entire season, while maintaining the integrity of the varsity in most cases. Very few changes occur once match play begins, but occasionally a player will knock a varsity player into the nonvarsity group and take that player's place.

Maintaining Involvement

The end result of using this type of system for team selection and position should be clear. Each player can progress on the ladder as far as her talent and desire allow. Even if a player doesn't attain match-playing status, she will be active in the sport and be part of a team she can identify with throughout high school.

When you cut a player, her season—and maybe her tennis career—is over. But you never know whether that gawky freshman will develop into a skilled player. The challenge process promotes competition within your team and helps players develop the competitive skills and sharpness to play hard consistently.

Your High School Ladder Rules

1. Letter winners are placed on the ladder in the order they finished the previous season.

2. New players are placed on the ladder in the order of round-robin finish below letter winners.

3. Before match season begins, a player may challenge up to three positions higher on the ladder (e.g., player number 9 may challenge player 8, 7, or 6). All preseason challenge matches will be pro sets.

4. After match play begins, a player may challenge only two positions up. These matches will be two out of three sets.

5. Once match season begins, challenge matches involving varsity members must be cleared through the coach and played at practice.

6. Players must accept a challenge from players below them on the ladder.

7. Players have one week to accept a challenge or forfeit their positions on the ladder. No excuses accepted except ill and out of school.

8. The top eight varsity players challenge once match season begins: Regular challenge of two out of three sets to take the place of number 6, 7, or 8 on the ladder. However, to take the place of one of the varsity singles players (top 5), challenger must win two consecutive matches against that player.

9. New players coming from another sport whose season had just concluded or new students to the school have one free challenge and may play any player on the ladder. If they win, they take that player's position and everyone moves down one place. If they lose, they are put at the bottom of the ladder. This applies only until dual match season begins.

10. If player number 9 beats player number 6 on the ladder, player number 9 takes ladder position six, number 6 moves to ladder position seven, number 7 moves to ladder position eight, and so on. If player 9 loses to player 6, the ladder remains the same.

11. If player number 9 challenges player number 6 but in the meantime player 6 beats player 4 and moves out of reach (more than three positions on the ladder), the match between players 4 and 9 must still be played as it was scheduled in good faith.

12. Players not in the varsity eight must play a minimum of one challenge match per week to remain on the ladder in good standing.

Figure 4.1 Rules for a challenge ladder.

There are many benefits to this system of maintaining a squad with as many players as you can manage, supervise properly, and give a positive experience to. A varsity team is established to compete. If your program allows, a separate junior varsity with an independent schedule can provide invaluable experience to future varsity players. If you must cut players, use a system that gives you time to assess each individual's potential, not just her current playing status. Once you have decided which players must be let go, talk to each one individually. Encourage them to continue playing tennis, to support this year's team, and to try out again next year. Following is an example of how you can handle this situation:

Coach: I know you're disappointed about not making the team, but we happen to have a very strong squad this year. Of course, we'll be losing several key seniors after this season, and spots will be open next year. I hope you'll try out again.

Player: I just don't know how to improve, Coach. I worked so hard this winter to get better and still lost to players I should have beaten.

Coach: I have two suggestions for you, Megan. First, you need to become a more consistent player and let your opponent take some of the risks. Give yourself more margin for error by hitting higher over the net and don't aim so close to the lines. Second, I'd like to see you play some tournament matches this summer in our local town tournaments so that you gain experience in match play. Next year at tryouts, you'll be a more confident competitor!

Player: Thanks, Coach. I guess I really thought just doing drills all winter at the indoor club would get me ready, but now I see that match play is more important for me.

TEAM POLICIES AND RULES

You must work out your personal philosophy of coaching, apply it to your coaching of the tennis team, and communicate it to players and parents. Your philosophy should be based on what you think is important in competitive sport and should reflect your values as a coach and as a human being. The simply expressed philosophy espoused by the American Sport Education Program

(ASEP) program, "Athletes first, winning second," is an excellent example of a coaching philosophy that is easily communicated. It is from your personal philosophy of coaching that team policies and rules should follow logically.

Rules

Be careful about making team rules that you can't or don't want to enforce. Coaches who make a lot of specific rules often find themselves bogged down trying to police them or frustrated with the fact that there are often extenuating circumstances that should be considered. A better path to follow is to keep rules to a minimum but consistently enforce the ones you do set.

Most schools have a standard set of rules to govern athletes in all sports (see figure 4.2). You should discuss these guidelines with your players at the beginning of the season, share them with parents, and give players and parents written copies so that they have no excuse to plead ignorance of them.

The next step is to develop some specific rules for your tennis team. Many coaches have found that this is best accomplished with input and discussion from returning players. If players are part of the process, they are much more likely to remember the rules and remind each other of them. Once these specific team rules are established, they too should be written down and distributed to all parents and players.

Common rules and their applications usually do not change from year to year. Typically they include issues such as lateness or absences from team practices and matches, behavior during team practices, and inability to play due to illness or injury. For most coaches, the essential player responsibility is to notify the coach *before* the absence occurs so that the team is not penalized by the absence of a player. You should give players some specific examples that illustrate absences that are considered excused and those that are unexcused. For example,

> ## Your High School Athletic Department Policy
>
> The athletic department strictly opposes the following actions by our athletes:
>
> 1. Possessing, distributing, or using illegal drugs or alcoholic beverages
> 2. Stealing
>
> *A player who violates these rules will be disciplined in the following manner:*
>
> **First violation:**
>
>   A. Player will be suspended for 20% of the team's regular schedule.
>   B. Player must attend at least one counseling session with the following groups of people in attendance:
>
>   1. Parents/guardians
>   2. Coach of the sport
>   3. Athletic director
>   4. Principal
>
> **Second violation:**
>
>   Player will be dismissed from all athletic teams for the remainder of that school year.
>
> Parent signature
>
> _____
>
> Player signature
>
> _____
>
> Date _____

Figure 4.2 Athletic department policy on rules and regulations.

players who claim illness over a period of time but decline to see a physician need to learn to be more responsible for their well-being. Claims of illness that linger without evidence of medical care fall under the "unexcused" category.

Minor infractions related to poor sporting behavior during practice can best be handled by sending the player off the court temporarily. Usually, when players lose the privilege of practicing and interacting with teammates for a little while, they will not repeat their offense. Your players need to understand that their behavior will be scrutinized in the off-season at tournaments, on the public courts, and around the school building. As members of a high-profile program, they should know that any individual misbehavior may be generalized to reflect poorly on all of the team's players.

However, you know that incidents will occur that require attention. Whether the infraction is minor or major, you can follow three simple rules in dealing with the player. First, try to make the player understand that you care about him no matter what he did. Second, the player must understand that he has to take responsibility for his bad decision. Last, and most important, the consequences for a player who makes a bad decision are not influenced by his position on the ladder. Stars don't receive special treatment!

Consequences

The consequences for player actions that are inappropriate should vary depending on the player, the situation, and the frequency with which the actions occur. Repeated infractions by the same player may signal more complicated problems and may require intense counseling. A first-time offense may simply indicate ignorance of the rule or lack of foresight by a young player. Experienced coaches who value the welfare of players take the whole situation into account before assigning consequences for infractions. You should take your time in reviewing the situation, talk calmly with the player as you investigate the incident, and give thoughtful deliberation before meting out punishment. It is often helpful to discuss these situations with your team captains to elicit another viewpoint. They will be able to influence other team members before other violations occur. Note: This should be part of the role of the captains depending on their maturity. They will often have a more complete understanding of the situation than you possibly can as a coach. Plus, they'll learn from the situation and head off future problems. You don't always have to take their recommendations; it is not a democracy, but it's a very good idea to listen to their opinions.

TEAM CAPTAINS

The word *captain* means leader. These are the keepers of traditions, veterans who have been through a season or two. By providing leadership within the players' ranks, they are indispensable to team morale. The captains' duties may include

- maintaining practice intensity and tempo when they are lagging,
- leading by example during conditioning work and drills,
- sharing their experience with underclassmen,
- helping the coach maintain team cohesiveness, and
- acknowledging good play or effort beyond expected levels at practice and during match play.

Some coaches appoint a team captain or captains, but most experienced coaches find better results by allowing players to choose their leaders. At the end of each season, it often makes sense to have your players vote on the captains for the coming year. Typically, the captain or captains have already exhibited some signs of leadership potential. The number of team captains is up to you and may vary from year to year depending on the number of upperclassmen on your team.

You will find that the role of the team captains also varies from one year to another based on their personalities and the overall team makeup. Some years, the captains may be the top players and therefore become helpful in evaluating talent, determining team positions, and assisting with coaching the younger players. Other years, the role your captains take on may be more of a social director and team spirit leader. Don't try to force your captains into a role that doesn't fit. Allow their role to develop naturally.

TEAM SPIRIT

Creating a focal point for team pride, spirit, and loyalty is essential to building tradition.

You, the coach, are the only constant in your program from year to year. Team pride must be instilled in every player each year.

One of the easiest ways to begin developing team pride is by having team uniforms. There are few things more intimidating to your opposition than your team arriving for a match with each player dressed in identical shirts, shorts, and sweatshirts. You might also include your team slogan on the shirts. The mental advantage uniforms provide your team will be apparent immediately. Too many high school teams allow their players to wear whatever they want to school matches. If complete uniforms are too expensive, at least have each player purchase a T-shirt monogrammed with your school's logo. During matches, team uniforms also allow spectators to identify your players.

Team traditions seem to develop on athletic teams, and you can suggest some team activities that become traditions. For example, a preseason trip to a professional tennis tournament or a nearby collegiate match can be a terrific instructional experience but also promotes team bonding. Team dinners before matches

Going to College Early

At one high school, a popular school tradition is the annual trip to the nearby state university to watch a match. Once the match begins, every player on the team picks a match to watch and is required to report back to the whole team on both players' strengths and weaknesses, tactics that were used, and their opinion on why the winning player was successful. They also watch other matches and get a good idea of the level of play in college. Kids are often impressed by the way the college kids root and cheer for each other, and thus come home a little less inhibited. The players also begin to see what they need to work on if they have hopes of playing college tennis someday. However, the best part of the trip is always the fun and the camaraderie established. By doing this early in the season, it sets a friendly tone for your team.

are also good mixers and encourage your players to spend time together off the tennis court. Year-end get-togethers are popular and give you a chance to highlight top performances, dispense lots of praise for your team's effort, laugh a bit at each other (including you), and set a good tone for the next year.

Simple rules can help promote discipline and team spirit. One such rule is requiring all team players to stay until the end of a match to cheer on those still playing. The last match can be lonely unless teammates gather around to cheer the players on.

Many tennis players are used to playing for themselves in tournaments. The spirit that builds through working within the team concept makes playing matches easier. Each player picks up his teammates with positive encouragement during a match. This team spirit can increase the confidence level of players who are struggling or players in very tight matches.

Players will be loyal to the program when they feel like important cogs in your machine. Treat each player with respect and provide generous praise—especially for outstanding effort and proper conduct. Treating your players this way will win and maintain their loyalty to your program.

SUMMARY

The keys to building and maintaining a successful program include the following:

- Assess the talent of prospective players each year and develop a flexible system of play that can maximize different skills and ability levels each year.
- Develop a feeder system within your community that exposes young players to tennis at an early age and keeps them playing.
- Nurture community support for your program, including support from school administration, faculty, students, and townspeople.
- Select the team using a system of round-robin play and ladder play. Be sure to look for potential doubles players as well as singles players.
- Develop clear team policies and rules, share them in written form with players and parents, and enforce them judiciously.
- Build team spirit, pride, and tradition through actions, events, and recognition of player accomplishments.

CHAPTER 5 ESTABLISHING SEASON PLANS

The joy of coaching comes from watching your players execute the skills they have been taught. The mundane tasks such as collecting player and parent forms will never compare favorably with on-court teaching. However, every successful coach realizes that many important responsibilities must be addressed before match play begins each season. These early-season tasks include

- verifying medical clearance, insurance, and eligibility,
- scheduling matches,
- providing proper equipment,
- formulating a master plan,
- conditioning your athletes,
- preparing for player injuries or illnesses,
- scouting opponents (discussed in chapter 13),
- arranging transportation to matches, and
- helping players with their college plans.

MEDICAL SCREENING, INSURANCE, AND ELIGIBILITY

No athlete should be allowed to attend practice until she has provided you with a medical clearance form. A local medical clinic may provide your athletes with a reasonably priced alternative to a private physician's physical examination.

A related task is the securing of proof of insurance for each player. Some schools do not provide insurance coverage for any students. Thus it is the parents' responsibility to show the school system that their child has insurance coverage.

The example form shown in figure 5.1 (Parent and Player Agreement form) combines the certification of the athlete's health and insurance. This form also grants the school permission from the parents to transport the athlete and seek medical care in an emergency. These medical and insurance forms should be kept on file at the school.

Parent and Player Agreement

School Board of (Your District)
Hometown, Your State 12345

Sport _____ Grade level_____ School year_____

Name of student (please print)

_____

Address

_____

Home phone_____ Date of birth_____

Place of birth_____

Parent's work phone_____ Other emergency phone_____

This application to compete in interscholastic athletics in (your school district) is entirely voluntary on our part and is made with the understanding that we have not violated any of the eligibility rules and regulations of the State Association or (your activities association). It is also agreed that we will abide by all the rules set down by the School Board of (your district), the State Association, and the school.

The School Board of (your district) and its school principals and coaches desire that athletes and parents or guardians of athletes have a thorough understanding of the implications involved in a student participating in a voluntary extracurricular activity. For this reason, it is required that each student athlete in (your district), and his/her parent, parents, or guardian read, understand, and sign this agreement prior to the athlete being allowed to participate in any form of athletic practice or contests.

1. I/We, the undersigned, as parent, parents, or guardians give my/our consent for the athlete identified herein to engage in athletics as a representative of his/her school.

2. I/We will not hold (your district), anyone acting in its behalf, or the (your state) High School Activities Association responsible or liable for any injury occurring to the named student in the course of such athletic activities or such travel.

3. I/We understand that no portion of the insurance premium for the player identified herein is to be paid from school funds.

4. I/We understand that school officials will complete required accident insurance forms after which all claims under insurance policy or policies for injuries received while participating in school athletics shall be processed by the player and his/her parents or guardian through the company agent handling the player's insurance policy, and not through the school officials.

5. I/We hereby accept financial responsibility for athletic equipment lost by the athlete identified herein.

(continued)

Figure 5.1 Parent and player agreement form.

6. I/We authorize the school to transport the student to obtain, through a physician of its choice, any emergency medical care that may become reasonably necessary for the student in the course of such athletic activities or such travel. I/We also agree that the expenses for such transportation and treatment shall not be borne by the school district or its employees.

7. I/We accept full responsibility and hereby grant permission for my/our son/daughter to travel on any school-related trip by bus or car. This statement remains in effect until the end of this school year unless canceled by me/us in writing to the school.

8. I/We know the athlete identified herein is in good health and physically able to compete in interscholastic athletics and has had no past illness or injuries that would prevent him/her from participating in said activities.

9. All parties should understand that in all athletic competitions there is the possibility of serious injury or even death to a participant. Consequently, all athletes must have insurance.

10. I/We undersigned, as parent, parents, or guardian, hereby agree to provide insurance coverage for the athlete shown above as indicated below:

(Check one or more, as appropriate)

❑ a. Basic 24-hour student insurance available through the local school for the current year.

❑ b. Supplemental senior high football insurance available through the local school for the current school year. (This covers other athletic activity. Student will also need basic coverage under *a* above.)

❑ c. Insurance coverage by insurance policy #_____ written on the _____ _____ company. I/We do not desire additional coverage and will assume all liability and responsibility for injuries received by said player in athletic participation not covered by the above identified insurance policy.

_____   _____
Student's signature   Mother/guardian's signature

_____   _____
Date   Father/guardian's signature

State of (your state)
County of (your county)

The above has been sworn to and subscribed before me this _____ day of _____ in the year of our Lord 20__.

My commission expires _____
Notary Public State of (your state) at Large

_____

Examining physician's certificate

I hereby certify that I have, on this date shown below, examined _____ and that based on his/her past history given to me and my physical examination of the athlete, I find him/her to be physically able to compete in interscholastic sports.

_____   _____
Date of examination   Examining physician

In addition, coaches must carry with them a notarized list of each player on their squad. This list grants any medical facility the right to treat an injured athlete.

Athletic eligibility is the last piece of the puzzle a coach must understand when screening athletes. Individual states, school districts, or leagues may have different standards. Most standards are based on grade point average minimums and in-district residency requirements (for the parents or guardians of the athlete). You should check with your school athletic director to ensure that the candidates for your team are all eligible. Prospective team members should also know what those standards are before the school year begins so that they can make academic plans to meet the standards.

SCHEDULING MATCHES

Scheduling team matches can be very easy if your school belongs to a conference or quite difficult if your school is independent. Even with conference affiliations, you'll be responsible for scheduling some nonconference opponents. Work closely with your athletic director to put together a match schedule that will help your team develop as the season progresses.

Your scheduling philosophy may depend on the relative maturity of your current team. If you have a young team, it may be wise to schedule a few matches at home early in the season against teams that you have a chance of competing with successfully. Veteran teams need to be tested early and on the road against the best competition available.

Balance your schedule with teams that are weaker and stronger than your squad. Road matches develop mental toughness that will pay dividends during your conference or district championship play. Remember that your scheduling strategy should be aimed at peaking your team for championship play at the end of the year.

It is usually a good idea to schedule some informal scrimmages with local schools, alumni, or local adult players early in the season. This gives that first taste of competition outside of your immediate team. Next in line would be some matches against nonconference opponents. After a few tests outside the league, your team will be better prepared for the matches that count the most—those within your conference. Near the end of the season should find you in competition with your archrivals or other schools who are competing for playoff positions. Although it may be hard to predict the top teams before the season starts, the traditional powers should schedule each other near the end of the season. This will allow the excitement to build and provide maximum time for their teams to develop.

PROVIDING PROPER EQUIPMENT

Unlike many other varsity sports, tennis teams are often responsible for purchasing their own equipment, including rackets, shoes, and uniforms. Depending on the background of your players, you will likely find that they have several rackets and tennis shoes of their own. For these items, your only responsibility may be to make arrangements for players to secure a discount through local dealers. Once the season is under way, the major expense for many players is to replace racket strings that break or loosen up. Again, you might be able to strike a deal for your team with a local store or local stringer. Some teams have found success in purchasing a stringing machine for team use and allowing players to learn to string on their own. Over time, this can save a lot of money if you have a tradition of well-motivated players.

Team uniforms are the primary equipment you need to worry about and become involved with. Many leagues require team uniforms, and even if your school will not provide them, you need to make sure your players purchase team shirts to at least forge a team identity. Booster clubs can be helpful here in assisting with the cost. Some teams will want to add a sweatshirt or a warm-up depending on the season of play. You and the team captains should plan the team uniform after gathering some suggestions from the team. Of course, once the decision is made, all team members must participate by wearing the uniform as instructed, and it should be theirs to keep at the end of the season.

Maintaining Your Courts

If your courts are on the school's campus, take pride in their appearance and become actively involved in their care. Although school budgets are often tight, regular maintenance of athletic facilities is crucial to prevent major repairs from becoming inevitable. Tennis court surfaces should be regularly cleaned to keep them free of dirt and debris, which can get ground into the surface by constant play. Nets, center straps, and windscreens need to be inspected regularly and repaired at the first sign of wear and tear. Regular resurfacing and repainting of lines should be scheduled with the advice of a reputable local tennis court builder. Many school administrators assume that once built, tennis courts simply exist on their own. However, the reality is that most hard courts need to be resurfaced at least every three to five years as the surface wears from use and weather.

The overall court environment can be enhanced by regular maintenance of the shrubs and grass. Your team may need to help clean up the area after matches to relieve your school staff a bit. Clean rest rooms should be nearby and accessible for players and spectators.

Essential Equipment

The addition of a ball machine to your facility can be a terrific investment. This piece of equipment enables your players to do repetitive drills to master stroke production. A machine can free you up to be on the same side of the net as the player, and it can also allow players to work on their own for extended periods to master a specific skill.

A videotape replay system can be another important piece of equipment for your team. Advances in technology and reduced costs make this tool affordable for any program (perhaps with some help from a booster club). Nothing is better for making points clear to players than allowing them to see themselves on videotape! For technique work, the video is crucial. For strategy and tactics, it can help hammer points home. For mental toughness, you can show players their typical body language and behavior.

A video replay is also particularly helpful when checking player behavior after a point ends. You can evaluate the positiveness of their body posture, the relaxation technique used (if any), and the ritual approach before the next point begins. Jim Loehr's video *30 Second Cure* is a terrific model to use and compare to your players on tape.

At much more modest costs, you should purchase a variety of barriers and targets to use as teaching aids. For barriers, use small red cones that can be found in most sporting goods stores. Use colored ropes and hula hoops as targets for drills. You also need equipment that allows you to string a line three to five feet above the net to help players gauge the optimal height for ground strokes, passing shots, and lobs. This critical teaching aid can be purchased, or you can make it yourself with a few poles at the net posts and some cord to string between them.

For official singles play, the tennis net is set at three feet six inches high at the singles sideline. Since most courts are set for doubles play, the net is often too low for official singles play. You may want to have your industrial arts department construct some single sticks to hold up the net at the singles sideline. If your players will be going on to tournament play, this may be a factor. For normal high school team matches, most people simply use the normal doubles height for both singles and doubles.

FORMULATING A MASTER PLAN

You should begin formulating a course of direction for the upcoming spring tennis season several months in advance of the season. This helps you coordinate all the organizational details of coaching and develop a monthly, weekly, and daily "to do" list as the season approaches. Once you have a master plan in place, it is simple to make any necessary changes to the plan during the season.

Begin your master plan by listing all the general topics that you anticipate will need to be dealt with during the season. From creating a preseason handout that informs each player of the important dates for your tennis team to summarizing the season when it is completed, everything that you will encounter must be addressed and planned for. Make your list as inclusive as possible, but expect to add to it after each season. Here are some of the items that may appear on your list for formulating a master plan:

- Preseason handout describing the team philosophy and policies
- Stroke production (incorporated into master practice plan)
- Physical conditioning
- Singles match strategy and tactics
- Doubles pairings
- Doubles strategy and tactics
- Mental toughness
- Coaching advice during crossover games
- Prematch and postmatch procedures
- Letter to players and parents summarizing the season

By having a master plan, you ensure yourself and your team a more fun and productive tennis season!

This planning will result in a well thought-out blueprint that gives structure to your entire season. In the next chapter, you'll see how to develop a master practice plan, weekly plans, and the daily practice content. Over years of coaching, you'll find that the fundamentals of your master plan need little change. But you need to adapt each year's plan to the players on that team, the team schedule, the weather, and other things that are out of your control.

CONDITIONING YOUR ATHLETES

Tennis requires athletes to be in top condition. During the high school season, conditioning should be part of the daily practice schedule. You will need to develop a plan for conditioning and proper nutrition to prepare your players for the dual match season. Your plan should also help them peak physically at the end of the season for conference or district tournaments.

Physical Conditioning

Ideally, your prospective players should be developing their aerobic base by running distances of several miles. A two-mile run in under 12 minutes is a reasonable target for most high school players. This training will build players' cardiorespiratory endurance and allow them to last during long practices and matches. If your athletes report for the preseason out of shape, you will be forced to spend time developing aerobic endurance during the first few weeks of practice.

A cautionary note: Be careful not to spend all your time building physical conditioning at the risk of turning off some terrific tennis players. This can also put them at risk of chronic physical injuries (e.g., shin splints) that are likely to develop in athletes who are poorly conditioned before the season.

Early in the season, before dual matches have begun, you should stress anaerobic development by having your players do interval training, which includes a long sprint followed by rest and then another sprint. The anaerobic system is the one that supports normal tennis match play, where there may be extreme physical demand for three to six shots by each player, followed by a 20- to 30-second rest. Along with the conditioning, you should be helping players develop their quickness, agility, flexibility, and anticipation. Once players have achieved cardiovascular fitness, maintenance of this conditioning level is the goal. Thus, during the middle of the season, sprints are shortened and distance running reduced.

Many coaches have found that circuit training is a perfect way to maintain proper conditioning. During match season, your team should train at least twice a week. In circuit training, players use circuit index cards to maximize their individual conditioning potential.

Each player uses an index card with seven exercises listed on it (see figure 5.2). At the beginning of the season, you should have a test day when each player goes through the circuit and performs as many repetitions of each exercise as he can in the time limit (for example, as many step-ups or push-ups as possible in 45 and 20 seconds, respectively). The test day results establish a player's baseline for each exercise. During the season, the circuit amount for each exercise is half what the athlete scored on test day. As figure 5.2 shows, Murphy Payne's circuit will be composed of 27 step-ups, 15 push-ups, 20 sit-ups, 10 lunges, 43 line jumps, 26 knee-chest jumps, and a line run. (These numbers represent half the amounts he performed for each exercise on test day.)

On the days that the players circuit train, stations are set up on the court for each exercise on the index cards (see figure 5.3). The goal for each player is to complete each exercise's circuit amount (specified on his index card) in the shortest time possible. Each player goes through the seven exercises twice to complete a circuit. When a player finishes his seven-exercise circuit twice, he

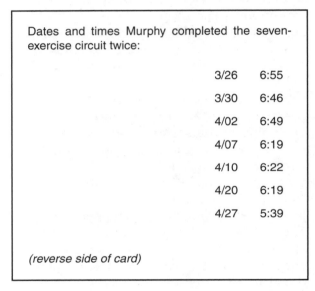

Player's name: Murphy Payne

	Test	Circuit
Step-ups (45 seconds)	53	27
Push-ups (20 seconds)	29	15
Sit-ups (30 seconds)	39	20
Lunges (30 seconds)	19	10
Line jumps (60 seconds)	95	43
Knee-chest jumps (30 seconds)	52	26
Line run twice across lines of 1 court (no test time)		

(front of card)

Dates and times Murphy completed the seven-exercise circuit twice:

3/26	6:55
3/30	6:46
4/02	6:49
4/07	6:19
4/10	6:22
4/20	6:19
4/27	5:39

(reverse side of card)

Figure 5.2 Sample circuit training card.

shouts "time." You should give the time in minutes and seconds, which the player will record (along with the date) on the back of the index card (see figure 5.2). Each player tries to better his circuit time as the season progresses.

The players' conditioning can be maintained at a proper level for dual matches through circuit training, intermediate distance sprints, and in-season strength (weight) training. The intermediate distance sprints typically include five 3-court sprints and three or four 440-yard sprints. The 3-court sprints are run at the beginning of practice and the more demanding 440s at the end of practice. As the championship part of the season approaches (two weeks before tournament play), you should fine-tune the players' conditioning by shortening the sprint distance and stopping the weightlifting. Shorter sprints include 1-court dashes and net-to-fence sprints.

Proper Nutrition

Adolescent tennis players often fail to realize the importance of proper nutrition in allowing them to compete successfully as athletes. Although the issues for boys and girls may differ, both genders need education, encouragement, and monitoring to ensure that they are getting the nutrients they need.

Eating and drinking the right things will decrease fatigue and cramps brought on by heat exhaustion. Hydrating by drinking plenty of water is essential. Remember that once a player is thirsty during play, it is too late. Players should begin hydrating by drinking six to eight 8-ounce glasses of water per day for the 48 hours leading up to the moment of competition.

Many high school athletes don't realize just how much nutrition can affect their ability to function properly during a strenuous season of practices and matches. Part of your role is to impress upon them the effect that the fuel they put into their body has on performance. Nutrient-rich food will help your players maintain good health and top performance. Players should try to get 60 percent of their calories from carbohydrates such as breads, grains, fruits, and vegetables. Protein, essential for building and repairing muscles, should comprise 15 percent of your players' diet. Protein-rich foods include chicken, fish, and beans. Your athletes should limit their fat intake to 25 percent of their daily total calories. Vegetable fat is less harmful than animal fat. A good nutrition game plan also provides your players with the vitamins and minerals their

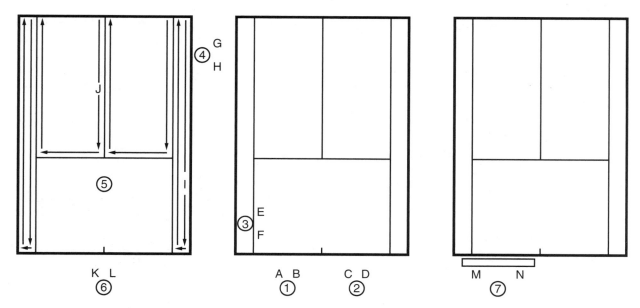

Figure 5.3 Example of circuit training on the court.

bodies need. An excellent resource is Nancy Clark's *Sports Nutrition Guidebook: Eating to Fuel Your Active Lifestyle.*

Nourishment prior to an event is a matter of personal preference. What works for one athlete might not work for another. The key is to eat foods that will prevent low blood sugar, help settle the stomach, and fuel the muscles (preferably far enough in advance to be stored as glycogen). Help your players discover which prematch foods serve them best. A daily diet of high-carbohydrate, low-fat meals will keep players' muscles fueled for action all the time, and they may not need to do anything special before a match. The day of a dual match or tournament play, an athlete should consume small amounts of food rather than big meals. This will provide the player with enough calories to supplement the built-up reserves without making her feel bogged down while playing.

Some athletes nearly starve themselves to maintain what they feel is the proper weight. Alarmingly, eating disorders among athletes continue to rise. If you suspect that one of your athletes has an eating disorder, don't ignore this threat to the player's health and well-being. Notify the athlete's parents or guardians and work with them to get the

athlete professional help. Be supportive and patient, for the healing process may be long and arduous. Another resource to add to your coaching library is *Helping Athletes with Eating Disorders* by Thompson and Sherman.

Off-Season Conditioning Work

The high school season is completed in three months. You should encourage your players to work on their physical conditioning during the off-season in order to prepare for the year ahead. After a period of rest and recuperation from the intensity of the past competitive season, physical training should begin anew with a different emphasis from preseason or in-season work. Strength training in particular should be accelerated in the off-season.

Some of your athletes will ask for your advice on how to prepare for tournaments during the off-season. Periodization, which simply means cycles of activity leading up to tournament play after some time off, has become an accepted training concept in tennis circles. The cycle of periodization outlined in appendix A may be helpful for your players to follow in the off-season.

Strength Training

The era of the underdeveloped tennis player is over. A quick look at the physical specimens on the professional tour will convince you that tennis players have learned that strength and power are essential to compete on the tennis court. Tennis doesn't require a bodybuilder's physique, so your strength program should stress building muscular endurance, not muscle mass. Appendix B illustrates a sample off-season (three days per week) and in-season (two days per week) strength-training program.

Progress in strength training is made in the off-season. When an athlete can perform two to three sets of 12 to 15 repetitions per exercise, it's time to increase the weight by 5 to 10 pounds. By contrast, in-season weight training is a maintenance program. Generally, during the season you should ask players not to increase the weight they are lifting for each exercise. If doing 10 to 15 repetitions starts to get too easy, the player should do as many reps as possible on the second or third set.

Proper strength training that accentuates muscle groups used in tennis provides players with strength and power. There are three major muscle groups frequently used in tennis. When it comes to strength training, tennis players should build from the ground up. Begin with the lower body. Push-off by the legs of a tennis player is accomplished primarily by these muscle groups: soleus, gastrocnemius, quadriceps, hamstrings, and gluteals. A second group of muscles provides trunk rotation for ground strokes and the serve and overhead. The muscle groups that a player uses to accomplish these tasks are the obliques and spinal erectors. The upper body muscle groups that help a player execute a stroke vary with the stroke, but players should be sure to train the pectorals, upper latissimus, rhomboids, middle trapezius, deltoids, triceps, biceps, shoulder external and internal rotators, and the wrist flexors. Strength and endurance, combined with speed and flexibility (gained from plyometric exercises and sprints), result in a properly conditioned tennis player. You can find details on strength training in the USTA publication *Strength Training for Tennis*. (See the resources section on page 193 for ordering information.)

Flexibility Training

A physical trainer, perhaps one on your school staff, can help you and your players understand the importance of maintaining and improving flexibility along with strength and endurance. Flexibility simply means the range of motion around the joints. A lack of flexibility can lead to muscle strains and tears, chronic soreness, and other overuse injuries. Lack of flexibility can also limit tennis technique due to a tight shoulder on the serve or tight hamstrings that affect movement.

You must be thoroughly familiar with the latest information on stretching and flexibility training. Generally, an athlete must warm up before stretching by performing light calisthenics or light jogging. Static stretching is recommended during the cool-down period after physical activity, while dynamic stretching, which may include tennis-specific movements, is generally recommended before actual play begins. Ask the physical training professionals at your school for help in this area and question them on the latest thinking you may hear about at coaching clinics.

PROVIDING MEDICAL CARE

Although few tennis players incur serious injuries on the court, an emergency plan for proper and immediate care of an injured athlete should be discussed with the athletic director to make sure it meets the standards. As a coach, preparing for emergencies can save your athletes valuable practice time and may keep you from being liable if litigation should occur.

Sprains and strains are common afflictions for any sports program but by treating them immediately you can reduce the risk of chronic injury.

At most high schools, every coach is responsible for a written emergency plan that adheres to the guidelines set by the athletic director. This plan states what will happen in the event of a serious injury. You should go over the plan with your team at the beginning of every season. The major considerations of the plan should include who will stay with the injured athlete, who will go to the nearest phone, and what the other athletes on the team will do. It's a good idea to do a "dress rehearsal" of the emergency plan with your team.

Most tennis programs will not have an athletic trainer present at practice. Thus, you will probably have to take care of minor injuries. Assemble a first aid kit for use at practice and matches. Your first aid kit should contain the items listed in figure 5.4.

In the case of a sprained ankle, which occurs quite frequently on the court, the availability of ice is critical. You should know where you can get ice so that it can be applied immediately. For a sprained ankle, ice, elevation, and compression of the injured limb are critical to suppress swelling. The quicker you treat these minor sprains, the sooner your athlete will be ready to return to the court.

Your school likely has a relationship with certain medical doctors in the community. If not, find a physician who has children at the school or an interest in athletics. The team doctor can get your athletes in for an office visit at a moment's notice. A strained back, pulled muscle, or torn ligament can be examined and diagnosed before it becomes chronic.

✚ Sample First Aid Kit ✚

- A list of emergency phone numbers
- Bandage scissors
- Plastic bags for crushed ice
- 4-inch and 6-inch elastic wraps
- Triangular bandages
- Sterile gauze pads—3-inch and 4-inch squares
- Saline solution for eyes
- Contact lens case
- Mirror
- Penlight
- Tongue depressors
- Cotton swabs
- Butterfly strips

- Bandage strips—assorted sizes
- Alcohol
- Benodine
- Antibacterial soap
- First aid cream
- Tape adherent
- Tape remover
- 1-1/2–inch white athletic tape
- Prewrap
- Sterile gauze rolls
- Insect sting kit
- Safety pins and elastic bands
- Disposable rubber gloves
- Mouth shield (for CPR)

Figure 5.4 Sample first aid kit.

TRAVELING TO MATCHES

Your school will have a transportation policy in place, and it is up to you to understand it thoroughly and abide by it. If you violate school policy, you will be putting yourself and your athletes at unnecessary risk.

Most schools try to provide transportation to away matches in school buses or vans driven by experienced professional drivers. This is the optimal situation since it frees you, your players, and their parents from the stress and responsibility of driving (and dealing with potential road emergencies or problems).

If you have to rely on parents for transportation, be sure to have them fill out the proper liability forms. These forms verify their insurance coverage and indicate their acceptance of the liability they will assume for your players.

Many teams travel together to amateur tournaments in the off-season. During the high school season, you may want to plan at least one away match that will require an overnight stay. These weekend tournaments and in-season trips provide valuable experience for adolescents. Bonds that are impossible to develop at home are formed among players living together over the weekend.

Seniors and other experienced letter winners can be given the responsibility of schooling the younger players in proper travel etiquette. Players should be reminded to be courteous in restaurants and hotels and at the playing site. They need to be well aware that they are representing their school and their team.

DISCUSSING COLLEGE PLANS

One of the most important decisions players will make while under your tutelage is choosing a college. This choice should always be made by the player and his family. However, you may be able to provide wise counsel if playing college tennis is important to one of your players.

During the years that players spend with you, you should have a reasonably good idea of their expectations for college. One of your responsibilities is to describe to them what might be expected of them on a college team at various levels of competition. Some top players will be attracted to very competitive college teams and may even qualify for a tennis scholarship. Other players may just be looking for a Division III level team that will allow them to compete without the pressure and time demands of a Division I program.

You should help your players judge the level of college tennis at which they have the best chance of being successful. Nothing is more disappointing for an eager freshman than being cut from a varsity team that is important to him. Nor is it any easier to take when a player makes the squad but is never quite good enough to crack the starting lineup. For kids who really want to play college tennis, help them understand the competitive level that suits them. You can do that by watching college matches, talking with coaches, and asking for advice from local teaching professionals.

Because you will often become a trusted adviser and teacher, many of your players will ask you for recommendations. Like other teachers in the school, you need to be comfortable making a positive recommendation in order to accept the request, and you must then be sure to complete it in a timely fashion for each student.

SUMMARY

Keep these things in mind as you plan for the season:

- Make sure all athletes are physically eligible.
- Work with your athletic director to provide a challenging match schedule that will allow your team to be successful.
- Provide your athletes with safe, proper equipment.
- Formulate a master plan for conditioning, nutrition, strength training, and flexibility training.
- Provide a plan for immediate medical attention should it become necessary in practice or during a match.
- Set a travel plan for away matches and establish rules of conduct for your athletes on the road.
- Work with athletes to continue their participation beyond the high school or summer league level.

CHAPTER 6 PLANNING AND CONDUCTING PRACTICES

There is a relatively new approach to coaching players that involves teaching aspects of the game in the following order: (1) the object of the sport, (2) the strategies and tactics of play, and (3) the skills to achieve strategic objectives. This approach is typically referred to as "game-based coaching."

GAMED-BASED COACHING

Game-based coaching reverses the usual learning sequence, but if you try it, you'll discover some terrific benefits. Instead of learning skills, strategy, and tactics and *then* playing the game, game-based learning allows your players to play the game, learn the strategy, tactics, and skills as they're playing, and become more complete players as they continue playing.

Children learn to play games by simply trying them. Rules are learned along the way, but the very first thing they learn is the object of the game. Maybe the object is to avoid being hit as in dodgeball, to avoid being caught as in a game of tag, or to complete a sequence of perfect jumps as in hopscotch. Once they understand the game, they quickly figure out

the best strategy for success by watching other players, testing their own theories, and adjusting their movements. The beauty is that they figure it out on their own by just trying it. This method of learning is often referred to as the "self-discovery" method.

Coaches often make the mistake of teaching people to play a game by having them spend the majority of practice time learning the skills first. Endless hours and days of repetition of skills may produce better skill performance, but it is soooo boring. And perhaps more important, people never get to experience the thrill of figuring out how to play for themselves.

Game-based teaching offers an alternative approach that will create new excitement in practice for your players, and it's likely you'll all have more fun. Gone will be the hours spent on convincing and cajoling players to change their technique to conform to your optimal picture of good mechanical form. Your players will also become natural, savvy players of the game of tennis more quickly.

Strategy and Tactics

The terms *strategy* and *tactics* are often confused or used interchangeably in coaching circles. Making some distinction between the two may help you understand the game-based approach to learning to play tennis. The terms have been used for centuries in warfare: Strategy is the overall plan for the battle, while tactics may represent the specific troop movements employed to achieve a particular strategy.

In tennis, an overall strategy may simply be to keep the ball in play and make the fewest errors possible. The tactics may vary, and they could include hitting higher over the net, hitting with less pace, using more spin, or aiming well inside the lines. Any or all of these tactics will help achieve the strategy of reducing errors.

The following are examples of typical tennis strategies for singles and doubles play:

Strategies for Singles Play

- Keep the ball in play
- Move your opponent side to side and up and back
- Hit to the open court
- Attack a weaker shot or use your strongest shot

Strategies for Doubles Play

- Hit down the middle
- Angle the ball away
- Play to the weaker player
- Use your strengths

The Four-Step Approach

Game-based coaching uses four distinct steps in the learning process:

1. Have players play the game or a modified game.
2. Stop play and ask the players to evaluate their success.
3. Structure practice of the skills that need to improve.
4. Return to playing the game.

In **step 1,** if you ask players to play a modified game (which is often called a lead-up game),

be clear about the strategic objective. These games should mirror actual game situations that are typically part of a point. For example, you could ask them to simply rally the ball in singles without making errors.

In **step 2,** you ask the players to evaluate their level of success. If many rallies ended after just a few shots, you might ask them why. They may respond with theories about the pace of their shots, the height over the net, the position on the court, or inconsistent technique. Once you've agreed on the cause of their errors, it is up to you to construct a drill for **step 3** that will improve their skill or choice of shots. This self-discovery method of learning involves your players in the process in a way that helps foster their independence as players and clearly requires their full attention. Because they have taken ownership of their learning, you will no longer have to constantly remind them of corrections they should make.

If you and the players agree that stroke technique is the problem, then you may need to start with some simply fed balls that allow the players to improve technique. As they progress, you'll want to gradually introduce a rally that is more like a game situation and assess their ability to reproduce acceptable technique.

Step 4 is to put them back into the rallying situation to see whether the adjustments you made have transferred to the game situation.

Selecting Game Situations

The games you use to teach your players should be based on the typical patterns of play that are used at all levels of tennis. In singles, for example, you can create a game where the server begins the point by serving to the outside of the service box to pull the receiver wide of the court. Once the return is made, the server has the option on the third shot of play to hit to the opposite side of the court to make the opponent run. If the receiver has anticipated that response, the server may choose to hit behind the receiver into the area from which she has come. In either case, the play stops after the 3 shots to force players to concentrate on just those first shots in a point.

You may invent competitive games like this by taking points or parts of points and assigning point values for success. In the example, the server could receive a point for hitting to the appropriate area based on the receiver's position. First player who reaches a score of 10 is the winner. These games are fun, they easily motivate players, and they transfer well to actual tennis play.

Depending on the skill level of your players, you may need only a few modified games for the typical patterns of play they are able to execute. A good way to choose the best patterns is to watch carefully for the typical patterns used in match play by your team and opposing teams. Of course, viewing videotape of professional players or taking a trip to watch a pro tournament will also reveal a variety of patterns. Watching a college match as a team can be equally effective. The temptation to imitate professional or college level players without the stroke technique to perform at that level is something you'll have to caution your players about.

If you are interested in learning more about the game-based approach to coaching, some helpful resources from the United States Tennis Association are available through Human Kinetics. These include the books *Tennis Tactics: Pattern of Play* and *Coaching Youth Tennis* and the video *The Games Approach to Teaching Tennis*. (See the resources section on page 193 for ordering information.).

Throughout the world, and particularly in Europe, the game-based approach is widely used and has been for some time. This approach is also used in other sports in the United States, and books and videotapes have been produced on how to use this approach in sports such as soccer, baseball, and basketball (all available through Human Kinetics). You may be uncomfortable at first using an unfamiliar style of coaching, especially since you probably weren't coached that way. Try it a little at a time, perhaps just one day per week. Experiment with it, and as you and

your players gain confidence in it, you'll likely look for more ways to integrate it into your practice.

Don't make the mistake of thinking that game-based coaching means you've abandoned working on tennis skills and technique. Not so at all. It simply means "playing the game or points first" and then working on the techniques used to achieve strategic objectives.

PLANNING PRACTICES

Preparation for the season must begin long before the first day of practice. Managing practice time efficiently and effectively will help your players improve their tennis and fulfill their potential. You should work from a master practice plan that varies little from year to year, add more detail and specifics in a weekly plan, and finally flesh out the schedule for each day in a daily practice schedule.

Most high school tennis seasons vary in length from 12 to 16 weeks. It's probably helpful for you to divide the season into three distinct units: the preseason, regular season, and championship season. The activities and priorities within each of these periods can change significantly, and separating them will help you focus practice sessions on specific instructional objectives.

The preseason is the time to focus on player fitness, including strength, power, flexibility, and endurance. Tennis technique should be evaluated, although major changes in style should be done in the off-season, not the preseason. Principles of percentage tennis need to be stressed in classroom sessions, drill situations, and simulated match play. This is the time for your players to make sure they understand and can apply the basic strategic concepts of both singles and doubles.

During the regular season, you need to develop a maintenance program for physical training (see chapter 5). Running should be for short distances, with emphasis on footwork, balance, and explosiveness. Emergency "first aid" (this is a typical coaching term) should be applied to tennis shots or strokes that cause problems in competitive matches. A major emphasis during this time is on dealing with the pressure of competition (winning and losing). You should also help players concentrate on performance goals rather than the outcome of matches and help them improve their skill in planning and executing a specific game plan.

During the championship season, you should shorten the length of practices and allow more time for rest. Your players should train physically by eating correctly, stretching often, and tapering their training load. This is not the time to improve or add strokes or skills; instead, players need to maximize what they can accomplish with the skills they already possess. Mental training skills and the competitive skills used in match play should be emphasized to help players cope with the excitement and pressure of important matches.

An overview of a comprehensive fitness plan is shown in figure 6.1. As you move through the year, different aspects of physical training should receive emphasis to allow players to peak physically during the weeks of championship play.

Special Circumstances

Planning for the tennis season is influenced by the time of year the matches are played. The time demands on your players may vary, too, depending on whether the school year is just beginning or ending. Another major factor for you to consider is the effect of cold, windy weather on preseason practice and early spring matches.

Practice mental preparedness with your players to help ease the competitive pressure of the championship season.

	Energy fitness[1]	Weeks	Muscular fitness[2]
Off-season			
Beginning	Aerobic training	•	
Middle		•	Strength
Preseason (4-6 weeks)	Anaerobic threshold	1	
		2	
		3	Endurance
		4	
		5	
		6	
Competitive (1st 4 weeks)	Anaerobic training	1	
		2	
		3	Power
		4	
Competitive (2nd 4 weeks)	Speed training	1	
		2	
		3	Speed
		4	
Championship (2-3 weeks)	Tapering	1	
		2	Tapering
		3	

[1]Energy fitness is the ability to store and use fuels to power muscular contractions. It includes both aerobic and anaerobic energy systems along with the respiratory, cardiovascular, and endocrine (hormonal) systems.

[2]Muscular fitness includes flexibility, strength, endurance, power, and speed. It also involves the nervous system that controls muscular contractions.

Figure 6.1 Sample fitness plan.

Fall Play

When there are only enough courts to accommodate either the boys' or girls' team, typically the girls' season is in the fall and the boys' in the spring. A fall season may require a preseason practice schedule in mid-August before school starts (similar to that of the football, soccer, or cross country teams). Two-a-day practices can be exceedingly effective if handled correctly, and the opportunity for your players to concentrate on tennis before school starts can produce terrific improvement.

The two-a-day practice pattern usually includes skill work and conditioning in the morning session when temperatures are cooler. Game situations or challenge match play is best in the heat of the afternoon or maybe early evening.

Cold Weather Play

Unfortunately, all tennis teams don't have the luxury of warm, pleasant weather in which to practice or compete. The typical northern-climate team that plays in the spring will find the weather just turning nice at season's end. How then can you get a team ready to play good tennis?

First, you have to be creative in seeking indoor court time, even if the hours are a bit unusual. Many club owners are glad to help school teams if coaches agree to practice times like 10 P.M. to midnight, 6 A.M. to 8 A.M., or on a weekend night. Modest court charges can be paid by your players (maybe two to five dollars each), a booster club, one generous donor, or through fund-raising events.

Second, if your school has a gymnasium, use it for conditioning, footwork and movement drills, practice against the wall, and volley and overhead practice. If the gym has a weight room, you can also teach your players the basics of strength training for tennis. Players should *not* practice returning serve or ground strokes on a wooden gym floor. Balls come off a wooden floor so fast that playing them off a bounce is frustrating and will likely produce poor stroking habits.

Third, use a classroom to teach mental training skills and the fundamental strategies and tactics of percentage tennis. Show videos and films of great matches (including high school matches involving past players) and spend time on team and individual goal setting.

Fourth, any day when the temperature is 32 degrees Fahrenheit or above, take the team out to the courts. Plan your practice activities to be vigorous and continuous, and insist on layered clothing for players and arctic wear for the coaches. Shorten the length of practice and end with some significant physical training before the players head for the showers.

If you blend indoor court time, gymnasium workouts, classroom sessions, and outdoor practices as weather permits, the preseason can be a very productive time. Make the best of your conditions and resources, and help your players enjoy the experience.

THE MASTER PLAN

The master practice plan (see the sample in figure 6.2) provides a blueprint for your tennis season and ensures consistency from year to year. You'll need to adjust your master plan a little each year to meet the needs of your players, but the plan should help you make sure nothing is left out when preparing for a season.

The natural flow from the master plan is a weekly plan that can be adjusted depending on the progress of your team, the results of competitive play, the weather, and other school events or community happenings. See the sample weekly plan in figure 6.3.

Daily practice plans (see the sample in figure 6.4) give you the opportunity to adjust each day and set aside the time you need for each component of practice. Be sure to include variety from day to day, frequently change practice partners and opponents, and allow time for some fun every practice. How much time you spend with a given player will depend somewhat on how she has been impacted by the outcome of recent matches and on how successful she has been in working toward the performance goals you agreed on.

Sample Master Practice Plan

	Technique	Physical training	Mental training
Preseason			
Week 1	Control of ball	Aerobic	Intrinsic motivation
	Percentage tennis	Endurance	Managing mistakes
	Baseline play	Flexibility	
	Ladder play	Strength	
Week 2	Midcourt play	Endurance	Goal setting
	Net play	Flexibility	Performance versus
	Defensive play	Strength	outcome goals
	Ladder play	Footwork skills	
Week 3	Consistency and accuracy	Endurance	Breathing techniques
	Offensive play	Strength	Watching the ball
	Develop weapon	440s	Review goals
	Ladder play	Movement skills	
Week 4	Review fundamentals	Endurance	Develop game plan
	Practice style of play	Strength	Handling line calls
	Doubles principles	220s	Sportsmanship
	Doubles positions	Movement skills	

(continued)

Figure 6.2 Master practice plan.

	Technique	Physical training	Mental training
Competitive first half			
Week 5	Serve and return	Strength	Match play behavior
	Serve and volley	Movement skills	Relaxation techniques
	Doubles receiving	Nutrition basics	Pace of play
	Stroke first aid		Doubles teamwork
Week 6	Doubles serving	Strength	Between-point behavior
	Poaching and signals	Agility drills	Coping statements
	Net play review	Hydration	Concentration skills
	Modified set play		Doubles teamwork
Week 7	Holding serve	Circuit training	Percentage play
	Breaking serve	Agility drills	Tiebreaker strategy
	Work on strengths	Sprints	Postmatch emphasis
Week 8	Patterns of play	Circuit training	Review performance goals
	Style of play	Movement skills	Coping with winning or losing
	Work on weaknesses	Sprints	
Competitive second half			
Week 9	Review baseline skills	Power	Relaxation training
	Consistency	Speed	Pressure drills
	Doubles skills		
Week 10	Review defensive play	Power	Concentration skills
	Serve and return skills	Speed	Pressure drills
	Work on strengths		
Week 11	Review midcourt play	Begin tapering	Between-point behavior
	Practice weapon	Movement drills	Review performance goals
	Play singles sets		
Week 12	Review net play	Rest and diet	Emphasize positive attitude
	Serve and volley skills	Movement drills	Build confidence
	Doubles skills		
	Play doubles sets		
Championship season			
Week 13	Review style of play	Continue tapering	Review game plan
	Review percentage tennis	Rest and diet	Review relaxation skills
	Practice strengths	Shorten practices	Deal with pressure
Week 14	Review doubles principles	Movement drills	Have fun
	Stroke first aid	Take time off	Emphasize teamwork
Week 15	Emphasize consistency	Rest and diet	Have fun
	Practice strengths	Quickness drills	Emphasize teamwork

Sample Weekly Plan

Week 5 out of 14

Day	Technique	Physical training	Mental training
Monday	Serve and return First serve percent	Sprints	Emphasize pace of play
Tuesday	Patience at baseline Doubles receiving team	Competitive sprints	Emphasize posture and coping statements
Wednesday	Match day		
Thursday	Stroke first aid	Fun ball skills	Discuss match results
Friday	Play points Tiebreaker matches	Light running and stretching	Relaxation concentration and pressure drills
Saturday	Match day		

Figure 6.3   Weekly plan.

Sample Daily Practice Plan

Week 2, day 2   *Equipment—Balls and targets*

Time	Activity	Key points	Drills
10 minutes	General warm-up Jog and stretch	Seniors lead	Basic 10 stretches Jog around 3 courts (3 times)
10 minutes	On-court warm-up	Use *one* ball	Hit all shots, especially serves
20 minutes	Review ground strokes	Emphasize consistency Height and depth	F to F, B to B Figure eight
30 minutes	Teach and practice approach shots	Use targets Underspin, down-the-line Do forehand and backhand Emphasize *depth*	Start with feed Add volley after approach off short ball
30 minutes	Competitive practice Modified game situation	Serve underhand Receiver must approach and follow to net	Weak serve
15 minutes	Conditioning	Record scores and times	Push-ups, sit-ups, and mile run
5 minutes	Cool-down	Announcements	

Note: Remind new players to turn in copy of birth certificates to AD by tomorrow . . . or else no practice!

Figure 6.4   Daily plan.

SETTING THE PRACTICE SCHEDULE

Short practices of high intensity and focus are far superior to long practices that drag on endlessly. Generally, you should plan for two-hour practices, perhaps a bit longer early in the season and certainly shorter near the end of the year. Gradually decreasing the length of practice helps keep players fresh and eager throughout the season. Your goal is to have your players at their peak for the end-of-season championship play.

CONDUCTING PRACTICES

Once you have established a seasonal, weekly, and daily practice plan, the key to success is making every practice fun. To do this, listen to and observe your players. Keep your drills and instruction moving and, above all, interesting. After a long day at school, your players' attention span will be limited, even for an enjoyable extracurricular activity. One foolproof way to stimulate interest is to add a competitive element to each drill. You can cater to your players' competitive spirit by constantly inventing new individual and team competitions to practice the skills necessary for match success. Also, don't neglect to use some competition against their own previous best scores, records, or times rather than just against the other players. When a practice appears to be dragging, don't hesitate to move on to another drill, even when the skill they're working on is being performed badly. Just plan to come back to that skill another time or day.

Players Get to Choose the Game

All players have their favorite games and drills that they love to do (and others that are not as much fun for them). A wise coach asks for player cooperation through most of the practice to work on things she believes need attention, but she always holds out the opportunity for "players' choice" near the end of practice if a good effort was put forth early. It's hard for you to predict what drills or games players will choose as their favorites from year to year, but they will always have them. The whole team doesn't have to agree on one drill either; let them choose a partner and do what they want.

Player Preparation

On normal school days, practices should start 30 minutes to 1 hour after classes are dismissed. This gives players time to see a teacher for extra help, get a homework assignment they missed, or change clothing and have a snack before practice begins.

Begin practice with several slow laps around the courts to raise the body temperature and begin the warm-up. Then all the players should form a circle and stretch the major muscle groups. After you have taught the team the proper procedures, you can appoint different exercise leaders for each week or for each day's warm-up and stretch.

The USTA has recently published a new guide to warming up and warming down which includes information on recommended dynamic and static stretching. Contact USTA publications department noted in the resources section (pages 193-194) for information on how to order.

Recent research in stretching technique has indicated that dynamic stretching is most important before play while static stretching is beneficial during the cool-down to prevent muscle stiffness and soreness. A dynamic stretch is simply a movement that simulates those movements used in the sport. This type of stretch will prepare an athlete's muscles to perform those movements repetitively after a warm-up. Typical tennis moves that can be simulated include agility moves that emphasize balance, quick shuffle steps, stretch and reach moves, and jumps for an overhead smash. Too much static stretching before play may slow player reactions, so the trend is shifting toward these dynamic moves.

Whether they are practicing, playing a competitive match, or playing for fun on the weekend, your players should get in the habit of warming up and stretching any time they step onto the tennis court. By helping them form this habit, you may prevent an unnecessary injury, especially in cold climates.

Take the Time

Late one fall afternoon, as the sun was setting, the JV players were patiently waiting to play once courts became available after the varsity match. Finally, it was Kathleen's turn. She rushed onto the court, hit a few ground strokes, and began her match without any warm-up or stretching. Within 10 minutes, the match had to be stopped and Kathleen had to be taken to a doctor for treatment. The result was a torn muscle—and a cast from hip to ankle for six weeks!

At the beginning of practice, let players visit with each other about events at school that day. If you want practice to be fun and players to feel a sense of camaraderie, you've got to give them time to chat, mingle, and enjoy being part of the team. Once the stretching is over, though, it's down to business.

Warm-Up

After the stretching period, it's time to set the tone for the day's practice. Begin by outlining the skills for the day and how you expect the team to work on them. Demonstrate what you expect for each activity rather than just describing it, and encourage any questions. If players truly listened, you shouldn't have to repeat directions once the drills or games begin. For players who have trouble listening, a few times sitting in the bleachers watching their teammates will help them pay closer attention in the future.

Next, players pair off and warm up on the court. This time is frequently misused. How often have you watched players try to impress a teammate by how hard they can smack each shot? During warm-up, shots should be kept under control as rhythm and timing are established. Wild, aimless hitting results in players wasting their time chasing balls. It can help to give each pair only one ball and to limit the total warm-up time to 5 to 10 minutes. Encourage them to hit all the shots at about half speed right back to their partners. The object should be to maximize the number of hits made in the 5 minutes.

Experienced players are accustomed to the following warm-up sequence:

1. Both players rally ground strokes from the baseline on their side of the court.
2. One plays at the net (volleys and overheads) and the other at the baseline (passing shots and lobs). After a few minutes, they switch positions.
3. Players alternate serving and returning.

Skill-Building Time

Skill-building time is the most critical time of the practice and is your chance to be a master teacher. This part of practice should begin with players reviewing the skills or shot combinations learned previously. This review time is often overlooked by coaches who are anxious to move on to new challenges. However, skills that are not constantly reviewed in practice will tend to break down under the pressure of competition. Set the habits by repetition, and as players demonstrate competence, step up the challenge a bit. For example, if you've worked on keeping ground strokes deep in the court, make a rule that all shots must land beyond the service line or the hitter loses the point.

If you are willing to try game-based coaching, this is the time to introduce a strategy or tactics within a game situation. As the players struggle to implement the tactical objective, you will likely find it necessary to isolate the specific skills needed and to work on improving those skills. Of course, if you have not bought into the game-based approach, it is normal to move directly into working on various tennis skills.

When introducing or practicing new skills or concepts, the topics are easy to choose because they naturally flow from your master plan and weekly plan. Usually, you will want to limit this time to 20 to 30 minutes of intense work on just one new skill. That is enough challenge for one day, and short, intensive work periods produce more efficient learning.

After a while, you may want to add the element of competition into drills to stimulate interest. Here are some ways to do this:

- Divide the squad you're working with into two teams by having different players choose sides each day. This is a perfect time to work on positive encouragement of teammates as players cheer on the members of their pickup team. Highlight any skill you want, such as the split-step and volley. After the player split steps, feed her a volley. If the volley lands crosscourt behind the service line, she has scored a point for her team. The teams try to win two out of three games to 10 points. You are the scorekeeper who awards points. Don't hesitate to stop the drill and point out deficiencies in technique as the drill progresses. Many variations of games can be devised, and you can structure the games for any skill level.

- Competitive situations can also be used very successfully in drills for individual players. Combine the split-step and volley sequence with an approach shot. Ask the player to hit an approach shot down the line from midcourt with cones or a rope as a visual target. After the player has hit the approach shot successfully, feed him a volley that must be hit crosscourt. The two-ball sequence of approach shot and volley earns the player 1 point. When one player earns 10 points, he moves on to the next court and a new activity. Players stay at the task until they achieve success. If you are feeding during the drill, adjust the difficulty of the feed to the player so that weaker players aren't stuck in one place all day.

- A third scenario would involve timing the drill. Using the approach shot, split-step, volley sequence again as an example, divide your players into two groups on opposite sides of the net. Feed a midcourt ball from the side of the court to player A, who must come in and hit an approach shot. Player B on the opposite side of the net tries to pass. The ball is played out until an error occurs. If player B passes player A cleanly, both players switch sides of the net. (If the passing shot is unsuccessful, the players remain on their side of the net and wait in line for their next turn.) Using a 10-minute time limit, all players caught on the side of the net where the passing shots are attempted suffer a penalty decided on before the drill begins. The level of intensity will increase dramatically as you inform the group that only 1 minute remains in the drill!

The final skill-building session in daily practice should be spent perfecting prescribed patterns of play, either by using modified play situations, or by simply playing normal sets with specific objectives agreed on for each player. Your players will look forward to this part of practice because it's fun to play games; however, you should watch out for the frustration that comes from their inability to

Eat to Win

One of the favorite activities of adolescent boys is eating. In an effort to get the boys to train harder, one coach came up with a foolproof contest. The team was divided up into two equal groups based on the preseason fitness test results. Then each group had eight weeks to train and improve their scores. The team that showed the most improvement would be the guests of the losers at a favorite local all-you-can-eat restaurant. The competition was a great motivator combining peer pressure and a tangible reward. It became a team tradition that lasted six years before a new group came up with a better (or at least different) idea.

transfer the new skills and strategies they've learned in drills to game situations.

Early in the season, expect players to focus on sound technique and strategy during play, and encourage them to try new ideas or modify ineffective playing styles. As you move into match play, it's better to emphasize match play skills and tactics and to reduce the emphasis on technique unless there is an obvious problem, such as late preparation. Having too many objectives will simply confuse any competitor, so try to focus match play practice on the one or two factors that will produce quick improvement and success in competition.

If you have players who compete in singles only or doubles only, practice plans and modified game situations should be specific to the skills they need. On the other hand, if your team members play both singles and doubles during the season, be sure to devote adequate time to the skills of each game.

Some examples of modified game situations or match play follow:

- Players are allowed only one serve. This exposes the lack of a dependable second serve.
- Players must attack the net any time the opponent hits a short ball. If they don't attack the net, they lose the point. This encourages getting to the net.
- Points count only after three shots are hit: serve, return, and first ground stroke. This helps players get into points without foolish errors too early in the point.
- Award two points any time the winning shot is hit from the net. This encourages attacking play.
- On all second serves, the receiver must chip and charge to put pressure on the server.
- Players lose the point if they try to change direction of the ball when standing behind the baseline. Instead, they should aim high and deep, and send the ball back in the direction from which it came.

- Encourage players to open up the court by hitting wide to one side with a short angle and following with a deep shot to the opposite side.
- Ask players to imitate a particular style of play—perhaps that of a famous player—and force the opponent to counter that style.
- Be sure to add pressure to some practice play so that players get accustomed to handling their nervousness in real matches. (Some ideas for how to do this follow.)

Here are some ideas for adding pressure to the play in practice:

1. Play best-of-three tiebreakers.
2. Use audience pressure by gathering teammates to watch the final game of a set.
3. Divide teammates into two teams and ask them to cheer on their assigned player.
4. Offer a tangible reward for winning the set, such as the chance to practice the next day with your team's top two players.
5. Ask one player to serve the entire set, and make it known that you expect him to win.
6. Ask one player to serve underhand, and make it known that you expect the opponent to win.
7. Start every game with the server behind 15-30.
8. Play no-ad scoring. (When a game is tied at 3-3, or the first deuce, the receiver chooses the side of the court to receive on, and the next point wins the game.)
9. Play handicapped scoring so that the player who trails in the set score is awarded a point in the succeeding game—one for every point behind. Example: Player A leads player B in games 2-0. In the third game, player B starts the game with a 30-love

10. Invite a team alumnus, local college player, or good adult player to practice. Let your young players cope with wily veterans in practice so that they will be ready for anything.

Physical Conditioning

Every practice should include some time for physical training near the end. Players need to improve strength, speed, power, flexibility, and endurance. You should vary the length of time and the stress level for this training based on the time of year and the schedule for matches.

It makes sense to schedule conditioning at the end of practice because you will usually not want to stress the athletes until just before you are ready to send them on their way (allowing for a sufficient cool-down period after the conditioning work). If you demand heavy physical work before skill work, players will become too fatigued to concentrate on skills, and their muscles won't respond.

Once in a while you might want to tire your players (perhaps with a long run before playing a set) to give them the challenge and experience of competing when physically fatigued. This is a great mental toughness test and may simulate what your players will face at year's end in district or state championship play.

Footwork and Movement

Footwork and movement drills are extremely important for tennis because they help players learn efficient movements and provide anaerobic training at the same time. Because short, powerful bursts of speed are the most typical moves in tennis, you should be specific in the types of sprints and agility runs you ask players to perform during the season.

The USTA has two outstanding videos on movement drills—*Movement Training for Tennis* and *Advanced Footskills for Tennis*—that show how to make these drills fun, cre-

ative, and competitive. (See the resources section on page 193 for ordering information.) Borrowing from basketball, football, and baseball, tennis coaches can take basic movement ideas and make them specific to tennis. The variety shown on these videos will let you try a new movement drill every day so that your players will never be bored and will never dread the prospect of wind sprints.

If you keep the following key points in mind, most high school players, both male and female, will enjoy fitness activities and take pride in their physical abilities:

- Keep training fun, emphasize the benefits, be enthusiastic, and expect a positive attitude.
- Never use physical training as punishment—you'll produce a mind-set that physical activity is to be avoided. That's just the opposite of your goal.
- Be creative and use great variety in physical training. New ways of accomplishing the same workouts will keep motivation high.
- Test your players periodically (every four to six weeks) on a few simple fitness

Tips for Effective Practices

- Take time to prepare for each practice by creating a practice plan.
- Keep each drill segment short and moving quickly. Concentration lags when drills drag for too long.
- Remain positive and be constructive with your criticism. If a player is having a hard time, praise a strength before picking on a weakness.
- Get into the moment yourself by having fun with your players and devising drills that allow them to practice a stroke in a matchlike situation.
- Use the pickup team method to get all the members of your squad involved in drills, with an equal chance at success.

tests and show them the improvement. They'll love getting stronger and faster!

- Be sure every player has personal fitness goals that are specific and realistic. Reminding players of these goals and having them share the goals with teammates can be powerful incentives to train harder.

- Use team competition and peer pressure to urge the less enthusiastic players to train harder.

SUMMARY

Here are the key planning points outlined in this chapter:

- Consider using the game-based approach by having your players play the game or a modified game, then learn the underlying strategy, next work on the skills needed to perform in the game, and finally play the game again.

- Have a plan in mind for each practice. Start with an overview for the season, then break your planning down into weekly and daily plans.

- Vary the emphasis during the preseason, competitive season, and championship season. Players need change depending on the challenges they face in competition.

- Remain flexible by using your daily practice plan to address needs that you couldn't foresee when you wrote a weekly plan.

- Keep your practices upbeat and competitive.

- Keep practices fun.

CHAPTER 7

STROKE PRODUCTION

One of your primary goals should be to provide each of your players with a biomechanically sound basis for each stroke; the stroke should be comfortable and not lead to overuse injuries. At the same time, each stroke technique must allow your players to accomplish the strategic aims or shot patterns that form the basis of winning tennis.

In game-based coaching, if you have effectively demonstrated what players need to do in a specific play situation, it will be clearer to them what type of shot will be most effective. For example, when the opponent is at the net, a passing shot with a good amount of topspin will keep the ball low and out of the power zone of the opponent at net.

Let your players maintain some individual style to their strokes. As you know from watching professionals, many different styles of play can be successful. Don't try to make the strokes of every member of your squad exactly the same.

The style you and a player choose should suit the player's physical and mental abilities on court. Maintain an open dialogue with your players as their strokes are taking shape, and listen to their feedback so that a cooperative exchange occurs. This makes learning much easier.

Use this chapter as a reference point for stroke production. Add your coaching flair and the players' individual style, and the result will be sound strokes that each player can rely on during match play.

COACHING TO LEARN VERSUS COACHING TO PERFORM

Every coach is faced with the problem of analyzing why a player didn't succeed during match play. Was it poorly learned racket skills, or was it just nerves? The easy way out for a coach is to blame the failure on the player's lack of effort or poor shot selection during a match. Assessing the failure as stroke related reflects badly on a coach's ability to teach.

To coach successfully, you must be able to assess a player's on-court problems correctly. If further basic training on stroke production is necessary, then you must "coach to learn," which is done by instructing the player to repeat the proper technique for the stroke that broke down during play. If nerves or poor shot selection was the reason for failure, then you must "coach to perform." This can be accomplished by talking to the player about shot selection and how to handle match pressure better so that strokes remain fluid and confident.

Learning

The learning process for motor skills can be divided into three primary stages (thinking, practicing, and performing) according to the objective of each stage, common characteristics of the stage, and how to maximize learning through the process. In the early stage, a great deal of conscious thought is required. On the other hand, great players who have reached the final stage seem to be able to compete "automatically" with almost no thought process. Your goal is to help your players through these stages of development to reach the "automatic" performing stage as quickly as possible.

1. **Thinking.** When a player first learns new tennis skills, a lot of thinking is required. The player must slowly process each step of a particular stroke as a new sequence of movements is ingrained. Be careful not to overload a player's mental circuits during this phase. Follow this advice for success:

- Simplify the basics of each stroke. The players can digest only so much at once.

- Correct one flaw in the stroke at a time. Overlook the minor details and concentrate on teaching the major biomechanical movements involved in the stroke.

- Give your players *positive constructive feedback* as often as possible. Resist the temptation to criticize early attempts so as not to discourage players or destroy their natural self-confidence.

2. **Practicing.** After learning the basic sequence of a stroke's mechanics, a player needs to spend quality practice time refining the skill. At this point, less conscious thought is necessary to execute the stroke, and this allows the player to concentrate on coordinating and refining the individual segments of the stroke until it is smooth and flowing. Many coaches refer to this practice as "grooving" a stroke.

Once the fundamental movements of a stroke become familiar to the player, errors decrease and performance becomes more consistent. You, the coach, are still coaching to learn, but now coaching feedback and dialogue with the player change. Rather than you having to point out errors in the stroke's execution, the player can begin to detect these flaws himself. Dialogue about error detection is no longer one-sided from the coach—the player can tell you what he should do to solve the error. Work closely with your player during this phase. Continue to use the player's feedback and opinions rather than asserting your view about what went wrong with a faulty swing. Doing this will allow your player to develop independent thinking so that he can correct a flawed stroke himself during play.

To plan quality practice time for a player during this stage of development, consider these factors:

- The player's capacity to learn. Everyone learns at a different rate. Allow the player time to absorb each phase of the stroke.

- The player's motivation to change or learn a new stroke. The desire for change must come from the player himself—not solely from you.

- Fatigue during practice. No one can learn a new skill on court if practice time lasts too long and causes fatigue. Players trying to master new skills need to be mentally and physically fresh. Generally, you should work on new skills or "grooving" shots early in practices when players are relatively fresh mentally and physically.

3. **Performing.** After much repetition and correction, the player will reach a point where she knows how to perform the stroke. As errors occur, she is capable of adjusting automatically. In fact, player overanalysis

in this phase usually interferes with stroke production. You can now coach the player to perform. Tell her to relax and let her stroke flow without dwelling on each movement required to execute it. Breakdowns in the stroke are now usually mental. Here are some things you can do to help players at this stage:

- If match pressure is causing stroke breakdown, inform your player that the stroke is not at fault. Once she can admit to being bothered by match pressure, you can help her adjust and overcome the problem (see pages 154-155).

- Shot selection from different areas of the court could be the problem. Watch the player during match play and suggest changes that will make each stroke more effective from different areas of the court.

- Offer suggestions about when your player should use a particular stroke to attack or defend her position on the court.

- Refocus your player on a specific tactic rather than the technique. Encourage her to just trust her body to execute the shot to her opponent's weakness.

- Be sure to teach your players the steps they can take to combat nerves and deal with pressure situations. Tried-and-true remedies for this include deep breathing, muscle tensing and relaxation, exaggerated foot movements, and bouncing on the toes. Different players will have favorites that seem to work for them.

- Create some pressure in practice so that your players can adjust to it. Use challenges with penalties or rewards, audience effect, or specific skill tests to create pressure. Example: Before a player can leave practice, she must hit five successful serves to the inside half and the outside half of each service box. If she misses, she must start over.

With practice, you'll become better at analyzing on-court problems correctly, which will allow you to decide whether to coach for learning or performance. As player confidence in you increases, don't be afraid to say, "I don't know." Then you and your player can solve the problem together.

If a player has entered the automatic (performing) stage of learning using incorrect technique, relearning the stroke can become very difficult. Players with self-taught strokes that include faulty mechanics must be taken back to the mental (thinking) stage of learning to relearn proper stroke production. Provide the player with simple cues to make the mental stage of learning flow more easily. Videotape is an excellent venue to point out improper technique to a struggling player trying to relearn a stroke. Relearning strokes is usually best left to the off-season when there is no pressure to perform in match play.

GRIPS

Much has been written about grips. Many coaches use terminology created to describe where the dominant hand is placed on the racket. Others use numbering systems, labeling the panels of a racket handle where the pad of the index finger and the heel of the hand should be placed. Generally, tennis players really don't care about artificial methods of achieving the proper grip—they just want a grip that works for them without having to think about it every time they prepare to hit a shot.

The best way to make this happen for your players is to give them simple parameters to use as a guide to a functional grip. (By now you may have recognized that the central theme running through this chapter is to keep instruction as simple as possible. If a stroke requires a complex sequence of movements, it is like a machine with too many moving parts—it will break down under pressure.)

Most players await their opponent's shot in the ready position with a forehand grip. Your players should experiment with whichever forehand grip feels comfortable. Whatever choice they make, it is a good idea to ask them to do two things before experimenting: keep the racket face perpendicular to the ground and keep a firm wrist. Doing so allows better contact with the ball through the hitting area. Achieving this racket position requires the dominant hand to be placed along the backside of the racket's handle, which results in an eastern or semiwestern forehand grip. Once a base forehand has been established, grip variations can be added to handle different situations.

Advances in racket technology and different playing surfaces force most players to use more than one grip during a match. Height of the ball's bounce and speed and trajectory of the shot must be considered in selection of a functional grip. The area of the court at which the shot is executed (baseline, midcourt, or net) will also determine what grip to use.

Because players will use more than one grip in a match, they need to be comfortable with how they are going to change grips quickly during a point. Grip changes should be accomplished by using the nondominant hand. The player cradles the racket at a point between the throat and the top of the grip (using the nondominant hand). As the shoulders are turning into the shot, the player uses the nondominant hand to turn the racket to the proper grip. The nondominant hand also aids in balancing the racket between points and allows the dominant hand some rest (see figure 7.1).

Different hand sizes and different racket handle shapes make it very difficult to standardize grips. With your assistance, each player should experiment to find what grip is most comfortable for each situation that develops during a point. For reference while discussing grips, refer to the following review of general grip terminology.

- Eastern forehand—The "shake hands" grip. To get this grip, place your palm flat

Figure 7.1 For this player, the top hand is nondominant.

against the strings and slide down the shaft to the handle (see figure 7.2a).

- Eastern backhand—From the eastern forehand grip, for a right-hander, turn the racket 90 degrees to the right. Left-handers turn to the left. (See figure 7.2b.)

- Western forehand—The "frying pan" grip. Put the racket flat on the ground and pick it up. Your palm will be further under the racket handle than in an eastern forehand grip (see figure 7.2c).

- Continental forehand—The "hammer" grip. The palm is on top of the racket handle, similar to holding a hammer before pounding a nail (see figure 7.2d).

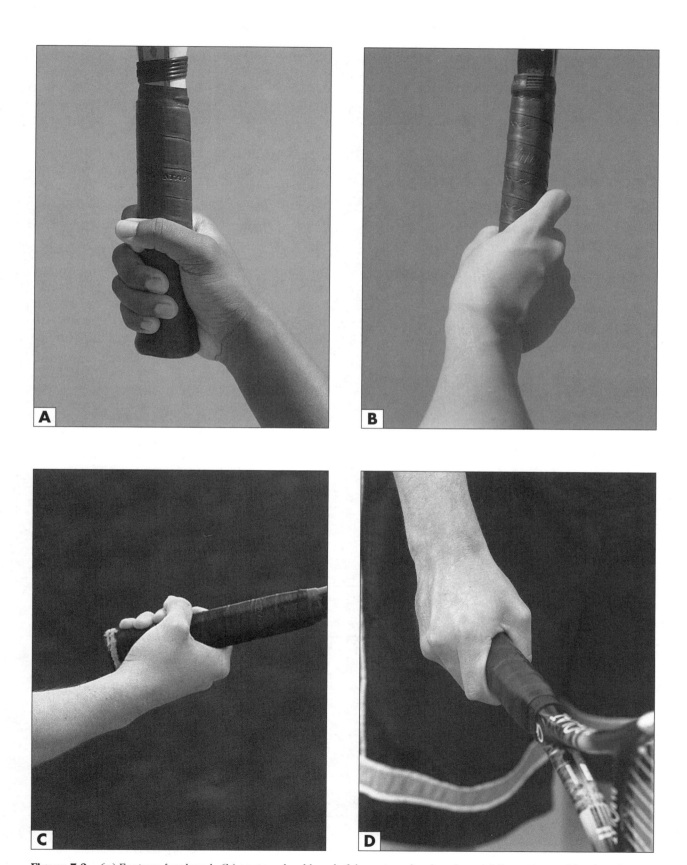

Figure 7.2 *(a)* Eastern forehand, *(b)* eastern backhand, *(c)* western forehand, and *(d)* continental forehand.

Another way of analyzing grips is shown in figure 7.3. Hand position for the eastern forehand, eastern backhand, continental forehand, and semiwestern forehand is determined by the alignment of the base knuckle on the panels of the racket.

Choosing the Right Grip for the Right Stroke

Each stroke requires a decision as to what grip will work best. Factors such as ball speed, height of bounce, and spin have to be instantly analyzed as the ball approaches. Occasionally these quick decisions will catch a player in the wrong grip. However, if a player knows which grip is best suited for her game in each circumstance, chances are she will be in the right grip most of the time before striking the ball. The following sections outline what to consider before choosing a grip for each stroke.

Forehand Grip

Hard-court play, which usually produces a consistent high bounce, has seen the forehand evolve into a powerful stroke. On hard surfaces, your players should consider a forehand grip somewhere between an eastern and semiwestern. Due to grip changes, the eastern forehand is usually picked by players with one-handed backhands, whereas two-handed backhand players are more likely to choose a semiwestern forehand. The eastern forehand grip requires less rotation of the hand when changing to a one-handed eastern backhand grip. A semiwestern forehand grip requires a severe grip change to achieve a proper one-handed eastern backhand grip; however, less adjustment by the dominant hand is required to achieve a proper two-handed backhand grip.

For an eastern forehand grip, the palm of the hand should be lined up with the racket face. To test your players, have them prepare for a forehand, freeze in the ready position, and then tell you without looking how their racket face is angled. If the palm of the hand is lined up with the racket face, the racket will be perpendicular to the ground. Presenting the racket face to the ball in this position creates a powerful and consistent shot. The grip allows the elbows to remain closer to the body and the wrist to be in a firm and comfortable position, which results in maximum power.

Slice Forehand Grip

The forehand slice (although fairly rare in today's tennis) requires an open racket face and an eastern forehand grip. Players who use

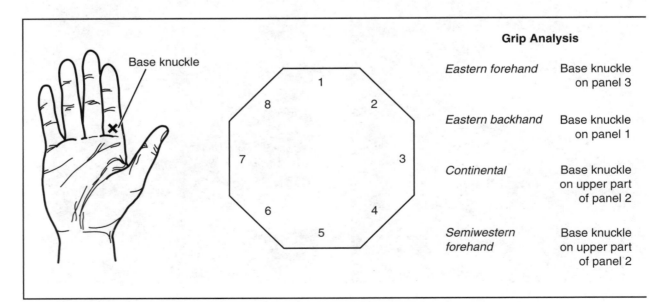

Figure 7.3 Grip analysis chart.

a western grip find this shot difficult if they are unwilling to change grips as they come in from the baseline. The western grip makes it difficult to open the racket face and slice the ball. This problem usually keeps players at the baseline rather than trying to approach the net on a low-bouncing ball at midcourt.

One-Handed Backhand Grip

This grip allows the most flexibility when reaching wide for a backhand. Midcourt backhand slices are usually achieved easier from this base backhand grip than from a two-handed grip. At the net your players will already have the second hand off the racket, unlike a two-hander, so the volley is usually easier because the best grip at net is the continental, which is easier to achieve with one hand on the racket.

The grip change from the forehand required to hit a one-handed backhand allows the player to present the racket face flat to the ball and keep a firm wrist. If the player doesn't change grips, then her wrist will be contorted. Keeping a firm wrist without a grip change will cause the racket face to be too open when presented to the ball. Thus a grip change is imperative.

For a right-handed player, the degree the racket should be turned to the right to comfortably achieve an eastern backhand grip depends on the strength of the player. However, as a reference point, the inside pad of the thumb on the dominant hand should be in line with the racket face (see figure 7.4).

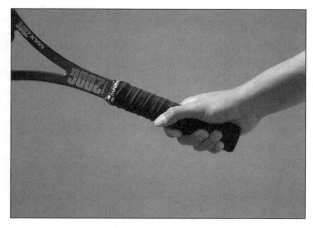

Figure 7.4 One-handed eastern backhand.

Two-Handed Backhand Grip

This is the most popular backhand grip for most junior players. Some coaches feel that this stroke restricts reach on the backhand side and forces the player to cover more court. However, the control and power most young players develop with two hands on the grip usually outweigh the lack-of-reach factor. Baseline players, especially girls, find this grip advantageous because the factor of wrist strength is negated with two hands on the racket.

Players who use a semiwestern forehand grip sometimes use the two-handed backhand grip without much noticeable change (from forehand to backhand) in the dominant hand's position on the handle. However, to present the racket face to the ball in a perpendicular fashion, the dominant hand should rotate to the top of the grip, resembling a continental forehand, and the nondominant hand should resemble an eastern forehand grip (see figure 7.5).

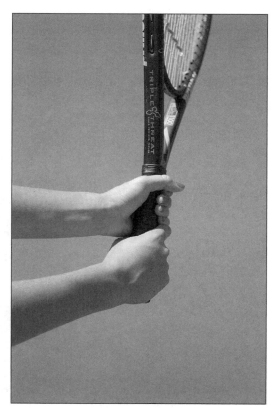

Figure 7.5 Two-handed backhand.

Slice Backhand Grip

When college coaches ask about players they may recruit, one of their first questions often is, "Can he come under the ball at midcourt or is he just another baseliner?" These coaches know that the ability to open the racket face up to slice an approach shot is crucial to having a complete game. To have a chance at the net, a player must be able to hit a sliced approach shot on a low-bouncing ball at midcourt. Once players are past the beginner stage, countless drills should be used to hammer home this important lesson in midcourt play.

For the slice, the grip will resemble a continental or eastern backhand grip. Tell players to think of delivering a karate chop with the base of their dominant hand. If a player has a two-handed backhand, try to convince him to take the nondominant hand off the racket to effectively hit the slice backhand (see figure 7.6). Doing so aligns the shoulders with the target as the racket moves from high to low to create underspin on the ball. This is achieved by pushing the dominant hand forward while the nondominant hand moves away from the point of contact.

Figure 7.6 Backhand slice.

Service Grip

Besides ground strokes, which include the return of serve, the most often hit shot is the serve. It's hard to convince a beginner that she should not use her forehand grip to serve. After all, she may be competing against other beginners who will not pressure her serve, so a flat serve is usually sufficient. But as players gain experience, they will need to add some spin to their serves for better control. To convince an advanced beginner to change her service grip to one resembling a continental, you should have her serve to a better player. Once she sees a few of her soft second serves blow back by her, it will be much easier to persuade her to try another service grip. A flat serve simply lacks the control of a spin serve. Once a player has adjusted to a proper service grip, first-service power can be tempered by the spin imparted.

The spin required for a reliable second serve also demands a continental grip. It may be difficult for an inexperienced player to grasp initially, but once she gains confidence in this service grip, she'll notice how much her control improves. It may be best to encourage players to make a gradual change from their forehand grip toward the preferred serving grip, and over time, the move to a continental serving grip will not seem so daunting.

Volley Grip

Quick exchanges at the net make grip changes for a volley impractical. Most beginners will attempt to hit volleys with their forehand grip, which usually means the player will have a very weak backhand volley. Convince your players that a continental grip should be used at net as soon as their wrist strength allows. The grip will resemble a continental with the heel of the hand rotated toward an eastern grip. This rotation is particularly evident on a high volley. If you have players who use both hands on the backhand side to volley, convince them to take their nondominant hand off the racket as soon as possible. This will allow them to keep the lead shoulder lined up properly and punch through the volley. Some players will be able to change grips on most volleys using the same technique described earlier and only resort to the one-grip continental in rapid exchanges.

The test of a good grip for any stroke is getting to the ready position and knowing how the face of the racket is slanted. Have your players prepare for and take a swing at an imaginary ball. Can they bring the face of the racket to the imaginary ball? Ask them if they feel that they are going to hit it nice and solid. A good grip makes the execution of a stroke easy. A bad grip makes proper stroke production nearly impossible. Impress on your players that failure to have a functional grip for all the strokes they must manage during play will cause glaring weaknesses in their game. Focus your players on proper grips as soon as you begin practice for the year. Without proper grip technique, all other stroke production work will be wasted.

SWING PATTERNS

Stroke production is a matter of individual style. Style, however, must be secondary to function if a player hopes to be successful in the game of tennis. How many players have you coached who wanted to look good on the court at all costs? They take an exaggerated backswing and huge follow-through, resulting in either a winner or, more likely, an unforced error. Unfortunately, style over substance is a pitfall young players get caught up in all too often.

Backswing

There are three basic ways for players to prepare their racket on the backswing. In the loop, the racket is brought back above head height and dropped below the waist during its forward motion to create a looping pattern. An elliptical swing requires the racket to be taken back across the face before dropping it down below the intended contact point. Players can picture the letter *C* with a upward rising tail to execute the elliptical backswing (see figure 7.7). Straight-back preparation is just that—the racket and arm are brought straight

Figure 7.7 The C-loop swing.

back below the level of the ball's bounce, then driven up and through the incoming ball.

Each type of preparation has its advantages and disadvantages, so players need to be able to use more than one type depending on the situation. For instance, on a fast-playing court surface where a short backswing is advantageous, a straight-back swing might be advisable. But on slow-playing court surfaces where more power needs to be generated, a longer backswing will usually work best.

Straight-Back Swing

Swing patterns that develop from a straight-back preparation may be easier for a beginner to grasp. The wrist is under control in most cases, and it's easier to handle pace. With this swing pattern, low to high ground strokes allow a beginner to achieve a better margin of error when the ball crosses the net. For the advanced player who uses this basic swing pattern, hitting the ball on the rise is easier to accomplish. During the preparation phase, the racket is close to the ground, which is where the ball must be contacted in order for players to "live off their opponent's pace."

Disadvantages associated with the straight-back swing pattern involve spin and pace. The path of the racket makes it more difficult to put topspin on the ball. Racket head speed is cut down because of the shortness of the backswing. If a player allows the ball to reach the top of the bounce before swinging, pace can be difficult to achieve.

Some players will use a looping or elliptical swing on their forehand but feel more comfortable with a straight-back swing on the backhand side. Andre Agassi is a good example of a player who uses more of a loop on the forehand and a straight-back swing on the backhand.

Looping Swing

The loop backswings are currently very popular. Most of the big hitters in today's game generate tremendous pace with these swing patterns. The freedom allowed the wrist maximizes racket head speed. Control is accomplished through spin. The loop should be smaller if the playing surface is fast or if the opponent is a big hitter. On a slower surface, such as clay, a player will have more time for preparation. The loop backswing is perfect to generate more power while maintaining control with topspin.

The disadvantages of the loop backswing are quite obvious. A young player can become power crazed and lose all semblance of control. For beginners, the freedom afforded the wrist coupled with a late contact point may further compound the problem of control.

Elliptical Backswing

For most players, the elliptical backswing combines the advantages of control and power. You would be wise to encourage this swing pattern for most of the players on your team. However, you must also allow for individual variation, especially for players who come to you with well-ingrained habits that are effective.

Regardless of which swing pattern is used, the key is to avoid excessive backswing. The problem of too much backswing usually occurs on the forehand side. (Excessive backswings are less likely on the backhand side because the player prepares by reaching across the body.) If the racket disappears behind the player during preparation, the contact point may be late, making control and pace more difficult to achieve.

Preparation to swing must be early enough so that the contact point is out in front of the player. For some players, this means using a short, compact swing. Therefore, when you are teaching swing patterns, moving from minimum swings to maximum is best. With a short, compact swing pattern, whether it's a loop or straight-back, your players are more likely to contact the ball out in front.

Once the players become comfortable with the swing pattern they are using, rhythm and flow can be introduced. The timing involved in hitting balls coming at different speeds and with various spins requires hours and hours of practice. Basic ground stroke drills are the ticket to developing a consistent stroke.

Movement Training

Tennis is a movement game. An excellent swing pattern will be of little use if a player's legs can't get her to the ball. In most sports, the arms are pumped to gain momentum while running. Tennis is different. Running to the contact point, a player's upper body must remain still as the legs work to get into position to hit the shot. An advanced player might pump her arms to gain momentum, but as she approaches the ball and initiates stroke preparation, her upper body is still. However, beginners are better equipped to execute a stroke if racket preparation is initiated as they run toward the ball and if they keep the upper body as "quiet as possible" until they execute the stroke.

Footwork

Footwork is actually the art of remaining balanced while anticipating an opponent's shot, running to the ball, and setting up to hit a shot. In the ready position, a player will feel balanced when her feet are shoulder-width apart and her knees slightly bent. The player should be on the balls of her feet, ready to move in whatever direction the ball is hit. Bending her knees slightly as she awaits the next shot will lower her center of gravity and prepare her to react (see figure 7.8). The best way to react to an opponent's shot and gain momentum quickly is by using a split-step, which is usually associated with approach shot–volley technique. However, many teams practice using the split-step before ground strokes as a means of developing explosive speed to the ball. To perform a split-step, the player takes a quick little jump step onto

Figure 7.8 Ready position.

the balls of both feet as her opponent takes the racket back in preparation for the next stroke. This action squares the shoulders, lowers the center of gravity, and allows the player to react quickly to an opponent's shot.

Balance and Recovery

As an opponent hits a shot, a player must maintain proper balance while reacting to the ball. Long strides are effective until the player gets close to the point of contact, when steps must be shortened. Shortening the steps as the shoulders rotate allows the player to lean into the contact point with a prepared racket, which makes recovery easier once the shot is hit. Recovery is the number of steps a player has to take to stop forward momentum past the point of contact after the ball is hit.

Many beginners make the mistake of bending at the waist to reach the ball at the point

of contact. This moves their center of gravity, which is the base of balance, away from the legs. The resulting stroke is all arms and does not use the body as a linked system. No help is received from the legs, hips, or shoulders.

To use the body as a linked system, the player must step into the ball. This allows the power generated by the legs to transfer to the hips and through to the shoulders as the player rotates into the shot. This power can then be used by the player's arms and hands to execute a stroke.

After completing a stroke, many players make the mistake of stopping flat-footed to see what happens to the ball they just hit. This loss of momentum makes working their way back to their opponent's possible center of returns more difficult. Teach your players to work just as hard between shots as during shot execution. If players bounce on the balls of their feet between shots, the time they'll need to prepare for the next shot will decrease considerably.

Footwork Tips

The following are some tips on footwork that you can give to your players.

- Maintain balance with a proper ready stance (on the balls of your feet, with knees slightly bent).
- Use a split-step to react quicker to an opponent's shot.
- Steps should be shortened as you get close to the ball.
- Use the body as a linked system. Power is generated first in your legs. Step into each shot so that this power transfers to the upper torso.
- Minimize recovery steps.
- Continue to work between shots. Don't stand flat-footed.
- When hopelessly out of position, gamble. If you hit a short ball, sprint to the side you think your opponent will most likely try to hit it.

Enhancing Footwork Drill

Purpose: To develop better footwork and balance.

Procedure: Set up pairs of red cones on opposite sides of the singles sidelines. Three players with their rackets are stationed in the middle of the court between the pairs of cones. On your command, players take a hop step and move toward a cone. Executing proper racket preparation and footwork as he approaches the cone, each player executes a shadow swing, recovers, returns to the middle of the court, and does another hop step before moving to the cone on the opposite side.

Coaching points
When properly executed, simulated shadow drills develop excellent footwork much quicker than drills where players must be concerned about hitting a ball after a feed. Try this drill to develop balance and footwork.

Three Stances

There are three stances a player can use to set up to hit a shot:

1. Square stance. This stance is the simplest way for young players to have good balance and weight transfer into their shots. The back foot lands first, and the front foot steps forward toward the net just before contact with the ball. The front foot is directly in line with the back foot. This classic style ensures good weight transfer and keeps the body sideways to the net at contact (see figure 7.9a).

2. Open stance. This stance may make it more difficult for players to establish good balance and weight transfer, although many top players use this technique successfully.

The back foot lands last and is closer than the front foot to the contact point. The back foot will generally be directly to the side or slightly behind the point of contact (see figure 7.9b). This stance is typically used by players who use a western or semiwestern grip. As grips have changed more toward the western forehand, many more players use an open stance almost exclusively, and your players will copy the professional players they see using it on TV. Your job is not to insist on a change in footwork, but to help players use the stance as effectively as possible. When you watch the top players use it, note their excellent balance and how they push off the back leg for power.

3. Closed stance. This stance is sometimes used by players with two-handed backhands. The back foot lands first, and the front foot steps across the body and beyond the point where the back foot landed (see figure 7.9c). This stance is seldom seen for a forehand except when a player is running all out for a wide ball and is forced to flick the ball back with his arm. The closed stance makes adequate hip rotation virtually impossible. Generally, you should try to get players to substitute a square or open stance for a closed one.

The square or open stance is acceptable for ground strokes. You should leave a player's open stance alone if he uses a western grip and can maintain balance and stability during the shot. However, for most high school players, the square stance is the best option. It allows a player to put his weight into each ground stroke, which transfers power from the legs into the upper torso. By stepping into the shot with this stance, the knees can bend during preparation and the player can stay down on each ground stroke. This total package of balance and weight transfer makes ground strokes easier to control and much more powerful.

Figure 7.9 (*a*) Square stance, (*b*) open stance, and (*c*) closed stance.

CONTROLLING THE BALL

Tennis is a game of restrictions. Specifically, the barriers are the lines and the net. If your players cannot control the ball when executing a stroke, no amount of power will do them any good. Once a player has arrived at the hitting area and is properly prepared to hit a ball, the moment of truth has arrived. She must be able to control the ball as she hits it. From this point in a stroke, ball control is a five-step process:

1. Mastering swing speed
2. Managing the contact point
3. Applying spin for control
4. Equating ball direction to angle of racket face
5. Following through to the target

Mastering Swing Speed

Control begins when a player determines how he will use the potential racket head acceleration provided by his legs and hips as they uncoil into the ball. At this point the player should line up the ball at a distance far enough away from his body to allow the shoulder and arm to move comfortably through the hitting area. A "slow arm" at this point in the swing will do wonders for control. No matter what the playing surface, if racket preparation is completed early enough, moving through the contact point with the arm under control will enhance the chances for success. Control implies guidance, which gives a player the image of taking care of the ball as he begins the swing. Players must understand that power comes from timing and rhythm, not necessarily arm speed. Managing racket head acceleration will determine the stroke's chances for success.

Managing the Contact Point

Each player must learn where the perfect contact point is for each stroke. Widening the base by spreading the feet apart in a square stance as the player strides into the shot creates a potentially longer contact area.

On the forehand side, the player should envision pushing the palm forward into the ball. Each player can determine her perfect forehand contact point by initiating an imaginary swing. The player should stand sideways to the net and stop her swing with her weight on the front foot and the racket face pointed directly forward toward the center of the court. This is the recommended contact point for a forehand that is just in front of the lead foot (see figure 7.10).

Figure 7.10 Forehand contact point.

For a one-handed backhand, the player should repeat the imaginary swing. Standing sideways, prepared to hit the ball, she should stop the swing when the racket head is slightly ahead of the front foot. The racket face again should be pointed directly forward toward the center of the court. This is the perfect contact point for a one-handed backhand (see figure

7.11a). For a two-handed backhand, the contact point should be virtually the same as for the forehand drive (see figure 7.11b).

- Ball and racket face should meet at the contact point while the player is balanced.
- Grip variations will vary contact point for each player.

Figure 7.11 (*a*) One-handed backhand and (*b*) two-handed backhand contact points.

Applying Spin

Putting spin on the ball is like applying the brakes to speed. Spin creates friction on the ball as it travels through the air. To impart spin, a player needs a firm but flexible wrist, which can be achieved by tightening the last three fingers of the hand around the racket handle before a stroke.

Three types of spin can be put on a ball. To accomplish these three spins, the racket head must accelerate through the hit as follows:

- Brush the back of the ball upward for topspin.
- Brush the back of the ball downward for underspin.
- Brush across the ball sideways for sidespin.

There are many reasons to use spin when executing a stroke. By applying spin, players can vary the depth, angle, height, speed, and bounce of a shot. If a player always hits the ball flat, he will be unable to hit some of the target spots, which makes it difficult to use the entire court. The six areas available to a player as target zones are the two baseline Ts, the two service line Ts, and the two drop shot Ts at the net (see figure 7.12).

Topspin

When topspin is put on a ball, the top of the ball spins in the direction of travel. The looping trajectory caused by topspin allows the ball to clear the net with a greater margin of error. This loop is effective in producing either a deep ground stroke or a sharply angled crosscourt shot.

To hit topspin, a player swings the racket from low to high. The top edge of the racket's strings should contact the ball first. The faster the racket head accelerates through the shot, the more topspin produced.

Underspin

When underspin is hit, the top of the ball spins away from the direction of travel. Because there is less air pressure under the ball, an underspin shot tends to stay in the air longer.

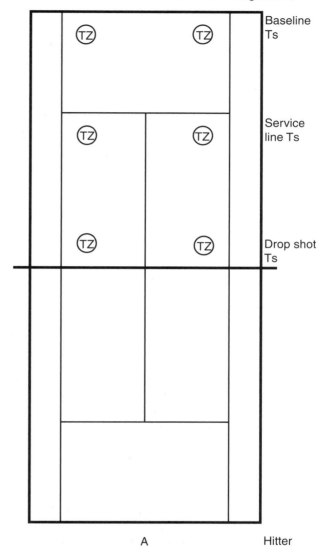

TZ = Target zone

Baseline Ts

Service line Ts

Drop shot Ts

A   Hitter

Figure 7.12   The six target areas.

An underspin shot that strikes the court at an angle greater than 45 degrees tends to "sit up" as in a drop shot. If an underspin shot strikes the court at an angle of less than 45 degrees, it tends to skid and stay low as in an approach shot. Underspin can also be used to control volley placement.

To hit underspin, a player swings the racket forward in a somewhat downward direction. The bottom edge of the racket's strings should hit the ball first. The swing pattern should begin slightly higher than where impact will occur.

Sidespin

When sidespin is hit, the side of the ball spins in the direction of travel. This is often referred to as "sliding" the ball. Sidespin is used to hit the ball at an angle off the court as in an approach or midcourt put-away. It can be used while serving to hit the ball wide and pull an opponent off the court. It is also helpful when attempting to change the direction of the incoming ball. To hit sidespin, a player swings the racket head across the back of the ball. The player contacts the ball close to the throat of the racket and drags the ball across the strings to the racket tip.

Ball Direction and Racket Angle

Elongating the contact point gives a player the time to tell the ball which direction he wants it to go. Ball direction is controlled by the angle of the racket face at impact. Once a player learns the contact point for the center of the court for each stroke, he can adjust slightly to hit the corners of the court.

Right-handed players standing at the center of the court hitting a forehand drive should picture hitting the ball at 6:00 for the center target, 5:00 for a crosscourt shot to the left corner, and 7:00 for a shot to the right corner.

Players need to realize that disguise is important when controlling the direction of the ball. To disguise direction as long as possible from their opponent, preparation should always look the same. Subtle variations of contact point and angle of the racket will vary the direction of the ball.

Clearance height over the net on ground strokes can be controlled by opening the racket face slightly or by imparting topspin. This will also cause the shot to land deep in the court. On a fast-playing court, the ball should travel over the net at about three to four feet. On a slow-playing court, the height over the net should be six to seven feet. If the choice of shot requires the player to hit a shorter ball into the opponent's court, closing the racket face slightly will help the ball travel in that direction.

Follow-Through

When hitting the ball, players must push the racket through the entire contact area, *with head still and eyes on the ball*. The follow-through should extend toward the target. Once the racket moves completely through the "hitting area," which points to the intended target, the speed of the swing often forces players to decelerate the racket as it wraps around their body or around the neck. This is not a problem as long as the hitting area was extended, and in fact, with today's light rackets and fast swings, an extended follow-through is required to have enough time to slow the racket down before ending around the neck or waist.

Players should have a target for a variety of situations. If an opponent stays back after serving, for example, the return should be deep in the court. If an opponent serves and volleys, the return should be low toward the feet of the opponent.

Your players should practice a progression of stroke production every day. If they follow a plan for each stroke, they'll quickly progress. The first priority should be getting the ball in play at all costs. Second, control needs to be gained over each stroke's direction—crosscourt or down the line. Third, your players need to learn to control the depth of each shot. Of course, baseline ground strokes are usually hit deep to the opponent's baseline. However, players should be able to hit short balls as well. Fourth, players should work on their ability to put the correct spin on each shot. Spin allows a ball to be hit with more power and still remain in court. Fifth, the players should learn to control ball speed, varying the pace of the ball during each point played.

SUMMARY

The fundamentals of tennis—strokes, grips, stances, footwork—are key to playing and competing successfully. As players practice each element, they should keep in mind how it affects their entire game. Each coach should become familiar with how certain grips are more effective with certain swing patterns and footwork. It's also important to allow your players some individual variation that falls within a "range of correctness" that is based on the principles of biomechanics. Form and style of play can be individualized as long as the laws of physics are understood and accommodated.

- Carefully analyze match play performance to determine whether poor play is the result of pressure and nerves or poorly learned fundamental skills. Structure practice time to address the cause of the problem.

- Help your players understand the importance of grips—how they affect the stroke and the limitations of each one. Assist players in choosing grips that fit their style of play and competitive objectives.

- Emphasize the techniques and skills of footwork, movement, and body balance for every shot. Court coverage, power, and consistency are all directly affected by player skill in these areas.

- Help your players solve the mysteries of controlling the tennis ball so that they can self-correct during play. Be sure every player knows how to adjust the height, side-to-side direction, depth, spin, and speed of the ball.

8 SERVES AND RETURN OF SERVES

Along with teaching your players the principles of proper grips, swings, and footwork, and the factors that control a tennis ball, you also need to help them understand key concepts for each stroke. Most coaches develop their own favorite concepts based on their experience and the skill level of players on each year's team. Chapters 8, 9, and 10 are devoted to teaching players the proper technique for serves and return of the serve, ground strokes and mid-court shots, and net play and defense against the netplayer.

COACHING TECHNIQUE

Working on player technique often requires individual attention from a coach to evaluate the player's current stroke and suggest improvement. However, for a coach trying to help an entire group of players, it is more efficient to present some general concepts for each type of shot and then organize a series of drills for practice of that stroke.

While players drill, the coach can troubleshoot by reinforcing proper technique and by making brief suggestions for improvement that do not interrupt the flow of the drill. Play-ers who are really struggling will need some individual attention, but you should schedule special help before or after a regular practice. Keep in mind that your role as coach during team practice is to coach all the players for the entire time.

TEACHING DRILLS

Helping players learn rapidly requires drills that isolate attention on a particular shot. This should include player repetition of the shot. The design of a drill should encourage players to perform the shot in a way that is similar to play during actual competition. The drills shown in this chapter and in chapter 9 and 10 are examples that you can modify or adjust to fit the needs of your team.

Over your years of coaching, you'll develop a repertoire of favorite drills that become the backbone of your practices. However, you should continually search for new ideas, make adjustments to old drills, and invent new drills to fit particular situations. When designing or choosing drills, it's helpful to think of the sequence in the development of a shot, as shown in the pyramid in figure 8.1.

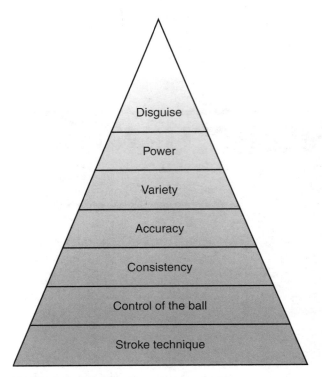

Figure 8.1 Shot development pyramid.

Here are some tips to help you use drills effectively in practice:

1. Begin by discussing the purpose of the drill and demonstrating it to your players. Identify the key points for players to focus on.

2. Remember to emphasize technique and control of the ball (e.g., height, direction, depth, and spin). As players' skills progress, drills should provide practice on consistency and accuracy. As often as possible, use live balls, rather than dead ball drills so that players learn to adjust to a ball in play. The coach should feed dead balls (i.e., a ball not in play) to players who are just learning a shot or a sequence of shots so that they can experience early success.

3. Whenever possible, simulate game situations and natural shot sequences so that your players begin to use patterns of play that transfer to playing points. Simulate the typical length of a point in drills so that players get used to playing out three to six shots in succession.

4. Use targets on the court when drilling for accuracy or consider targets above the net when emphasizing control of direction and height.

5. Challenge your players by using a variety of drills each practice, and change drills before players become tired and bored of the repetition. Adjust the purpose of a drill by performing the drill for a certain amount of time, for a certain number of trials, until there is a winner, until players master the skill, or until the coach blows the whistle.

6. Maximize court space by using some drills that can accommodate six to eight players on one court, thereby freeing other courts for singles drills or game situations.

7. Adjust drills to the ability level of players on each court. Although all players may be performing the same task, you can make the drill more difficult for your better players by adding the challenge of depth, accuracy, or increased penalty for errors.

8. Integrate frequent rotations and enough movement into each day's drills so that your players are getting a good physical workout without even noticing it. Make sure players do not have to stand in line for a turn more than 30 seconds—nothing is more boring.

9. Look for opportunities for positive reinforcement while players are drilling. Try to catch them doing something right. If you need to correct their technique or performance, do it clearly, concisely, and without emotion.

10. Above all, remember to make drills fun. Players like challenges. They like competition and love to beat the coach. Plan some time each day for fun—especially after periods of intense concentration and hard work.

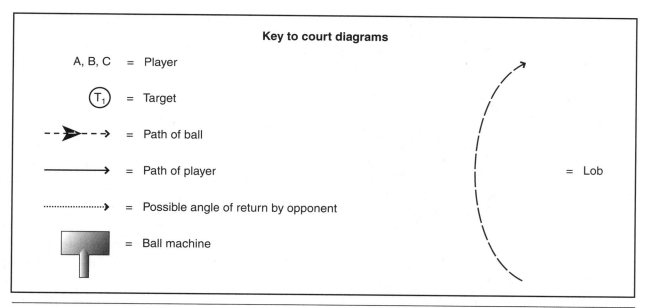

Key to court diagrams

A, B, C = Player

(T₁) = Target

- - ▶- - → = Path of ball

——————→ = Path of player

··············→ = Possible angle of return by opponent

[ball machine symbol] = Ball machine

= Lob

Use this key to decipher the diagrams.

SERVES

Since every point in tennis begins with a serve and the return of serve, it would seem players and coaches would place more emphasis on perfecting these two shots. In fact, if you chart match results, you'll find that many points never get beyond these first two shots before ending. Most players spend a large majority of time practicing their "rallying" skills and rarely do they focus on the serve and return. It's your responsibility as the coach to make certain they give equal attention to these two shots that begin every point.

Teach your players the wisdom of adopting the following priorities when serving:

- Get the serve in the court consistently, even under pressure.
- Vary the placement to the opponent's backhand, forehand, or at the body.
- Adjust the amount of spin—if serves are long, add more spin; if serves fall short, use less spin and aim higher.

After players master these skills, they can work on adding speed and power to force a weak return. You should urge players to take some time before each serve to perform a ritual (before beginning the serving motion). The ritual should include a deep breath or two to relax, a few bounces of the ball, and a decision on the placement of the serve and the type of serve to be delivered. One of the telltale signs of nervousness and choking is rushing between first and second serves. The pre-serve ritual should help to relax and focus the server by slowing the process.

The aim on the service toss should be in line with the tossing shoulder and out in front of the body. The distance in front will vary depending on the service motion of each player and the type of serve being hit. For example, a flat serve will be hit farther in front than a kick serve.

Power on the serve is generated from the ground by bending the knees and then straightening them during the reach to contact the ball. A 20 percent turn of the shoulders away from the starting position provides good body rotation and, when combined with a continuous swing of the racket arm, allows for maximum velocity.

Players should use a pre-serve ritual to calm themselves before serving.

Second serves should be hit with exactly the same motion and speed as first serves, but the margin of safety should be increased by adding quite a bit more spin to bring the ball down into the court. Help your players resist the temptation to push the second serve, which risks an attacking shot from the receiver, especially if the serve lacks depth.

Pressure Serving

Purpose: To test serves in a pressure situation.

Procedure: Ask each of your players to imagine herself in the following scenario: "It's the third set of a tough match, and you're up 6-5. Odds are if you hit four first serves in you'll win the match." Then have each player attempt these four serves in succession (see figure 8.2):

1. Serve to the outside half of the deuce court.

2. Serve to the inside half of the deuce court.

3. Serve to the outside half of the ad court.

4. Serve to the inside half of the ad court.

If all four serves land in, you've got a winner. If a player misses on the first serve, she must go and hit 40 practice serves before trying again. For a miss on the second serve, the penalty is 30 practice serves, and so on.

Coaching points

Remind each player to take time for her serving ritual and to focus on the task at hand. If your players try to ensure success by hitting serves too softly, simply add the rule that the ball must pass the baseline on the second bounce. You can increase the pressure on the server by gathering an audience of cheering players, which often happens at the end of a crucial match. An excellent variation of this drill—a variation that promotes cooperative teamwork—is to assign a receiver to work with each server. They work together to accomplish four serves and four returns successfully (the returns are required to land crosscourt beyond the service line).

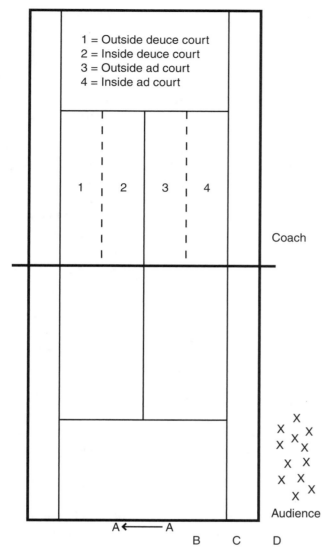

Figure 8.2 Pressure serving drill.

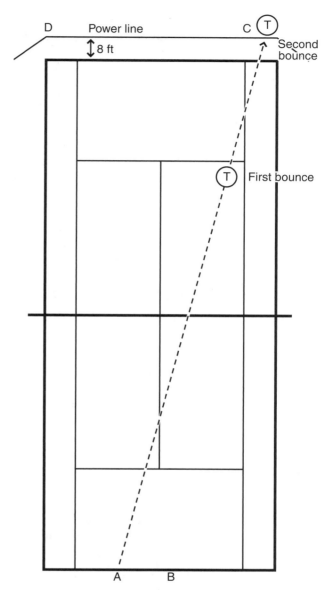

Figure 8.3 Serving power drill.

Serving Power

Purpose: To measure the depth and power of the first and second serves.

Procedure: Players serve 10 serves from the serving position. A partner marks the spot of the second bounce of all serves that land in the service box with enough power that the ball's second bounce lands behind the power line 8 feet beyond the baseline (see figure 8.3).

Serve and First Volley

Purpose: To practice the serve, split-step, and first volley.

Procedure: Servers line up at the baseline. One at a time, they try one serve to the service box straight ahead, perform a split-step as the receiver begins the forward swing, and then volley the ball beyond the service line. The purpose of serving straight is to maximize space and allow the identical drill to proceed simultaneously on the other half of the court. This will free other courts for singles drills or play.

Coaching points

Emphasize getting the serve in (faults cause a loss of turn), perfecting the technique and timing of the split-step, and hitting the first volley deep. After players achieve repeated success, let them play the point out using the center line and doubles sideline for boundaries. Because the playing area is limited, the ball tends to stay in play longer, and the serve-and-volleyer will gain the confidence to move in for volleys or retreat to hit an overhead smash.

RETURNING SERVE

Although every point requires a return of serve, this is probably the least practiced shot in tennis. Emphasizing the following points with your players will help them improve their service returns.

Players should adjust their position on the court based on the speed and depth of the opponent's serve. They should move inside the baseline to attack a weak second serve and move behind the baseline to counter a hard first serve.

Tell your players to watch the ball as the server tosses it, split step just before he contacts the serve, and begin their return with a quick shoulder turn. If the serve hits the net, they should check to see if their shoulders are turned.

Because there is usually less time for the swing on a service return, the length of the backswing should be shortened from that used on normal ground strokes. Most returns should be hit crosscourt or deep down the middle to increase the margin for safety. If the serve is weak, a player should attack it by going to the opponent's weakness. The receiver's position should bisect the angle of possible serves from the opponent. If the server varies his serving position, the receiver should adjust to the left or right accordingly.

For most players, you might suggest waiting with the forehand grip if that is their preferred shot. This way they'll only have one possible grip change to make (to the backhand) when the serve comes. Waiting with a grip between forehand and backhand is inefficient because there are then two possible changes to make. If the server is hitting a high percentage of serves to the backhand, it may be wise for the receiver to adjust by starting out with the backhand grip.

The key to an early reaction to the location and type of serve is for the receiver to watch the ball closely during the service toss, then look and listen to pick up the spin and direction of the ball just after the server contacts it. Some servers provide clues unknowingly by varying their stance or service toss for different types of serve. The receiver must watch closely for clues as the server begins his serve.

If the server hits a spin or kick serve that bounces high and kicks up to shoulder height, the receiver may be forced to play a return out of his preferred hitting zone. The most common counterstrategy is to move forward and take the serve on the rise before the spin takes full effect. Many players find it easier to chip or slice a serve with a lot of spin on it. Whether driving or slicing, however, the key to success is to move forward to attack the ball and close the racket face a bit or to cover the ball to control the upward movement that results from the heavy spin.

The safest return with the best margin for error is returned at the same angle it was hit from. On serves that are less difficult to handle, players may want to change the angle of return and hit to the opponent's weakness.

Practicing service returns should start with a series of drills that emphasize consistency. A modified game that focuses on the serve and return can be structured by limiting each point to those two shots. Keep score the same way as a normal set but end each point after the service return. Increase the difficulty of the task by limiting the placement of serves and returns. If the players in the drill are of uneven ability, you can increase competitiveness by limiting the choices for one player and not the other.

Because many points are ended during the first couple of shots, you may want to use modified games that emphasize the importance of consistency early in the point by requiring a serve, return, and one ground stroke before the point begins. This will help your players grow accustomed to playing their way into each point.

Service Return to Targets

Purpose: To promote consistency, depth, and accuracy on returns.

Procedure: Players return serves to a predetermined target area of the court. Targets 1, 2, and 3 emphasize depth of the return against a baseline player, whereas targets 4, 5, and 6 are valuable for practicing returns against a serve-and-volleyer (see figure 8.4). Balls

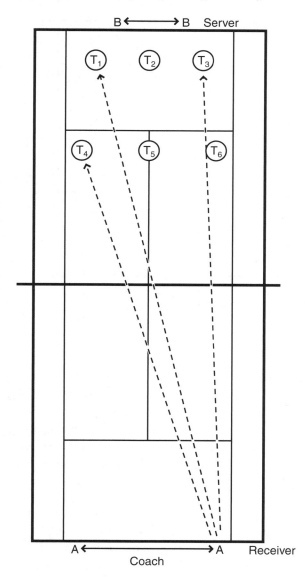

Figure 8.4 Service return to targets.

returned to targets 4 and 6 will also force a defensive baseliner to move forward and sideways away from her more comfortable home position behind the baseline.

Coaching points
After players gain consistency in placing the return, add the element of competition by using conventional scoring or some adaptation. Another twist is for the coach to assign the target area for each return.

Punish the Server

Purpose: To develop an offensive, punishing return of serve.

Procedure: The receiver assumes his normal position for returning serve. As the server begins his service toss, the receiver quickly runs around his weaker stroke to hit the return with his favorite shot (typically a forehand drive). The objective is to hit an aggressive return out of the server's reach (see figure 8.5). Normally, this strategy is useful against second serves, so you should limit the server to hitting second serves.

Coaching points
Be sure your receivers practice this shot from both the deuce and the ad courts. You can add a competitive element by scoring two points for an outright winning return, two points for hitting the return deep to the server, and one point for eliciting an error from the server on the first ground stroke.

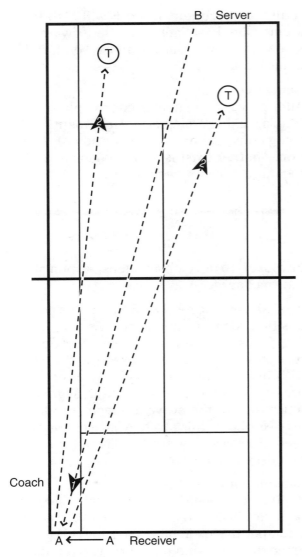

Figure 8.5 Punish the server.

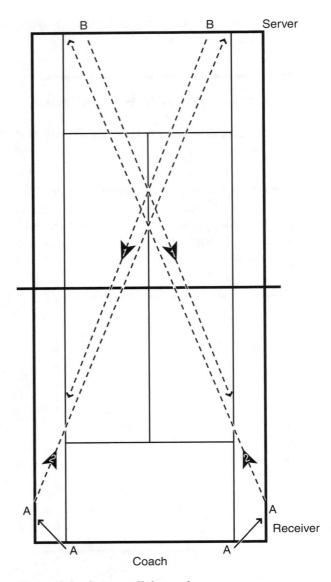

Figure 8.6 Cutting off the angle.

Cutting Off the Angle

Purpose: To practice moving forward on the diagonal to defend against wide serves.

Procedure: The server is limited to serving to the wide angle on the outside of the service boxes. The receiver must cut off the angle by moving forward at 45 degrees to intercept wide serves. The return should normally be played crosscourt to prevent the server from hitting the next shot to a wide open court (see figure 8.6).

Coaching points

Insist that the receiver think forward first and sideways second to cut off the angle. The most common errors with this return result from a lateral movement that requires more steps and then a crossover step with the inside leg that blocks the hip rotation during the hit. This shot is usually critical against a left-handed slice serve in the ad court or a right-handed slice serve in the deuce court. It is often a particularly troublesome return for two-handed players due to their problems in reaching for wide balls. Vary the drill by letting the server serve to either the inside or outside corners of the service boxes. This will keep the receiver from cheating to the outside in anticipation of a wide-angle serve.

SUMMARY

Serving and receiving skills are typically underpracticed even though they begin every point in tennis. Be creative in drills and games with serving and receiving since players are easily bored working on these skills. Keep records during match play of the number of mistakes made on serves or returns to emphasize their importance to your team.

CHAPTER 9 GROUND STROKES AND MID-COURT SHOTS

After the serve and return, most points begin with an exchange of ground strokes. Keep the following concepts in mind as you work with your players on ground strokes.

- You should stress steadiness on ground strokes. Players should generally hit ground strokes crosscourt and deep to prevent the opponent from taking the offensive.

- Ground strokes should be hit more aggressively when players move inside their baseline to play a shot.

- Players should vary the height, spin, and pace of their strokes to keep the opponent a bit off balance—just like a baseball pitcher changes speeds and types of pitches.

- Aiming for target areas well inside the lines will give players a good margin for error. The target should be established at the intersection six feet in from both the baseline and the sideline.

GROUND STROKES

A key to consistent and accurate ground strokes is keeping good balance while moving to the ball and during the stroke. Explosive longer strides are necessary for covering long distances to reach the ball, but short adjustment steps are required as players position for the shot. The footwork options—square, closed, or open stance—were discussed in the previous chapter, and the choice of a stance should be based on the grip, swing, and technique of each player's shots. Urge players to get to the ball early so they have time to set up properly for their next shot rather than having to hit on the run.

Early preparation of the racket is important to produce smooth, relaxed ground strokes. As players begin the small adjustment steps before the stroke, they should turn their shoulder to prepare the racket for the shot. Encourage players to begin preparing their racket about the time the ball crosses the net. If they wait until the ball bounces to begin their swing, they will most likely be too late.

Once your players have improved their consistency and accuracy from the baseline, they should experiment with playing the ball on the rise after the bounce. This will reduce the time the opponent has to prepare between shots and is the foundation shot for an aggressive baseliner. Because the ball is moving upward after the bounce, a slight closing of the racket face at contact is required to cover the ball and counteract the upward flight.

Alley Rally

Purpose: To promote steadiness and accuracy on ground strokes.

Procedure: The alleys are used for this drill, so four players can participate on a single court (two players on each side of the court). Two players compete against each other at each alley. To begin the drill, one player puts the ball in play by a self-drop and hit, and the two players begin a rally. All shots must land in the alley to be considered good. After an error, the same player begins the next point until she has begun play five times. The other player then initiates the next 5 points, and the game continues until one player reaches 21 points.

Coaching points
Players are positioned on the court side of the alley, and players A and C are allowed to hit only forehands, whereas players B and D may hit only backhands. This drill is fairly difficult because the alley is only four and one-half feet wide. Tell players to keep their strings to the target (alley) as long as possible. Doing so will lengthen the stroke. At the end of the game, players switch to the other side of the net for a new game.

Wipers

Purpose: To practice moving along the baseline and hitting ground strokes deep in the court.

Procedure: Feed six balls to each player, alternating forehands and backhands. Players move to the ball and drive it crosscourt and deep. After six hits, the player runs around the net to retrieve the six balls and then rejoins the line to wait for his next turn.

Coaching points
Stress the importance of aiming the ball high enough over the net to achieve good depth.

Two-on-One

Purpose: To develop good court coverage and consistency.

Procedure: Two players at the net volley balls to a baseline player. Any player can begin the point, but the volleyers must hit every ball crosscourt, and the baseline player must hit down the line (see figure 9.1).

Coaching points
After three minutes of nonstop action, players rotate positions. After all three players have had a turn as the baseline player, they repeat the sequence but now the volleyers hit down the line and the baseline player hits crosscourt.

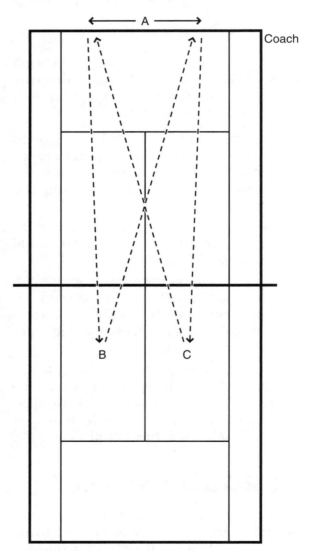

Figure 9.1 Two-on-one.

Figure Eight

Purpose: To work on directional control of ground strokes.

Procedure: Player A begins the rally by hitting crosscourt to the forehand of player B. Player B returns the ball down the line to the backhand of player A, who again plays the ball crosscourt to the backhand of player B (see figure 9.2). The sequence continues with the ball in play until an error occurs and a new point begins. Player A may hit only crosscourt, while player B must hit down the line.

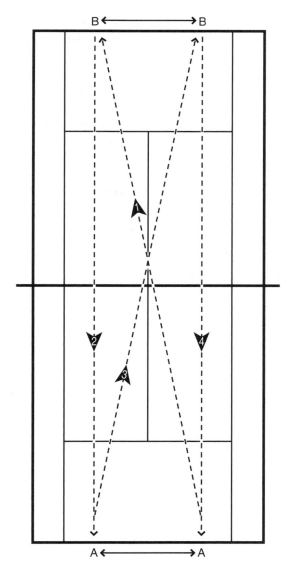

Figure 9.2 Figure eight.

Coaching points

After a few minutes of play, switch the players' roles. You'll notice that the player assigned to hitting down the line does the most running, which reinforces the value of a crosscourt shot. A good variation when court space is limited is for each player to have a partner who takes over the play after every six hits.

Scramble

Purpose: To promote court coverage and fitness.

Procedure: A coach stands at the T (service line) and feeds balls in rapid succession to various points of the baseline. The baseline player must get to each ball, prepare, and return the shot into the court. Each player hits 10 shots, but if he misses a ball, 3 more shots are added.

Coaching points

Adjust the level of difficulty to the skill of your players by asking them to hit to target areas or by changing the interval between feeds. Your intention is to tire players enough to reveal stroke breakdowns and to encourage them to be mentally tough even when fatigued.

Moving Your Opponent

Purpose: To learn to vary the spin, speed, and trajectory of ground strokes.

Procedure: Player A begins the play from his forehand side of the court and varies his shots to player B by moving him around the backcourt. Player B must return every ball to the forehand quadrant of A (see figure 9.3). When B makes an error, C takes his place.

Coaching points

Encourage players to change the speed, spin, and trajectory on every shot. This drill practices topspin drives, slices, moon balls, and angles. Because this is a ground stroke drill, neither player is allowed to approach the net.

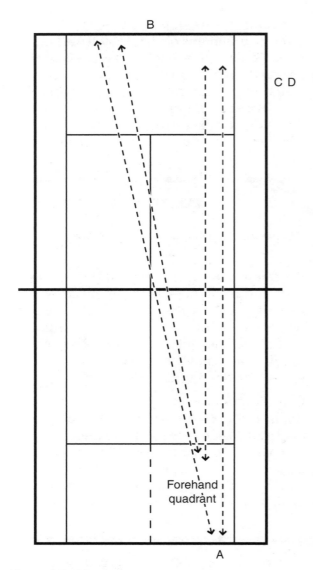

Figure 9.3 Moving your opponent.

MID-COURT SHOTS

Mid-court shots require major changes in stroke technique. The most important decision a player has to make at the midcourt is whether to play a safe shot and move in to volley or to go for an outright winner. There are several concepts you should keep in mind as you work with your players on mid-court play.

Players should go for a winning drive from the midcourt when

- they can contact the ball above the height of the net,
- their opponent is out of position, or
- they are balanced and prepared to hit the shot.

Most of the time, players should hit an approach shot down the line to reduce the angle of the opponent's passing shot. They should aim the ball deep and low by keeping the trajectory flat and adding a little backspin for control. Players can also use an occasional drop shot to confuse the opponent, who may be looking for a deep attacking shot.

To disguise their intention, players must prepare exactly the same for a winning drive, approach shot, or drop shot. However, as they move closer to the net, they may want to shorten the length of their backswing a bit.

Because of the range of options available to players in the midcourt, it's helpful to establish some rules for choosing which shot to play. The most important rule and first lesson to be learned is that balls that bounce even with or lower than the net should be sliced as an approach shot and followed to the net.

A second rule of play is for balls that can be taken above the height of the net. In this case, consider the capabilities of each of your players and choose the shot with the best percentage for success for that individual. For some it will be a winning forehand or backhand drive; for others it may be a sliced approach. Consider, too, that the same player may be better off driving the forehand but slicing the backhand. The key point is to choose the option that makes sense and then practice it so that it becomes automatic during match play.

A third rule is to decide how often to use drop shots. For many players, the drop shot is too delicate a touch shot to hit on hard courts or in pressure situations. Drop shots with the wind at the player's back are also risky. It is probably wise to stick to a very limited use of drop shots for the majority of high school players.

Body balance and movement are vital to successful mid-court play. Teach your players to move forward at a controlled speed, to keep good balance during the shot, and to move through the shot upon contact. Unlike baseline shots in which you want players to plant their feet firmly before the shot, approach shots should be played while moving to the net.

The length of the backswing on most shots from midcourt should be reduced from the normal length on baseline ground strokes. Because the player is closer to the net and moving forward, the ball will tend to carry deep into the court even with a shorter swing. Tell your players that mid-court shots should have a backswing that is longer than volleys but shorter than baseline ground strokes.

One vital shot to learn in the midcourt is a half volley, especially for serve-and-volley players. Teach your players to avoid this shot if possible, but when they have no choice but to play a ball at their feet, they should use a shortened backswing with a long follow-through to guide the ball deep into the opponent's court.

Approach to Targets

Purpose: To practice the technique of the approach shot.

Procedure: Players form two lines on either side of the court with the first player in each line in three-quarters court. The coach feeds a short ball alternately to the lines on the left and right. The first player hits an approach shot down the line to the target and rotates to the opposite line (see figure 9.4).

Coaching points
The main point of this drill is to allow for multiple repetitions of approach shots on both sides of the court. Players hit forehand approach shots from the right side of the court and backhands from the left. Coaches should feed balls rapidly to keep the drill moving. (A coach may also designate two players as feeders to free himself to coach on the same side of the net as the hitters.) After several trials for each player, the coach may add a finishing volley after each successful approach shot.

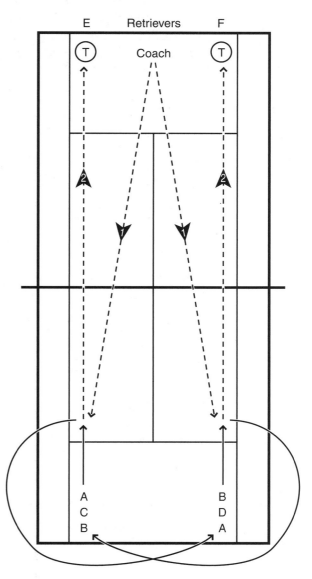

Figure 9.4 Approach to targets.

Continuous Approach

Purpose: To develop control and rhythm during a baseline rally followed by an approach and volley.

Procedure: Two players form a team on each side of the net at the baseline. Player A begins the drill with a crosscourt forehand to C, who returns short to the forehand of A. Player A hits an approach shot to C's backhand, and C hits a passing shot down the line. Player A volleys the ball crosscourt to D, who repeats the sequence with B as her partner (see figure 9.5).

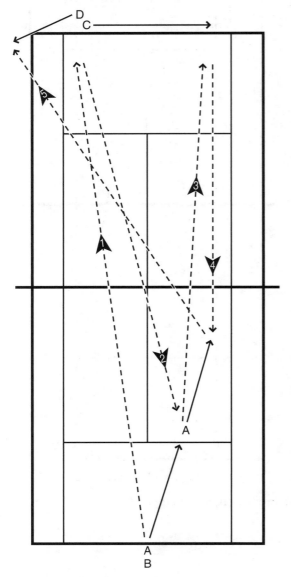

Figure 9.5 Continuous approach.

Coaching points

This drill promotes consistency and control of midcourt shots to simulate a typical game situation. Players should be encouraged to keep the ball under control and in play by hitting at about three-quarters speed in the beginning. Each player should have an extra tennis ball in her pocket so that if she misses a shot she can quickly put another ball in play at the same spot and continue the drill. After a set amount of time, repeat the drill using backhand shots.

Winner or Approach

Purpose: To practice choosing whether to hit a winner or an approach shot based on the height of the ball.

Procedure: Players line up to take turns from the baseline. To begin the drill, a coach puts a ball in play, and the player hits a ground stroke on this first ball. On the second ball from the coach, the coach varies feeds above the net and below the net. Players must choose the correct shot—winners off high-bouncing balls and approach shots off low-bouncing balls (see figure 9.6).

Coaching points

Mix up shots to the forehand and backhand sides. Reinforce players who choose the right shot even if they miss.

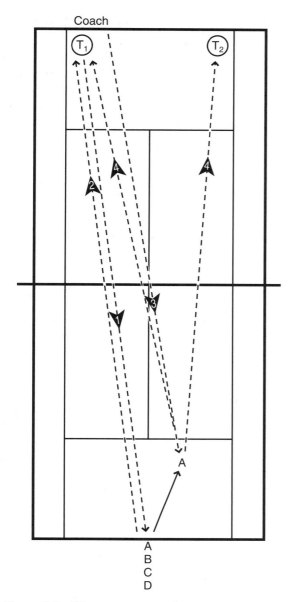

Figure 9.6 Winner or approach.

Approach From the Air

Purpose: To practice approach shots taken in the air.

Procedure: Player A is fed a ground stroke that must be hit deep in the opponent's court. The opponent answers with a moon ball, which normally gives him time to recover. Player A steps in to midcourt to play an approach shot out of the air, takes the net, and plays the point out.

Coaching points
This is an essential drill to help players learn to pressure defensive baseliners. The technique for the approach shot is the same as is used on a bouncing ball, but it may be a bit more difficult to time the hit correctly.

Half Volley Deep

Purpose: To practice hitting half volleys deep down the line.

Procedure: Player A feeds a ball to player B, who is just behind the service line. Player B half volleys the ball down the line, aiming for depth and closing in to the net. Player A may try a passing shot or a lob, and the point is played out. The next player, C, repeats the sequence, followed by D, and so on. Player A is always the feeder and passing or lobbing until the coach makes a switch.

Coaching points
Be sure that players work on both sides of the court so that they can practice half volleys using the forehand and backhand. Emphasize a short backswing and a long, controlled follow-through to produce depth on the half volley.

SUMMARY

Use the following points to help your players develop sound stroke mechanics:

- Establish several key concepts for each tennis shot that every player should understand. Consistently reinforce proper application of these coaching tips during practice.

- Be creative in planning and developing drills to practice specific shots or sequences of shots. The purpose of each drill should be clear to players so that they can transfer their knowledge and skill to game situations.

- Solid ground strokes are the key to staying in the rally. Steadiness, control, and consistency should be stressed.

- On the other hand, depth, variety, and pace can help elicit a weak shot from the opponent and present an opportunity to attack.

- Once players are lucky enough to receive a ball in the mid-court, they need to be trained to automatically take advantage of it by punishing the opponent, or hitting an approach shot and save the punishment for net play.

CHAPTER 10 NET PLAY, PASSING SHOTS, AND LOBS

Once players have reached the net position, the goal is to end the point decisively. It is possible to hit the ball down at the net, and even more likely is that sharp angles are exposed to put the ball out of reach of your opponent. Volley skills include balls hit deep to drive the opponent back, angle volleys to end the point, and drop volleys that land just over the net as a change of pace. Of course, every player loves the chance to hit an easy overhead smash and end the point with a bang!

VOLLEY

Play at the net requires quick responses and decisive movements by players in order to end the point in their favor. This chapter describes the key concepts for net play. All volleys involve a short, compact movement with a follow-through toward the target. Players should prepare for the shot with a quick turn of the upper body and align the racket face behind the flight of the oncoming ball. Balls that players can hit above the net should be angled off to the open court (offensive volley). On balls below the net, players should play the shot safely deep down the line and wait for the next shot (defensive volley).

As the opponent strikes the ball, a player should close in quickly to volley or retreat to hit the overhead smash. Closing in makes passing shots difficult and opens up more angles for winning volleys.

For low balls, players should bend from the knees, keeping their shoulders and back relatively straight. On wide balls, they should move diagonally toward the net to intercept the shot.

Volley technique must be efficient because there is less time to react to the oncoming ball. The racket head should be above waist level and out in front of the body. Advanced players prefer a continental grip because it requires no grip change from forehand to backhand. If your players must change grips, be sure they do so by using the nonracket hand at the throat of the racket to change the angle of the racket face and grip.

Two-handers should usually be encouraged to convert to a one-handed volley to extend their reach and to defend against balls at the body. This is probably a change to make in the off-season because it will take time.

Good balance is essential at the net to allow quick recovery for the next shot. Players should maintain a relatively straight upper body and bend from the knees for lower shots. When possible, the volleyer should transfer weight forward by moving diagonally toward the net and stepping into the shot with a crossover forward step.

The primary objective at the net is to end the point, and normally the flight of the ball is down into the opponent's court. Most winning shots are achieved by angling the ball away from the opponent, which is done by setting the wrist angle and maintaining a tight grip and firm wrist upon ball contact.

Balls directed at the body are best covered by the backhand from waist to face. Encourage your players to hold their ground or step forward on every volley rather than stepping back. During drills, a good way for you to prevent the backward step is to stand directly behind a player as she prepares to volley.

Keep the head and chin up throughout the hit.

The overhead smash is a spectacular shot that is hit with a grip and swing similar to the serve. The first move should be to turn sideways and retreat to a position just behind the expected contact point. Both arms should be raised together. The non-racket arm's role is to help maintain balance. At the same time, the racket arm bends and then straightens to reach up to meet the ball at full extension. The contact point is about a foot in front of the body so that the ball will be directed downward into the court. The head and chin should stay up throughout the hit to avoid pulling the ball downward into the net.

On very high defensive lobs or on windy days, urge your players to let the ball bounce before they try an overhead smash. Because the ball picks up speed as it falls, very high lobs are difficult to time correctly.

Volley to Targets

Purpose: To develop accuracy on eight possible volleys.

Procedure: Use a ball machine or feeder to give each volleyer eight shots in a row. Begin with forehand volleys deep crosscourt and down the line (targets 1 and 2 in figure 10.1). Follow with short-angled volleys to the short crosscourt angle and finally down the line (targets 3 and 4). Repeat the sequence using the backhand volley.

Coaching points
Tell players to move forward on the diagonal to cut off the ball. If you notice that a player has difficulty with one of the eight shots, allow some time for individual help and practice as soon as possible. Be sure that every player uses some underspin on each volley to control the depth of the shot. Short volleys may prove especially troublesome for players who take too big a backswing. Teach them to "soften" their hands and simply deflect the ball to accomplish the short angles.

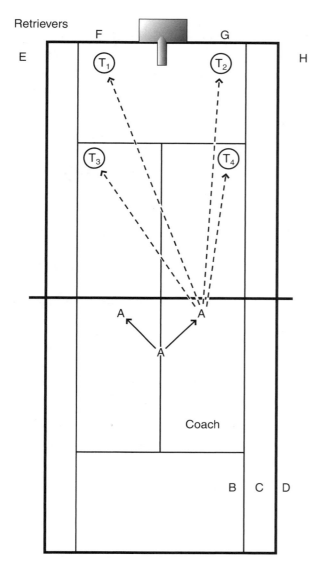

Figure 10.1 Volley to targets.

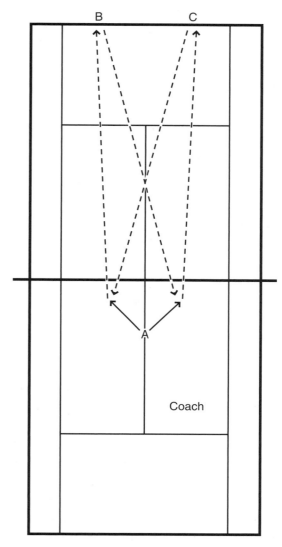

Figure 10.2 Two-on-one volleys.

Two-on-One Volleys

Purpose: To work on consistency and directional control of the volley.

Procedure: Two players at the baseline feed ground strokes to the volleyer. Any player can begin the point, but the baseline players must hit every ball crosscourt, and the volleyer must hit every ball down the line (see figure 10.2).

Coaching points

After three minutes of nonstop action, players rotate positions. After all three players have had a turn as the volleyer, they repeat the sequence, but the volleyers now hit crosscourt and the baseliners hit down the line. A good variation is to ask baseliners to mix in lobs occasionally to prevent the volleyer from crowding the net.

Kamikaze Volleys

Purpose: To practice closing in to the net and reacting quickly to the speed of the oncoming ball.

Procedure: Two players, one on each half of the court, begin the play from three-quarters court. Either player puts the ball in play, and both players must volley the ball out of the air back to their partner straight ahead, take one step toward the net, and then split step to prepare for the next volley. The object is for both players to close in to the net while the ball is in play.

Coaching points
Encourage players to keep the ball under control and to reduce the size of their backswing as they move closer to the net and have less time to react.

Overhead Countdown

Purpose: To promote teamwork and add pressure during practice of overhead smashes.

Procedure: Begin the drill by assigning four to eight players to a team. Multiply the number of players by 10 to arrive at the number of successful smashes to be hit. For example, six players multiplied by 10 equals 60 smashes.

The first player in line begins to smash lobs from the coach while the group chants backward from 60 with each successful smash. If the first player misses after 7 successful smashes, the next player in line replaces him, and the group takes up the count at 53. Once the second player misses, the third player replaces him. Continue until all six players have had a turn.

Of course, you hope to reach zero smashes before you run out of players. If not, assign every player in the group to hit the remaining number of smashes before they leave practice that day. For example, if the countdown ended at 17, each player must perform 17 successful smashes at the end of practice.

Coaching points
Because you are feeding the lobs, you can vary the difficulty according to the ability of the group and particular players. Challenge the best players with difficult lobs and boost the confidence of less-skilled players with easy chances.

PASSING SHOTS AND LOBS

Defensive play against a net player involves hitting the ball past her to the left or right or lobbing a shot over her head. Players should think of passing as a two-shot sequence. First, they must get their opponent in trouble, and after a weak volley, they should pass her on the second shot. Heavy topspin should be used on passing shots to keep the ball low, and topspin or backspin should be used on lobs to control their depth in the court.

Players should choose a lob when

- their opponent is close to the net,
- their opponent has an undependable overhead smash,
- the wind is in their face or the sun is in their opponent's eyes, or
- they are deep in the court behind their baseline.

Players should choose a passing shot when

- their opponent does not close in to the net,
- their opponent has an undependable volley,
- the wind is at their back, or
- they are inside their baseline.

Because the objective is to prevent the net player from hitting a winning volley, passing shots should be hit lower to the net than normal ground strokes. Ask players to aim one to three feet over the net and apply plenty of topspin to the ball so that it dips downward after crossing the net. The extra topspin can be achieved by emphasizing the upward path of the racket from low to high and accelerating the racket head through the hitting area.

The most important concept to stress with your players is to keep the ball low so that the net person must play a defensive shot. Although most young players tend to slug away when the opponent reaches the net, speed and power alone will not produce successful passing shots. Of course, the key to defensive play is learning to disguise and integrate lobs along with passing shots.

Lobbing is the only answer to counter the attack of the volleyer who closes in very tight to the net. Many players are vulnerable to a lob over their backhand side, so urge your players to aim that way most of the time.

To disguise the lob, its technique should look identical to that for ground strokes. The loft of the ball can be achieved by opening the racket face just enough through the hitting area. Using backspin on lobs to control the depth of the shot is the first order of business for your players. Topspin lobs are more offensive and may require more touch and practice to gain good control. However, some players who use semiwestern or western grips and apply heavy topspin to their ground strokes may find topspin lobs to be an easy addition to their repertoire.

Defensive lobs are hit high in the air to allow recovery for the next shot. Because the ball will fall rapidly from a greater height, the opponent will be faced with a more difficult shot if the lob is hit at least "three stories high." Tell players to aim high defensive lobs to land just behind the T at the service line to allow plenty of room for error.

Perfect 10

Purpose: To learn to adjust the height and depth of ground strokes for effective passing shots.

Procedure: Players are fed four balls in succession, which they try to hit in sequence to the following locations: deep crosscourt, short crosscourt, deep down the line, and short down the line (see figure 10.3). Each

successful shot earns the point value shown in the figure, and all four shots hit correctly earns a perfect 10. After their turn, players retrieve the four balls they hit and replace them in the feeder's basket.

Coaching points
This is a basic drill to help your players learn to adapt their normal ground strokes to passing shots. Emphasize two changes that must be made to hit the shorter balls: apply more topspin to the ball and aim lower over the net. You might try stretching a rope three feet above the net and asking players to aim over it for deep shots and under it for short ones.

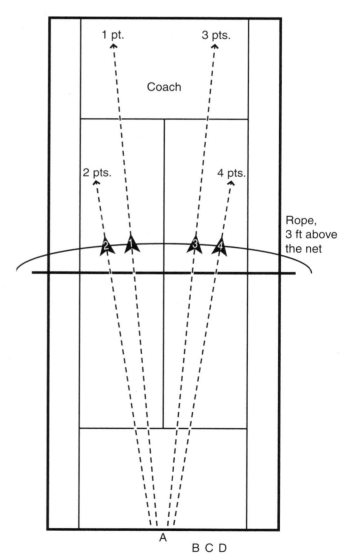

Figure 10.3 Perfect 10.

Passing Shots

Purpose: To develop the feel of crosscourt angled passing shots.

Procedure: Players A and B put the ball in play from the service line and stay right there for the returning shot. Players C and D try to hit a topspin passing shot aimed at the short crosscourt and angled low to the net, and the point is played out (see figure 10.4). Players A and C work together at the same time that B and D are performing the drill on the other side of the court. Perform this drill on the forehand side first, then switch to the backhand side.

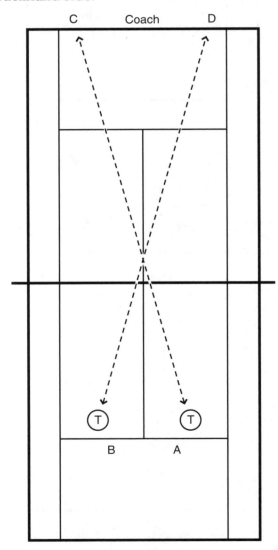

Figure 10.4 Passing shots.

Coaching points
Although players A and B are forced into the unnatural position of remaining at the service line instead of closing in, they will get good practice at digging out low volleys and half volleys. After about three minutes of work, players should rotate clockwise to the next position until they have practiced from each of the four spots.

Two Balls Across, One Wide

Purpose: To develop better ground strokes and defensive lobs.

Procedure: Players line up on one side of the court to wait for their turn. When the drill begins, the player moves across the baseline as you feed two balls in succession across the baseline. You then feed a third ball to the opposite side of the court so that the player has to sprint back and throw up the defensive lob (see figure 10.5).

Coaching points
This drill allows ground stroke work as well as practice in the art of hitting a high defensive lob that allows the player hitting the lob time enough to get back into the center of possible returns.

Lobs and Smashes

Purpose: To develop the touch and technique of defending against the smash with high defensive lobs.

Procedure: Player A tries to put away overhead smashes anywhere within the doubles court. Players B, C, and D defend by lofting defensive lobs and trying to return every smash (see figure 10.6). After two minutes, players rotate clockwise to the next position.

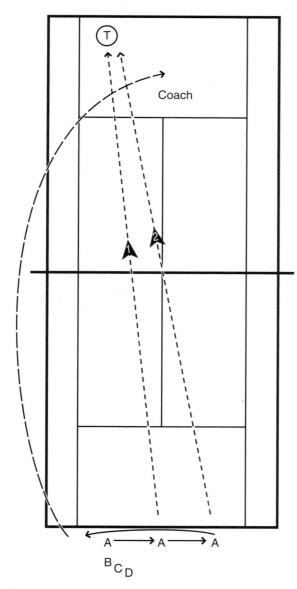

Figure 10.5   Two balls across, one wide.

Coaching points: Add the element of competition by scoring a point for each successful smash.

SUMMARY

In both singles and doubles play, learning to play shots at the net is critical for all levels of

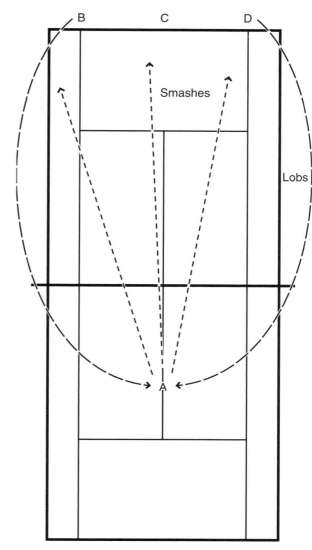

Figure 10.6   Lobs and smashes.

play. Emphasize the opportunity to end the point at the net and allow your players to enjoy the exhilaration of smashing a winner or volleying a cleverly angled touch volley. Don't neglect the defensive shots against net play, passing shots, and lobs. They often hold the key to matches due to poor strategy or poor execution. Emphasize the use of spin on both passing shots and lobs to control the ball and increase the difficulty for the offensive player.

CHAPTER 11 SINGLES STRATEGY

At the most fundamental level, singles strategy is simply hitting the ball over the net and into the court once more per point than the opponent. After just a few sets, most players realize that it is also a good idea to aim the ball out of the opponent's reach or hit to an obvious weakness such as a suspect backhand. At the same time, you want your players to hit their favorite and most dependable shot as much as possible while covering up their weaknesses.

A good framework for teaching singles strategy is to help your players understand it as a combination of these basic features:

- The principles of percentage tennis
- Your players' strengths and weaknesses
- The opponents' strengths and weaknesses

Your first task as a coach is to teach your players the principles and applications of percentage tennis while they are developing their skills. This approach will help them understand the reasons for learning certain shots or the necessity for changing an inadequate stroke. During this time, you should introduce players to various fundamental shot sequences (such as opening the court) and allow them to experiment using each pattern.

Eventually, your second task is to help each player analyze her personal strengths and weaknesses. Once the two of you agree on the analysis, you can begin to fashion an

Tennis players each have their own unique style of play. Work with them to develop their strengths and overcome their weaknesses.

individual style of play that makes sense to both of you and that the player enjoys. Tips on building a style of play are covered in the next section of this chapter.

The final task for you and your team is to learn to analyze the opponent's game and tailor a game plan for each match. Sometimes it's possible to collect information by scouting opponents before a match. But if that's not possible, your players will need to perform a quick study during the warm-up period and during the first few games of the match. It's up to you to help them learn to take a quick inventory of each opponent's strengths and weaknesses and then factor this information into their game plan for the match. Scouting is discussed further in chapter 13.

PERCENTAGE TENNIS

The height of the net, the dimensions of the court, and the rules of the game provide consistent parameters for all players. To those limitations you must add the collective wisdom accumulated over a span of more than 100 years by the coaches and players of the game. Once your players have a good grasp of the principles of percentage play, they will be launched on a steady path of improvement throughout their high school career, collegiate tennis, and even during adult and senior tennis years.

Use all the teaching aids and methods at your disposal to help your players learn the principles quickly and retain the knowledge for years. Classroom talks, reading assignments, videotapes of the great players, and periodic written examinations are all appropriate tools.

Some coaches have collected and constructed test questions on the principles of percentage play. After a few weeks of preseason practices, players are given a series of questions to answer in writing during a classroom session. You should vary the difficulty of the test from year to year and among team members depending on what they could be expected to know at that point in their career. A passing grade of 80 percent is required, or you might ask them to repeat the test each day until they earn a passing grade. Your players should know that you take their learning of percentage play seriously. Maybe the best part of the experience is watching them help each other study for the test.

On the tennis court, you should use carefully planned demonstrations by skilled players to support your points. Follow each demonstration with a series of drills that progress from simple to more advanced and focus specifically on the concept you just demonstrated.

Check each drill you plan to use in practice to be sure it replicates the correct shot or series of shots strategically. If your drills mirror a game situation and provide plenty of repetition of the right shot at the right time, your players will quickly improve in match play. All the drills presented in the book will be helpful to improving match play on one level or another.

Finally, during "set play" practice, you should stop play to reinforce good use of percentage play and good choice of shots. On the other hand, if players make poor choices, resist the temptation to dwell on the mistakes they make. For example, if you notice two players sparring from the baseline with shots landing near the optimal aim points well inside the lines, stop play and call attention (in front of the entire team) to their good percentage play. It's natural for onlookers to notice and be impressed by shots that land on a line, but you have to emphasize that line shots are poor risks and not deserving of applause.

Generally, players make a poor play for one of these reasons:

- They don't understand the correct shot.
- They understand what to do but use poor technique.
- They are affected by the pressures of match play, a loss of concentration, or fatigue.

Take the time to determine which of these reasons produced the poor play and help your players find an alternative. A few gentle but direct questions will produce better results than orders, sarcasm, or negative criticism. Your job is to help your kids become their own coach on the court and learn from each mistake. Your conversation might go something like this:

Coach: I wonder whether that was the best choice of shots, Jim?

Player: I dunno, Coach. I thought I had him dead at the net.

Coach: Did you notice where he was in the court?

Player: I'm not sure . . . I guess he was kind of close to the net.

Coach: What might have worked better?

Player: I should have tried a topspin lob like we practiced yesterday.

Coach: Good idea. Next time he comes in, try the lob and see what happens.

Tennis Is a Game of Errors, Not Winners

At almost every level of play, 85 percent of tennis points are lost as a result of an error. It follows that 15 percent of points are earned by a winning shot. Understanding that statistic will help your players realize that a smart strategy is to get opponents in trouble and force them to take a risky shot. A well-coached team will practice using a singles strategy that will be obvious even to the casual spectator. From every position on the court, your players should automatically choose the shot that will put them in the best position to stay in the point or result in an error from the opponent.

Of course, many errors in high-level tennis are forced by the placement or power of the shot. Errors that are not forced are the result of poor choice of shots or faulty technique. Naturally, the player who can force errors from her opponent while limiting her own unforced errors has a great chance for success. The few winners she collects will be icing on the cake, but they really won't win matches because they will be so rare.

Keys to avoiding errors involve playing each shot with a low risk of error. Here are some specific suggestions:

- The first objective on every shot is to clear the net. When both players are at the baseline, ground strokes should be aimed about three to five feet over the net. This will not only ensure clearance but will also tend to keep the player's shots deep in the opponent's court.

- The second objective is to direct the ball inside the lines. Smart players aim well inside the baseline and sidelines for a comfortable margin of safety. Measure six feet in from the sideline and six feet in from the baseline and use that intersection as the target for most ground strokes (see figure 11.1).

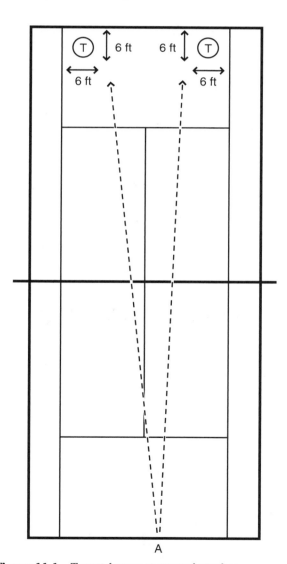

Figure 11.1 Target for most ground strokes.

- Any time your players are in trouble or are forced to play the ball from behind their baseline, outside the sideline, or on the run, they should hit the ball high and deep to allow themselves time to recover for the next shot.

- When in doubt, a shot hit deep and down the middle of the court reduces the chances for making an error and keeps the opponent from attacking.

- It is generally safer to play a ball back to the same direction it came from rather than trying to change its direction. For example, a crosscourt forehand is easier to return crosscourt. If a player tries to change the angle of the racket face at contact, even just a few degrees, the timing is delicate and risky.

- Early preparation for each shot is the key to consistency. Urge your players to get in position early, set up for the shot, and aim to hit every ball in their strike zone (about waist high) while maintaining good balance.

- Most errors occur early in a point, especially in returning serve. Your players should develop a mind-set to begin each point from a neutral position and "work" the point before attacking, particularly on slower courts.

POSITION ON THE COURT

Strategy is influenced significantly by the area of the court where a player is positioned. Most tennis coaches divide the singles court into four general areas:

1. Baseline
2. Three-quarters court
3. Midcourt
4. Net

The closer players get to the net to play a ball, the more angles they have available to hit a winning shot. Figure 11.2 shows how the angles increase closer to the net.

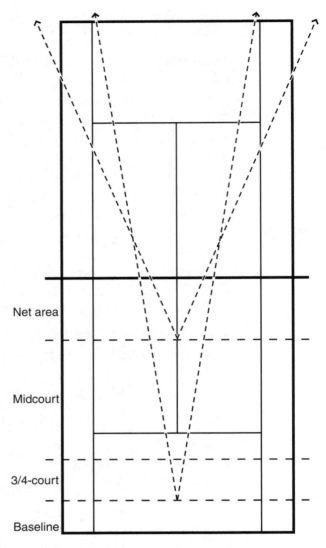

Figure 11.2 Angles to the net.

Baseline Play

The objective of players at the baseline is steadiness. The flight of the ball should be upward from the racket to achieve net clearance and depth. A crosscourt shot is safer than a shot down the line because the net is lower in the middle (three feet) than at the sidelines (three feet, six inches), and the diagonal shot from corner to corner adds about four feet to the length of the court.

Players must learn to bisect the angle of possible returns. This doesn't mean the player returns to the center of the court each time but that he stays diagonally opposite the ball. Figure 11.3 shows the proper baseline positioning for court coverage based

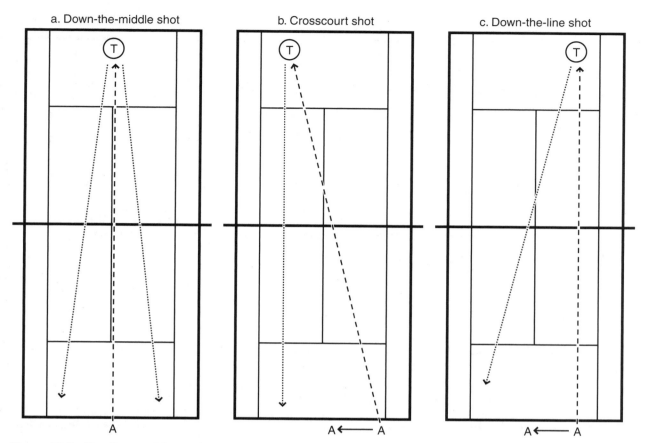

Figure 11.3 Baseline positions.

on the possible angles of return by the opponent.

Stress to your players that a position on or behind the baseline is a defensive one. Their objective should be to remain steady; stay in the point; vary the shots by changing the spin, speed, and trajectory; and wait for a short ball from the opponent.

Notice in figure 11.3a that the player is positioned in the middle of the court when his shot is hit down the middle. In figure 11.3b, the shot is crosscourt, so the returner's position is just to the right of center, diagonally opposite the ball. If the shot is hit down the line, as in figure 11.3c, the player should move to the left side of center to bisect the angle of possible returns.

Bisecting the Angle Drill

Purpose: To practice bisecting the angle of returns.

Procedure: Feed three balls to a player who hits the first ball down the middle and recovers to the middle (see figure 11.4a). The player hits the second ball crosscourt and makes the recovery to the right of center (see figure 11.4b). The third ball is hit down the line, and recovery is to the left of the center mark (see figure 11.4c).

Coaching points

After players are recovering correctly each time, add a second shot. For example, the player hits the ball crosscourt and recovers; you then hit a second ball angled sharply back crosscourt. If the player has moved too far to the center, he will not be able to reach the second shot.

Three-Quarters Court Play

The objective from three-quarters court is to force an error from the opponent. This is the time for the player to hit her favorite

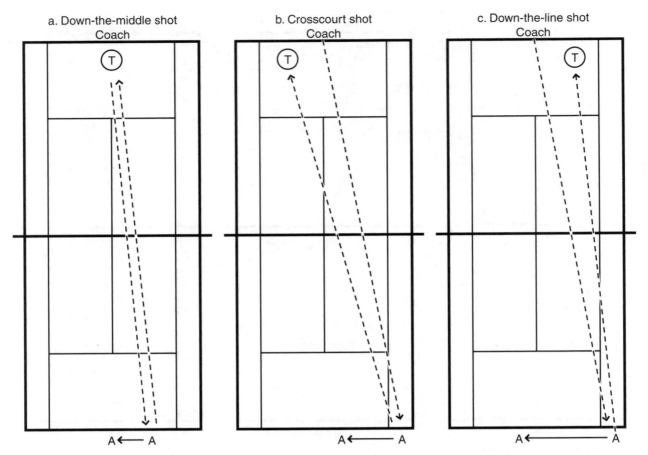

Figure 11.4 Bisecting the angles.

shot, such as the inside-out forehand. Playing a ball from three-quarters court opens up better angles to move the opponent. A good combination of shots is for the player to hit sharply crosscourt to one side and then follow up with a deep shot to the opposite side. The opponent will have to cover a lot of ground to catch up with both shots. As the skill level of your team improves, advise your players to take the ball early off the bounce (as it is rising) to reduce the time the opponent has to recover position.

On shots of medium difficulty, a good play from three-quarters court is for the player to run around a weakness and hit her favorite shot. For most players this means a forehand. If the opponent is quick to cover the open court area, your player should direct the ball back to where the opponent came from and force her to change directions.

Inside-Out Forehand Drill

Purpose: To develop an attacking inside-out forehand.

Procedure: Players line up at the baseline on the backhand side. From behind the service line, feed the ball short and high toward the center of three-quarters court. Players move up in turn and hit aggressively with a forehand drive to target 1. This shot should be hit firmly, and the path of the ball should exit the court across the singles sideline, not the baseline (see figure 11.5).

Coaching points

For variation, players can add a forehand down the line by hitting the outside of the ball and hooking it down the sideline. The ball should land deep in the corner (target 2). After a number of trials, let players choose their best shot.

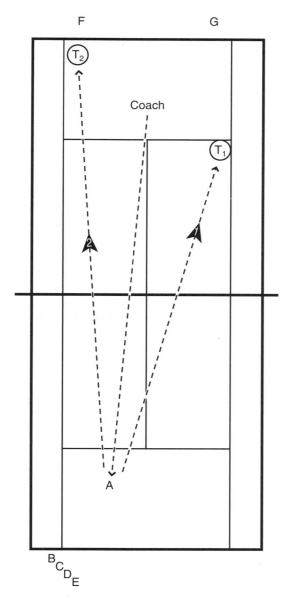

Figure 11.5 Inside-out forehand.

Mid-Court Play

Balls that land in the midcourt are an invitation for the player to hit a forcing shot or an approach shot. On these shots, the flight of the ball should be straight, and the player should aim for good depth.

A ball in this area of the court can be hit for an outright winner if the player can play it above net height. He should play it flat with just a little spin for control, using either topspin or backspin, whichever works best for him.

On balls below or even with the net, the player should slice an approach shot down

the line and follow the path of the ball toward the net. This allows him to bisect the angle again by keeping him on the same side of the court as the ball.

A crosscourt shot forces the player to move across the center line as well as forward to bisect the angle. It's a risky play unless the opponent has a significantly weaker shot on one side, in which case the player should simply approach to the opponent's weakness.

To keep the opponent guessing after a series of approach shots down the line, the player should hit a deep shot to the other side. If he disguises the shot well, he'll catch his opponent deep in the opposite corner.

Three-Ball Drill

Purpose: To develop the habit of approaching the net on a short ball.

Procedure: Feed a deep ball to the player, who drives it deep crosscourt. The second feed should land short, and the player should hit an approach shot down the line and move through the shot to the net position. The final shot is a volley angled crosscourt (see figure 11.6). The next player performs the same sequence.

Coaching points
After players achieve some success, add a fourth ball that should be fed as a lob. The player should hit an overhead smash to the backhand side of the court.

Net Play

Once the player has reached the net position, she should end the point by hitting the ball down into the court, using the angles to put it out of reach of her opponent. To eliminate the chance of hitting into the net, and to open up wider angles, she should close in to the net with at least two forward steps so that there is little risk of error as the opponent tries to pass. If the opponent counters with a series of lobs, the player should hang back until the opponent is committed to a shot.

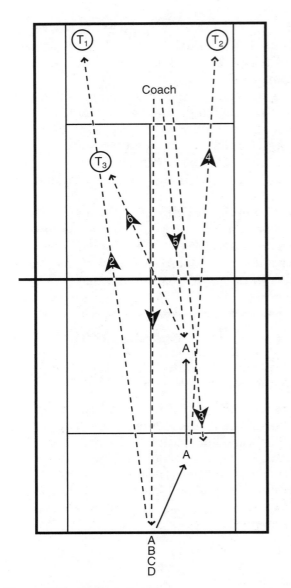

Figure 11.6   Three-ball drill.

On balls below net level, the player should push the ball back deep down the line and wait for a better opportunity to angle it off. (See the closing to net drill and figure 11.7.)

Quick opponents will often race to cover the open court area. Your players should try hitting behind opponents once in a while to keep them honest. Once a player is at the net, she should expect to move two steps forward to volley or three steps back to hit an overhead shot. To prepare for the next shot, she should split step and get her balance just before her opponent begins the shot, then "explode" forward or backward to the ball.

(See the two steps up or three back drill and figure 11.8.)

Closing to Net Drill

Purpose: To learn to play balls below the net back down the line and those above the net crosscourt for a winner.

Procedure: Feed to the player at net. If the ball is above the net, the player closes quickly and angles it off crosscourt. If the ball is below the net, he plays it back down the line and waits for the next ball (see figure 11.7). After trying a winning volley, the player goes to the end of the line, and the next player comes to net.

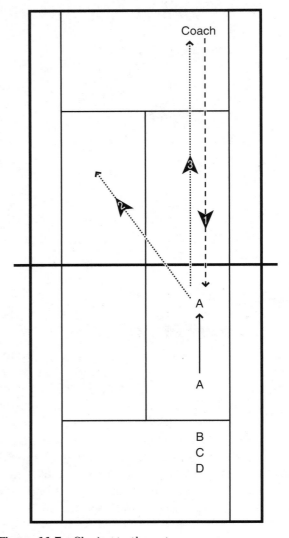

Figure 11.7   Closing to the net.

Coaching points

It's a good idea to start with several low shots to get players used to making a defensive volley. When they do get a high ball, they should pounce on it for the put-away.

Two Steps Up or Three Back Drill

Purpose: To practice moving up or back at the net.

Procedure: Players A, C, E, and G use half the court, and players B, D, F, and H use the other half. Be sure players stay on their side of the center line to prevent collisions. The player at the net puts the ball in play underhand, and the baseline player either lobs or drives the ball, trying not to make an error. The net player moves two steps in before each volley and three steps back before each overhead smash, both of which are directed back to his baseline partner (see figure 11.8). The ball should stay in play for several hits before the next player, E or F, becomes the net player.

Coaching points

Because players defend only half the court, the ball will stay in play. Emphasis should be on quick, explosive steps by the net player to move up or back. Ask net players to watch the baseliner for clues as to whether he will drive or lob.

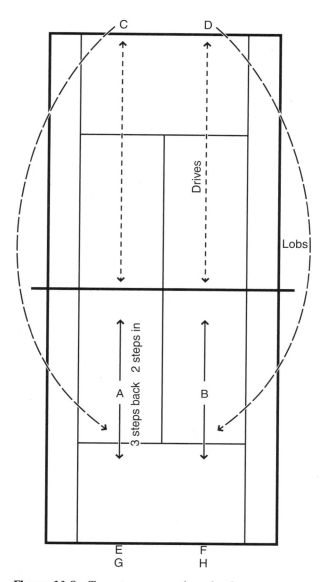

Figure 11.8 Two steps up or three back.

PRINCIPLES OF PERCENTAGE TENNIS

There are several more principles of percentage tennis that apply to match play. You should share the following principles with your players. Although there will be exceptions to the rule, each of these principles is sound advice the majority of the time.

Never Change a Winning Game

The adage "never change a winning game, but always change a losing one" is pretty sound conventional wisdom, but there are exceptions. If the score is close well into the match, your players may be better off staying with their strengths and reducing their errors just a bit. Abandoning a sound game plan late in a close match is risky, even if your player is a little behind.

Get Your First Serve In

Getting the first serve in is always a good idea, especially for players who tend to double-fault under pressure. To help them improve their percentage, urge your players to add more spin to their first serve rather than reducing the speed.

Use the Elements to Your Advantage

Most tennis players are annoyed by bright sun, wind, heat, humidity, and cold. Train your players not only to tolerate the elements but to use them to frustrate opponents. This means your players have to practice in those conditions and adjust strokes and strategy accordingly. Strokes may have to be shortened on gusty days, and players may need to use more spin to control the ball in the wind.

Use Your Strengths on Important Points

There's no question that you'd like players to go with winning combinations in a tight match. Drop shots, touch volleys, and cute angles should be outlawed when the score is close. It's simply too risky to rely on a fine touch under pressure.

The Last Game Is the Toughest to Win

This is often true, especially when playing an opponent who has been committing unforced errors throughout the match. Suddenly faced with losing, she becomes steady as a rock and refuses to make errors. This calls for patience, and perhaps the element of surprise. Just be sure your players have a plan that makes sense and emphasizes their strengths and the opponents' weaknesses.

STYLES OF PLAY

As your players become comfortable with the principles of strategy and can execute the concepts in practice, they should develop an individual style of play based on their particular strengths and weaknesses. Although there will be variations on the theme, styles of play generally fall into one of four categories:

- Counterpuncher
- Aggressive baseliner
- All-court player
- Serve-and-volleyer

Your task as a coach is to help each player choose a style that suits her and then plan practice time to develop the skills needed to use that style in match play.

To select a style of play, spend some time with each player to analyze her physical abilities, racket skills, and competitive personality.

Most young players will have one or more players on the professional tour whom they admire. Unfortunately, their choice of role models is not always based on style of play. You need to help them choose players who use a style that would be good for them to imitate. Encourage them to watch videotapes of favorite players in action so that the visual images become strong and clear. Figure 11.9 can be used to help players think about their role models and what qualities they admire and strive for.

Counterpuncher

Counterpunchers often develop from a retrieving style and make it a point of honor to return every shot. In junior tennis, these players are referred to as "pushers" because they usually hit with little pace and use high, arcing moon balls as their bread-and-butter shot. As players mature, they can progress from a pushing style into a legitimate counterpuncher.

The physical characteristics necessary for this style are excellent movement skills and

Date_____ Name_____

My role model(s) include _____

_____

_____

_____

What style do they use—Aggressive Baseliner (AB), Counterpuncher (CP), All-Court (AC), or Serve-and-Volleyer (SV)? _____

What are their strong points? _____

_____

_____

_____

What are their weaknesses? _____

_____

_____

_____

What are your strong points? _____

_____

_____

_____

What are your weaknesses? _____

_____

_____

_____

What are your goals for playing more like your role model? _____

_____

_____

_____

Figure 11.9 Role model questionnaire.

quickness. Physical conditioning is also a key because long points and matches are likely. Defense is the strength of a counterpuncher, so steady ground strokes, accurate passing shots, and well-controlled lobs are essential skills. Counterpunchers often feel most comfortable playing behind the baseline and have more success on slow-playing courts, particularly clay.

The competitive personality of a counterpuncher is marked by patience, determination, and a "never say die" attitude. These players are fighters who love the battle but typically do not take risks. Role models have included Michael Chang on the men's side and Martina Hingis, Arantxa Sanchez-Vicario, and Amanda Coetzer for the women. On the professional tour, there are very few players of this style left among the top-ranked players. The emphasis on power, which has developed because of enhanced racket technology, and stronger, faster athletes in the sport has virtually eliminated counterpunchers from the very top levels of professional tennis. However, counterpunchers probably dominate high school tennis throughout the United States.

To develop the counterpuncher style, use drills that emphasize consistency and concentration on ground strokes, such as the counterstroking drill. Another simple drill is to ask your players to keep a ball in play for 100 shots without an error and then challenge them to break their previous record. Targets on the court should be used to aim for depth and improve accuracy of ground strokes. You also may want to stretch a rope above the net six to eight feet from the ground to get players used to aiming high. Naturally, the lob is a key weapon for a counterpuncher, so drills that require lobbing over the outstretched racket of a net player are helpful, particularly over the backhand side.

Counterstroking

Purpose: To practice defensive play.

Procedure: Two players begin at the baseline, and the counterstroker (A) puts the ball in play with a self-drop and hits from anywhere on the court (see figure 11.10). The aggressive player (B) looks for the opportunity to take the net via an approach shot or to hit a winner off a short ball. The counterstroker must defend the baseline and cannot approach the net. The winner is the first one to win 21 points.

Coaching points
This is a long, grueling drill that requires patience and concentration. Although this drill may not fit everyone's style, all of your players can benefit from it because there will always be points in a match when they must

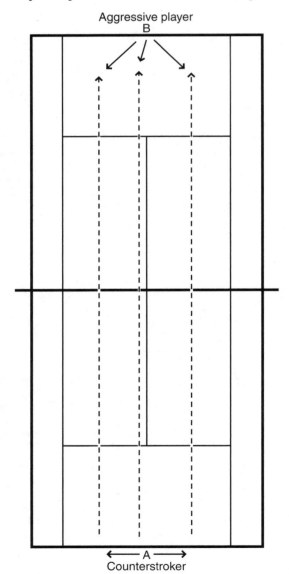

Figure 11.10 Counterstroking.

rely on their defensive skills to get them out of trouble.

Strategies for playing against a counterpuncher require patience in setting up shots because players can expect to see a lot of balls come back over the net. They should take advantage of short balls and get to the net so that they can end the point, but they must vary their approach shots to keep the counterpuncher guessing. Players can dictate the play because the counterpuncher's style is to react rather than mount an offense himself. Another effective ploy is to draw him in to the net, where he is probably uncertain, and exploit his lack of familiarity and confidence with volleys and overheads. The counterpuncher loves side-to-side running, so players should challenge him instead with up-and-back movement.

Aggressive Baseliner

Some players will progress from counterpunchers to aggressive baseliners as their skills and strength improve with practice and through the natural maturing process. This style requires quickness in setting up for shots and the muscular strength and endurance to hit the ball with pace when there is an opening.

An aggressive baseliner is typically positioned on or just inside the baseline to take advantage of balls that land short and are begging to be attacked. It's not unusual for this player to have a forehand grip more toward a western and a two-handed backhand. Crosscourt drives with heavy topspin are the foundation of the aggressive baseliner's game, along with the ability to hit winning shots down the line. At least one shot must be a weapon that she can count on in any situation.

Her competitive personality includes calculated aggression and a willingness to take some risks. These players delight in going all out for a winning shot, but only when the odds are in their favor. Current role models in professional tennis include many of the top players, such as Serena Williams, Venus Williams, Lindsay Davenport, Jennifer Capriati, Andre Agassi, Leyton Hewitt, and Andy Roddick.

The aggressive baseliner must develop penetrating baseline ground strokes that land deep in the court. She should work on precise footwork and steady balance so that she can hit forcing shots off high balls, low balls, short balls, and against all types of spin. A simple but effective drill is to ask the aggressive baseliner to hit 90 percent of her shots to the opponent's backhand corner. This will improve her ability to exploit an opponent's weak stroke.

Another good drill is to have one player hit crosscourt and the other player down the line for points. First one to earn 15 points wins. Players then switch the direction of their shots for the next game. Because aggressive baseliners are building at least one shot into a weapon, they must practice that shot thousands of times, until they own it. Most players prefer to develop the forehand, but they shouldn't overlook the potential of the backhand, especially two-handed backhands.

Using Your Weapon

Purpose: To teach players to open up the court and use their weapon to hit a winning shot.

Procedure: Feed the ball to player A, who hits a forehand deep crosscourt. A second ball from you lands moderately short, and A rolls a sharply angled shot crosscourt with topspin to pull the opponent wide. A second player, B, stationed at the baseline, hits the third ball with her backhand crosscourt to A, who steps in and hits a winning two-handed backhand down the line (see figure 11.11).

Coaching points
By opening up the court and moving her opponent outside the singles sideline, she has set up her favorite down-the-line backhand. Be sure to emphasize excellent footwork and balance on this shot. As your player gains confidence, she should take the ball early on the rise to reduce her opponent's recovery time.

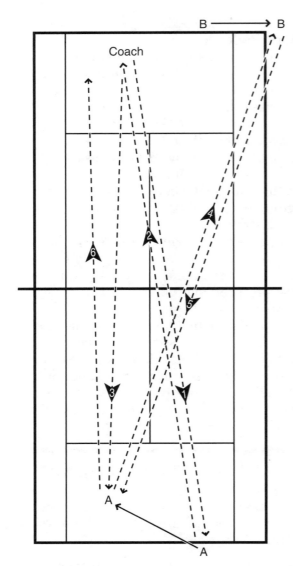

Figure 11.11 Using your weapon.

All-Court Player

Players with the all-court style are athletic, quick, and have excellent movement skills. The demand for all-court coverage and shot making requires endurance and a high level of fitness. Racket skills are weapons of precision for all-court players, who tend toward eastern grips and compact elliptical swing patterns. Because of the variety of their shots, they need to learn to become complete players, so it often takes longer for these players to develop. Don't be surprised if your players with this style begin to play their best tennis near the end of their high school years.

All-court players are shot makers who love to make something happen. They shift easily from defense to offense and like the variety of shots. Usually armed with a flexible game plan, all-court players probe until they expose an opponent's weakness. On the professional tour, all-court players tend to compete well no matter what the court surface. Typical role models include Patrick Rafter, Marat Safin, James Blake, Amelie Mauresomo, and Justine Henin.

The all-court player's toughest decision is which part of his game to emphasize. Most of the time he'll play offensive tennis and try to take the net on every short ball. Sometimes against particular opponents he may find it more productive to use a game plan that counters his opponent's strengths. Many all-court players do not have one outstanding weapon but balance that by having no obvious weaknesses. They play well from every part of the court.

An excellent modified game situation for all-court players is to have them play a regular set but reward them with two points instead of one for every point they win on a volley or overhead smash. This will encourage them to get to the net as quickly as possible to end the point.

The primary focus of drills for the all-court player should be shots from the midcourt. These players must develop solid approach shots off both sides and a winning drive for at least one side, because they can often run

Against an aggressive baseliner, the key for your players is to keep the ball away from her big shot by varying the pace and spins of their shots. She likes power, so they should take the pace off their shots and mix low slices with high, arcing moon balls to the center of the court to avoid giving her angles to hit a winner. Because aggressive shot makers usually rely on one shot as a weapon, your players may need to hit to her strength first to open up the weaker side. An aggressive baseliner wants to dictate play, so players need to mix up the play and seize control of the point as soon as possible.

around to hit their favorite shot on a short ball. Drop shots from both the forehand and backhand are good additions as long as they are not overused. All of their midcourt shots should be hit with identical racket and body preparation to disguise the shots. Because all-court players typically want to take the net whenever possible, drills that emphasize midcourt shots (e.g., the weak serve drill) are excellent practice and fun to play.

Weak Serve

Purpose: To test the ability to execute midcourt shots and win the point.

Procedure: Two players compete in a regular set with normal scoring except that the server (A) gets only one serve that must be played underhanded out of his hand and below waist level. The receiver (B) must play the ball with his forehand on the deuce court (if he is right-handed) and with his backhand on the ad court. The receiver must hit the return and rush the net for the next shot or else lose the point. Naturally, he should try approach shots, winning drives, or drop shots (see figure 11.12).

Coaching points

This game will quickly reveal weaknesses in the transition game. Players should be expected to lose their serve. Once your players get the idea, they'll love this game. What better way to practice the "chip-and-charge" technique that you want them to use against a weak second serve?

Because they try to play a well-rounded game, all-court players usually have some weakness in shot making. Strategies for playing against all-court players should include playing to their weaker side and aiming for depth on ground strokes to prevent them from attacking at net. A player should also try to increase the percentage of first serves in to counter the attack on the weaker second serve, and he must be sure his own returns have good depth. He can use sharply angled ground strokes to open up the court and then direct the ball to the other side to force the player to cover the entire court.

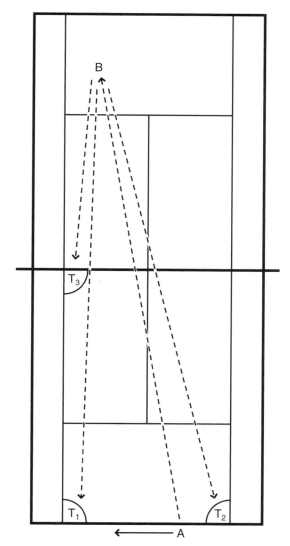

Figure 11.12 Weak serve.

Serve-and-Volley Player

Serve-and-volley players are usually tall, with good reach and agility, powerful overheads, and a soft, deft touch. Clearly a big serve is crucial to the serve-and-volleyer, as is a punishing overhead smash. Quick hands and penetrating volleys are essential at the net. Because these players are most comfortable at net, they should practice dependable midcourt and approach shots. Shallow or weak second serves should be attacked and followed to the net.

Serve-and-volley players tend toward eastern or even continental grips because grip changes must be very quick (and serves, volleys, overheads, and sliced approach shots are often hit with the same grip). These players need to have an aggressive on-court personality and the resolve to make something happen. Points tend to be short and risks high, so there is no room for the fainthearted. Role models on the professional tour include Pete Sampras and Tim Henman. Past role models included Boris Becker, John McEnroe, Martina Navratilova, and Pam Shriver.

To develop the serve-and-volley style of play, players have to start by creating a serve that is truly a weapon. They will need to have command over a hard, mostly flat serve that stays low after the bounce, a slice serve to hit the wide angle or curve into the receiver's body, and a dependable spin or kick second serve. Each type of serve is effective if it consistently lands deep in the service box with varied placement.

Convince your players that speed alone will not produce aces or weak returns. Teach them to serve wide to pull the opponent out of the court. Show them the advantage of a serve to the inside corner of the service boxes to reduce the angles of possible returns. Point out that an occasional serve right at the receiver will jam her and often produce a weak return. Of course, the most damaging serve is simply one hit to the opponent's weakness.

Eventually, you should expect a serve-and-volleyer to have command of 18 different serves, including slice, flat, and kick serves to each of the six target areas shown in figure 11.13. Make up games and contests among players similar to Around the World in basketball. Each player in rotation tries to hit the 18 different serves consecutively. When someone misses, the next player takes a turn. You might also try playing Horse, another basketball playground game. One player executes a serve, and the next player in line must imitate the same type of serve to the same location. If she misses, she has the letter *h*. The first player to spell *horse* loses and drops out of the game.

The bread and butter for a serve-and-volleyer is to execute the serve, follow the

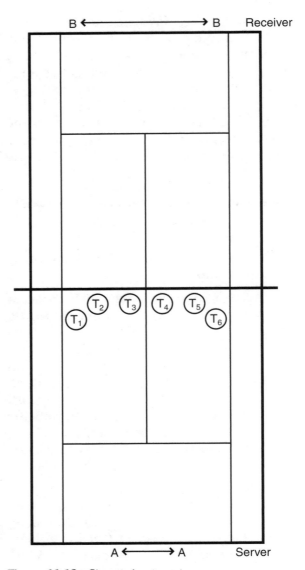

Figure 11.13 Six serving targets.

path of the ball to the net, split step to gain balance as the receiver begins her forward swing, and then make the first volley. These three skills require an enormous number of repetitions in practice. The chances are excellent that if your serve-and-volleyers can perform the serve, split-step, and first volley with consistency and confidence, they'll win their service games decisively.

In your eagerness to work on serving and volleying, don't overlook mastery of the overhead smash. In fact, players who rush the net and close in to angle volleys away are likely to be tested by lobs. No shot in tennis tests the athleticism of your players more, is more fun to hit, and is more demoralizing to miss than the smash. Use the overhead 10 drill as the basis and vary the difficulty level by requiring placement deep in the court or alternately to the left or right side.

Overhead 10

Purpose: To practice recovering from the net and smashing a winning overhead.

Procedure: The player starts at the normal net position halfway between the service line and the net. She runs forward and touches the net with her racket as the coach or feeder puts a lob over her head. She retreats three steps, jumps (using a scissors kick with her legs to maintain balance), and hits the overhead smash (see figure 11.14). She recovers immediately and runs forward to touch the net again and repeats the sequence until she has hit 10 smashes.

Coaching points

As players improve their skills, you can increase the difficulty of the lobs. It's also a good idea to require players to aim the smash at a target crosscourt to practice taking advantage of the longer angle and reducing the chance for error. This is a great drill for conditioning, team competition, and dealing with pressure. Several sets of this drill are a physical and mental challenge!

Against a serve-and-volleyer, points develop quickly, so players need to seize the advantage early in the point. They should drive or chip their returns at her feet as she rushes the net and hit the majority of their returns and passing shots down the line to give her less time to cut the ball off. They can lob early in the match to slow the serve-and-volleyer's attempts at closing to the net. If her serve is a real problem for players to return, they can vary their position at the baseline by moving in and chipping a few returns low, or retreating a few steps to gain time to drive or lob their return.

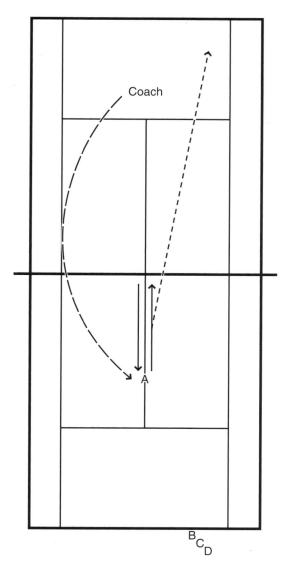

Figure 11.14 Overhead 10.

PRACTICING VARYING STYLES

Players on your team will have different styles of play, so practice sessions must be structured to work on the different skills and shot patterns they need to develop. This is where you'll need to be creative in pairing people for drills. During the learning stage, players with the same style of play should be paired together to work on specific skills that define their style. As they gain in skill and confidence, provide them with opportunities to test their style against players with different styles.

The natural next step is to help players analyze how two opposing styles of play relate in match play. They need to learn how to adjust their game plan on the basis of an opponent's style. If all four styles of play are not represented among your team members, recruit some adult players in your community to prepare your team to face a type of game they may see in match play. It's a good idea to include a left-hander, too, so that each of your players has faced one in practice before the season begins.

SUMMARY

The key concepts of singles strategy presented in this chapter are as follows:

- Help your players understand that singles strategy is based on the principles of percentage tennis.

- Teach your players to analyze the strengths and weaknesses of their game and their opponents' game.

- Create a plan for each player to help him develop a style of play that fits his physical ability, racket skills, and competitive personality.

- Provide opportunities for your players to practice using their skills to combat each of the possible styles of play of their opponents.

CHAPTER 12 DOUBLES STRATEGY

From the high school level to professional circles, most successful doubles teams share two components: compatibility and good communication. Compatibility begins with the players' strokes complementing each other's as the team applies sound doubles fundamentals. Communication allows the doubles team to implement tactics as a unit and support one another whether the tactics succeed or not. A good doubles team can become even greater by playing together for a long time. Covering for each other as a point unfolds becomes automatic for members of a veteran doubles team.

COMPATIBILITY

It is no secret that the most successful doubles teams at any level of play usually get along well as competitors and are often friends off the court too. Bob and Mike Bryan, who are currently ranked number one in the world on the men's tour, are an example of the ideal doubles team. They are identical twins who have played together since they were young. One is a left-hander and one a right-hander, their skills complement each other, and they are best friends.

Since you're not likely to get many "twin teams," the next best thing is to encourage your players to pair up with people they would like to play with. You might ask them to write down their top three choices and hand it to you confidentially. This procedure helps you pair people who at least want to play together. Since you want doubles players to treat their partners kindly—like a best friend—it's best for them to start out with someone they'd like to play with.

Many coaches also like to pair a freshman who shows promise with an upperclassman who has more experience. This can work well, but it doesn't allow teams to stay intact year after year. A lot may depend on whether your league restricts players to singles or doubles only, or whether players can play both. In leagues where players can only play one, the doubles players are often the younger players, and they work their way up the lineup over the years. In this case, keeping teams together year after year usually doesn't work.

Although complementary styles of play are important, it may be even more important to have emotional and competitive personalities that blend. A highly anxious, excitable player definitely needs a calm, steady partner and vice versa. Two personalities that are identical may not make the most successful team.

COMMUNICATION

On the court, all good doubles teams communicate between games, between points, and even during points. If this doesn't come naturally, you have to insist that your players talk at these times. Nothing causes a doubles team to fall apart more quickly than a lack of communication, particularly if one player starts to play poorly. The struggling player is embarrassed, her partner is annoyed, and the team is headed for defeat. A few kind words from her partner may pull her out of her streak and give her a dose of self-confidence.

During the point, players need to call out on lobs or shots down the middle to prevent the momentary hesitation that will doom them. They also need to help each other out on service line calls when the opponent serves. A third time to talk is when they are certain a ball is going long or wide—they need to let their partner know.

Between points, partners need to agree on their plan for the coming point. Depending on who the team leader is, the net player may say, "Serve wide and I'm poaching on the first serve." When receiving serve, a player may say, "I'm going to lob over the net player, so be ready to take the net."

At the changeovers between games, partners should discuss any change in tactics that might make sense. They can also remind each other to be aggressive, steadier, quicker getting back, or other similar quick tips. After a minute or two of pure rest, it's often a good idea in doubles to get emotionally excited again before play begins. A little enthusiasm and excitement usually help team play and can be an effective motivator.

Although you can't force players to spend time off the court with their doubles partner, you can encourage them to work together during physical training time and to practice together in addition to regular team practices.

You can also assign them team duties such as working at a fund-raiser together. If they choose to spend time together at school or socially, so much the better.

HIGH-PERCENTAGE DOUBLES

Doubles teams give themselves the best chance of success if the stroke production they use during play minimizes unforced errors. Employing high-percentage shots during play allows a team to develop positions of strength on the doubles court. These positions can be capitalized on when the opposition is pulled out of position, allowing for a point-ending ground stroke, or by getting to the net as a team first and winning the point with a volley.

First Serve In

In doubles, 75 percent of the points are won by the serving team when the server gets the first serve in. Teach your players to use a three-quarters-speed spin serve as a first delivery when serving. This will allow the server to get a high percentage of first serves in play. A spin serve's chances of landing consistently deep in the box keeps the returner back while giving the server more time to move forward to execute a successful first volley.

Teach your players to resist the temptation to hit a big, flat first serve in doubles. The server should use his "big" first serve as a change of pace, to occasionally surprise opponents and keep them off balance. Remember that the more first serves your doubles team gets in play, the greater its chances are to hold serve.

Taking the Net First As a Team

Doubles play is most effective when a team takes every opportunity to get to net. Both members of the team should always be looking for ways to close in. Once a team has established net position, they are capable of hitting down into their opponent's court, which usually results in a high-percentage winner. Don't let your players fall into the trap of forcing their way in to the net. Instill in your doubles teams the instinct to sense opportunities to close to the net without rushing headlong into disaster by charging the net foolishly at the wrong time.

Play Down the Middle

Doubles is often described as a game of angles. However, the first principle of doubles is to play as many balls as possible into the middle of the court. Teach your players to resist hitting too many balls down the line or at sharp angles. The doubles alleys increase the width of a tennis court, and although there are two players covering this expanded court area, the highest percentage target area is down the middle.

An occasional down-the-line shot can serve as an excellent change of pace to keep the net person from moving into the middle too frequently, but caution your players to use this tactic sparingly, even if their opponents are tempting them to hit up the line. Hitting up the line means the shot crosses the net at its highest point and with the smallest target area to land in.

Trying to create angles by forcing shots crosscourt can present the same pitfalls as up-the-line shots. When your players hit angles, they should maintain a safe margin of error by aiming for a target area well inside the doubles sidelines.

Tell your doubles players to patiently work the point. They should wait for opportunities to establish a position of strength at the net and put away volleys down the middle. Or they can move out of position occasionally to execute a winning ground stroke down the middle. Doubles teams who keep most shots in the center of the court and resist the temptation to go down the line or create sharp angles give themselves a much better chance of success.

Force the Opponents to Hit Up

Many high school doubles players react to the threat of an opponent at the net by overhitting their ground strokes. Remind your players that slow and low is much more effective than hard and high. Establish a tactical priority of trying to make opponents hit up so your team can close and hit down. The best way to accomplish this is by feeding the opposition low shots at their feet whenever possible, but especially on the return of serve. This tactic can also be employed when volleys are being exchanged. A soft, low volley often produces a high volley that's easy to put away.

PLAYER RESPONSIBILITIES

Each doubles player has specific responsibilities on court to maximize the team's chance for success. Veteran doubles teams not only know what their primary responsibilities are, but can also anticipate how their partner will react in most situations and respond accordingly. Teach your doubles teams how to react to the situations they'll face as the server, server's partner, receiver, and receiver's partner. Once your players have learned their primary responsibilities, focus on communication between partners so the team works as a unit.

Server

A properly executed doubles serve immediately projects the serving team into a position of strength. Once in this position, exploiting the opponents' tactical or stroke production weakness becomes much easier. Here are the server's responsibilities in doubles:

- Taking a service position at the baseline between the center notch and the singles sideline to cover his half of the doubles court.

By communicating and practicing individual responsibilities, you increase your chance of winning at doubles.

- Getting a high percentage of first serves in play, with depth and spin.
- Varying service placement.
- Moving forward to bisect the returner's possible angles.
- Executing a firm, low, and deep first volley.
- Covering the open court if his partner poaches.
- Communicating verbal instructions to his partner as necessary.

Server's Partner

Communication between the server and the partner before the serve allows the team to work in unison. Once the server hits a successful serve, mobility at the net by the server's partner is key to success. The responsibilities of the server's partner are as follows:

- Positioning himself between the singles sideline and the center service sideline, about halfway up in the service box.
- Using hand signals for serve placement and to indicate his intention to poach or stay.
- Reacting to any short, soft returns by volleying them down the middle or at the feet of the receiver's partner.
- Moving closer to the net to poach.
- Remaining as active as possible by using head and shoulder fakes to distract the receiver.

Receiver

A seemingly poor return of serve placed in the court is better than a perfect return that misses by inches. Teach your players to look for offensive opportunities after returning serve. Here are the service receiver's responsibilities:

- Positioning himself as close to the service box as possible, while ensuring that he can still return the serve consistently.
- Getting as many returns in play as possible—making the other team play.
- Returning primarily crosscourt.
- Keeping returns low to make the volleyer hit up.
- Moving forward whenever possible.
- Chipping and charging any short second serve.
- Calling serves on balls wide of the service box singles sideline.
- Covering the open court if his partner poaches.

Receiver's Partner

The receiver's partner should attempt whatever will aid the receiver in making a successful return of serve. Here are the responsibilities of the receiver's partner:

- Positioning himself at the service line, halfway between the singles sideline and the service box center line.
- Calling all serves for his partner in the area of the service line and the center service line.

- Cutting off any floaters within reach at the net.
- Covering the alley, especially after a wide serve.
- Covering the middle when a weak return by his partner opens up the court.

Before each point, a server's partner and the server can communicate with each other verbally or by using hand signals. Common tennis hand signals are described in table 12.1. The server, of course, can verbally disagree with any sign by saying no; however, if the server agrees to hand signals given by his partner, he must acknowledge each sign given. If the server disagrees with the signal given, the players should communicate verbally before beginning the point.

DOUBLES STYLES OF PLAY

There are many successful styles of doubles play. When the styles of the two players on a doubles team blend well, the chances for success are much increased. A lot of successful doubles teams are composed of one player whose style and temperament are steady and another whose style is aggressive. The steady player moves the ball around, while the aggressive player looks for a way to end the point. Also, the aggressive player, who may have a more volatile personality, can

Table 12.1 Common Tennis Hand Signals

Hand signals	Message
For poaching	
Open hand behind the back	Player is poaching
Closed fist behind the back	Player is staying
One finger extended down behind back	Player is faking a poach
For service placement	
One finger behind the back	Serve out wide
Two fingers behind the back	Serve into body
Three fingers behind the back	Serve down the middle

keep the team emotionally charged, while the steadier player keeps the team's feet on the ground. Thus an emotional balance is achieved.

Of course, this doesn't mean that two baseliners or two extremely aggressive players can't team up in doubles and find success. However, the tactics they employ during match play must accentuate their strengths. If both members of the team are willing to do whatever it takes to make the team a winner, any two styles of play can blend together well.

Parallel Play

A doubles team should attempt to play side by side whenever possible. Parallel play eliminates the gaping hole created when one player is up and the other is in the backcourt. This is why the server or service returner should seize every opportunity to move forward and join his teammate at the net. Not only should the team play shoulder to shoulder, they must also move right or left together as they track the ball when it's in the opponent's court. If a shot is hit to the left corner of the opponent's court, your player on the left side should shuffle in that direction to cover the alley, while his partner moves into the middle to bisect the possible angle of return.

Parallel play should also be employed when the net team is driven away from the net by a defensive lob. Both players should retreat, with the player tracking the lobbed ball retreating the farthest. With both players now at the baseline, no hole is created between the players for the opposition to attack.

Both Players Up

When a doubles team with solid volleys and overheads seizes every opportunity to get to the net, that team's chance of winning the point increases to 65 percent. Once at the net and employing parallel play, a team can isolate an opposing player at the baseline. A triangle can be created so that all volleys are hit back to a single opponent at the baseline until a weak return allows the net team to end the point. This two-on-one concept allows the two players at the net to continue to close toward the net. If both members of the opposition are playing back, their returns will eventually allow the team at net to angle off a winner. If the opposition is playing one up and one back, eventually their returns will allow the closing team to volley a winner down the middle or at the net person's feet.

Serve and Volley

The server should deliver a spin serve down the middle (or inside corner) of the opponent's service box as often as possible to cut down on possible angles of return. Depending on the skill level of the opponent, serving wide to their weaker side can also create opportunities to serve and move forward. After serving, the server should move forward until the returner begins preparation to hit her stroke. At that time, the server should split step to increase her potential for lateral mobility. A first volley is crucial to the server's chances of joining her teammate at the net. The first volley should be hit firmly so that the opponent's net player can't poach, and it should be hit deep enough so that the player at the baseline is pinned there. Once at the net, the server can join her teammate in parallel play.

Chip and Charge

A weak second serve delivered short in the service box is a great opportunity for the receiver to join his teammate at the net. If the receiver anticipates a weak second serve, he should move inside the baseline, drive or chip the return deep into the opponent's court, and move in behind the return. The chip (a sliced return) usually bounces low. The server then faces a low ball, which is usually hit up to the team at the net. The slice puts backspin on the ball, slowing the ball down and giving the net rusher time to assume a good volley position.

Players must use caution when trying the chip and charge. A lot of high school players rush headlong into trouble because they haven't perfected the slice return of serve. If the player returning the serve uses topspin (instead of backspin), the opponent at the baseline will have a good ball to hit back and can often catch the net rusher off balance. So, when employing the chip-and-charge maneuver, it is better to use a slice to keep the ball low and give the net rusher time to get to the net.

Playing Against Two-Up Teams

If your doubles teams tend to be defensive, or often find themselves retreating from the net, they need to develop some sound strategy to cope with an aggressive team that constantly takes the net. The basic play to move a team away from the net is to employ a defensive lob. But caution your players to try not to lob just barely over the heads of the net team, because this usually results in an easy overhead. Practice hitting high, deep lobs with the primary purpose of moving the offensive team away from the net, which allows your team to move in and take a position of strength.

If the net team plays at the service line without closing in, the best play is a soft ball at the net team's feet, which usually makes them return the ball up into the defensive team's court. This should allow the defensive team to move forward and win the point with a ground stroke. If the net team volleys short, the baseline team can hit a soft dink wide to create an opening that it can then exploit by hitting a winning ground stroke down the middle. Practice these scenarios often so that your doubles teams are prepared to execute them during match play.

One Up and One Back

As mentioned earlier, playing one person up and one person back is dangerous because it exposes a huge hole down the middle where most shots are played. However, if your play-

ers' skills are at the advanced beginner level, this formation may be your only choice. Many high school doubles teams lose matches because they are unable to serve and volley. Unsuspecting coaches read about proper doubles techniques and require their players to try to serve and volley even when the players are not ready to do so. If your players lose more points than they win by forcing their way to the net, they should try playing one up and one back.

By playing one up and one back, doubles teams avoid rushing the net and losing points.

Serve and Stay Back

If your players cannot consistently hit a spin serve deep into the service box, or if their first volley is still in the formative stages, they should deliver the serve and stay back. Even if the server has no intention of rushing the net immediately, she should be taught to step inside the baseline after serving. By stepping into the court, she gives herself the opportunity to move forward. Because this tactic of staying back after serving invites the service returner to move in to the net, the server's subsequent shots must be kept crosscourt and deep. If the returner's partner frequently poaches, the serving team can try lobbing. This means the returner must retrieve the lob, which creates a hole down the middle that can be exploited by the serving team.

Return and Stay Back

The tactic of returning serve and staying at the baseline can be productive if your doubles teams are strong off the ground but have relatively weak volleys. When the returning team stays back most of the time, they are susceptible to angled volleys from a team that closes to the net. Thus, the primary task of returning teams that rely on baseline tactics is to keep the opponents as far away from the net as possible. Soft, low returns at the incoming net rusher's feet often produce a short volley return that can be exploited by the baseline team. Lobbing and hitting angled dink shots, as well as strong ground strokes, are skills required of doubles teams that remain on the baseline. Retrieving lobs and being pulled up and back by the baseline team can be tiring and frustrating to an aggressive doubles opponent. As the match progresses, such tactics can produce unforced errors by the aggressive doubles team as the baseline team patiently remains deep in the court.

Play Down the Middle

The natural weapon against a team that plays one up and one back is to volley down the middle between the two players, which can be done by getting to the net as quickly as possible. Once at the net, either player can cut off crosscourt returns and win the point with an easy volley down the middle. Instruct your net team to position in the middle of possible returns. They

should bait the baseline player into trying to hit a low-percentage shot up the line or a sharp angle crosscourt that might produce an unforced error. The tactic of creating a triangle between your two net players and the opposition's baseline player makes it relatively easy to elicit a soft or high return that can be volleyed at the opposing net person's feet.

Both Players Back

Doubles play will occasionally dictate that both players remain at the baseline—a defensive tactic usually employed when things aren't going a team's way. However, sometimes this different approach can change the course of a match. An advantage of this tactic is that it can take the pressure off a server or returner whose weak play has exposed his partner at the net. Although you should use this look primarily as a change of pace, if your doubles players are beginners who are uncomfortable at the net, a baseline formation might make the difference between success and failure.

Serve With Partner Back

Keeping the server's partner back on the serve is a formation that is most often used by a team with weak serves. Soft serves can expose the server's partner at the net to returns she cannot handle. If your player has a decent first serve but a very weak second delivery, play her partner up at the net on first serve and back her up to the baseline on second serve. With both players at the baseline after the serve is hit, they must move together as a team across the baseline while playing ground strokes.

Receiving Serve With Both Players Back

The tactic of playing both back to return serve can be used by any doubles team to give the serving team a different view. However, this tactic is most often used when the returns of serve have been too high, creating easy volley put-aways for the serving team. With both players on the returning team back, the pressure is taken off the returner whose partner has been a sitting duck at the net. The returner often regains emotional security without the pressure of having to protect his partner at the net with a crosscourt return.

Playing Against Two-Back Teams

When your team encounters a good doubles team that plays both back, the key word is *patience*. Defensive doubles teams are willing to wait for the aggressive team to make an unforced error. Many high school doubles matches have been lost by teams that felt they used the correct strategy by heedlessly charging the net at every opportunity.

Instruct your players to keep returns low, preferably with slice, so that the baseline team has to hit the ball up. Tell them to approach the net with caution. If the baseliners lob frequently, your players should stop just inside the service line rather than getting closer to the net. This will allow your team to turn short lobs into overhead winners. If the baseline team hits powerful ground strokes, your players should close to the net so that volleys down the middle or angles are easier to achieve. Your players can occasionally hit short drop shots when the baseliners execute soft shots at their feet. This moves the baseline team in, where they are not as comfortable.

The "I" Formation

The serving team should use a conventional alignment most of the time. However, when the serving team encounters a returner with a great crosscourt return, the "I" formation might be the answer. In the "I" formation, the net person straddles the center line of the service box and stays as low as possible so the server doesn't hit her. Communication between the doubles partners employing the "I" formation is very important. The net person signals which side she will cover and where she wants the server to deliver the serve. After delivering the serve, the server must cover the area vacated by the net person.

This formation distracts the returner and makes the low-percentage down-the-line return more attractive. It also makes a solid crosscourt return harder to accomplish because the net person may move in that direction and volley the return for a winner.

When playing against the "I" formation, your players should return down the middle more often than against a conventional service alignment. The net person who begins the point in the middle will move one way or the other as the serve is delivered, which opens up the middle for the return. If your players are distracted by the movement, they should lob a shot that the server will have to retrieve, negating any advantage the moving net person might have.

DOUBLES DRILLS

The following drills will help your doubles teams improve their game.

Half-Court Doubles

Purpose: To practice doubles serves, crosscourt returns, crosscourt first volleys, and closing to the net.

Procedure: This drill simulates doubles play between two players. The two players are positioned at opposite baselines. One is the server and the other the returner. They can only play shots crosscourt as they play out the point (see figure 12.1).

Coaching points
Instruct the server to serve and volley, because the returner will try to chip and charge any serves that land short in the service box. This drill eliminates the distractions of all four doubles players being on court and allows two players to concentrate

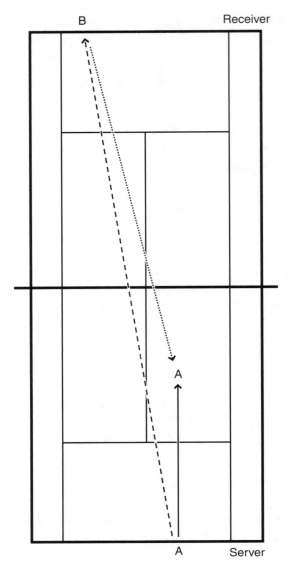

Figure 12.1 Half-court doubles.

on crosscourt doubles fundamentals without worrying about a poaching net person entering the picture.

The Doubles Drill

Purpose: To develop a better transition game as a doubles team.

Procedure: Two players are a team at net, and another two players are a team at the baseline. From the middle of the court behind the net team, you feed the ball short

down the middle to the baseline team. As the baseline team comes forward, they return the feed down the middle. The point is played out as all players try to close off the volley (see figure 12.2). As soon as the point is finished, the next baseline team is fed another ball and the sequence is repeated.

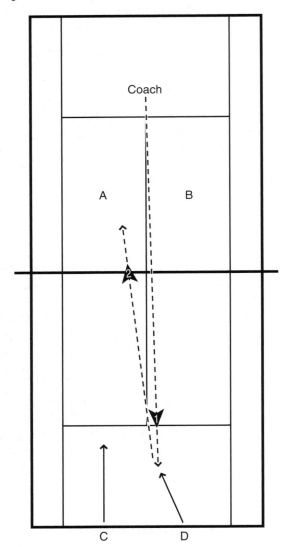

Figure 12.2 Doubles drill.

Coaching points

Returning the short feed low to the team already at the net provides excellent practice for the team moving from the baseline to the net. This also simulates match situations where volleys must be closed off at the net.

Baseline Doubles

Purpose: To practice transition play for a doubles team moving together from the baseline to the net.

Procedure: All four players that comprise the two doubles teams start at the baseline. One player starts play by feeding a ball out of her hand to the team on the opposite baseline. Players can come forward only when a short ball is hit by the opposing team (see figure 12.3). The first team to score 15 points is the winner.

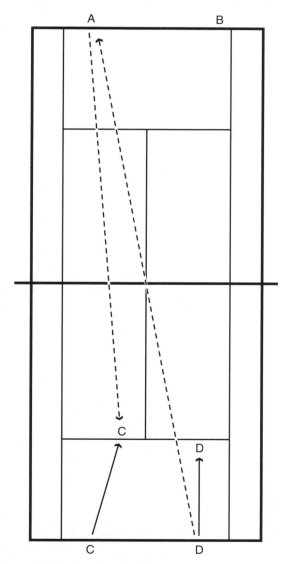

Figure 12.3 Baseline doubles.

Coaching points
This is an excellent drill to get doubles teams to come forward together. Emphasize communication by the team as they approach. The players should call the ball by saying "mine."

Doubles Offense-Defense

Purpose: To practice transition play for a doubles team from the baseline to the net.

Procedure: The squad is paired off by teaming the number one player on the ladder with the lowest player on the ladder, and so on until all the players have a partner (e.g., 1-8, 2-7, 3-6, 4-5). Divide the teams evenly on opposite baselines. The coach stands behind teams on the defensive baseline and feeds short balls so that the team on the opposite (offensive) baseline must come forward together and play. The point is played out as the defensive team tries to move the offensive team away from the net and take the net themselves (see figure 12.4). Points can be scored only by the team that comes forward to play the short feed (offensive team). If the team that began at the baseline (defensive team) wins the point, they switch baseline places with the offensive team they defeated. If the offensive team wins the point, they score 1 point for their team. The game ends when one team scores 10 points.

Coaching points
This is a great game to conclude practice with on days when you're focusing on doubles. Stress to your players the importance of teamwork. Make the higher player on the ladder responsible for communicating positively with her partner no matter what the score of the game might be.

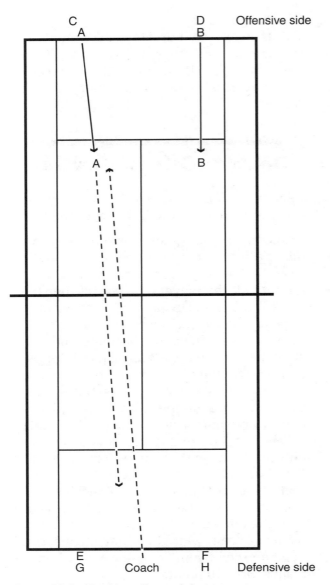

Figure 12.4 Doubles offense-defense.

Figure 12.5 Defensive lob.

Defensive Lob

Purpose: To practice doubles situations with all four players back.

Procedure: The first doubles pair (A and B) enters the court at the service line and comes forward to the net, which they touch with their rackets. You feed a lob over their heads, and they both retreat to retrieve it. One of them hits a return lob (see figure 12.5), and the point is played out against the second doubles team (E and F). The second doubles team, positioned at the opposite baseline, can't come forward unless the lob is short. If the retrieving team wins the point, they exchange places with the team that began at the baseline. The next team enters the court and play continues.

Coaching points
Remind the team retrieving the deep lob to hit a deep lob back to their opponents. Encourage players to come forward as a team if a short lob or ground stroke is hit.

Inside-the-Baseline Doubles

Purpose: To practice taking all shots from inside the baseline and not retreating behind the baseline to a position of weakness.

Procedure: Two doubles teams position at opposite baselines. One player begins the exchange by feeding a ball just behind the service line to the opposing team. Players cannot retreat behind the baseline for any reason (see figure 12.6). The point is played out until an error is made or a short ball allows one team to move forward and end the point with a volley.

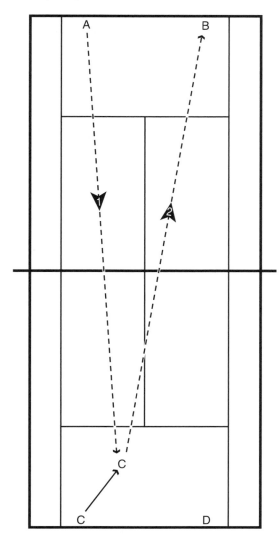

Figure 12.6 Inside-the-baseline doubles.

Coaching points

This drill makes the doubles teams conscious of holding a position of strength on court and not retreating. Encourage the teams to move forward when possible and to practice calling for each shot with a loud "mine." Calling for doubles shots this way establishes a commitment by the player taking the shot.

King- or Queen-of-the-Hill Doubles

Purpose: To practice doubles skills and promote competition in practice.

Procedure: Doubles teams compete in a practice "tournament" where the goal is to work toward court 1—where the top doubles team plays—and rebuff all challengers. Doubles action begins on three courts. Four games are played to determine the winner on each court (this allows each player to serve one game). If both teams on a court win two games, a tiebreaker is played to determine the winning team on that court. Play stops on each court when a winning team has been determined on court 1—whichever team on courts 2 and 3 was ahead when play stopped on court 1 is the winner. This prevents slow matches from keeping the other two courts waiting and allows rotation of the teams to occur all at once. The losing team on court 3 stays there if no teams are waiting to enter play, or it rotates off the court to the end of the waiting line if there are teams waiting. The winning team on court 3 moves up to court 2. The losing team on court 2 stays on court 2, but the winning team on court 2 moves up to court 1 as the top challenger. If the top challenger beats the kings (or queens) of the doubles hill, they become the new rulers. The dethroned team moves all the way to the end of the waiting line of teams.

Coaching points

Encourage partners to move right and left in tandem when retrieving ground strokes so that there is no hole down the middle.

SUMMARY

Remember the following coaching points as you are working with your doubles teams:

- Compatibility and communication are the ingredients of a good doubles team.

- Employing high-percentage shots during doubles play develops positions of strength on the court.

- Servers should try to get as many first serves in as possible by using a three-quarters-speed spin serve.

- The team should move forward toward the net whenever possible.

- A doubles team should play a high percentage of shots down the middle of the doubles court.

- As they close toward the net, doubles teams should try to make their opponents hit up.

- The doubles team, not the two individuals who comprise the team, must be the players' first priority.

- Parallel play by a doubles team eliminates a defensive hole in the middle of the court.

- Instruct your doubles teams to place the majority of serves down the middle unless the receiver has a stroke deficiency on either side.

- Teach your doubles teams to slice most approach shots in order to keep the ball low and to force the opponents to hit up to the incoming team.

- A doubles team should primarily use whatever doubles formation best fits the team's natural style of play.

- The I formation can be used to take away a receiver's crosscourt return.

CHAPTER 13 PREPARING FOR COMPETITION

After several weeks of intense practice on tennis skills and mental skills along with physical training, it's time to prepare for matches by helping each player develop a specific game plan. As mentioned in previous chapters, that game plan is built on the principles of percentage tennis and your player's strengths and weaknesses. You've had time to teach and practice the skills and strategies of percentage play as well as evaluate individual strengths and weaknesses. Now you need to know what you're up against in your opponents.

KNOWING YOUR OPPONENTS

Information on your opponents can be collected by you, your team members, or assistant coaches. You might also seek out knowledgeable tennis friends who can lend a hand by scouting nearby teams when you have a team match or other conflict.

Try to create an atmosphere in which everyone associated with your team knows that he or she can make a real contribution to team success by supplying accurate scouting data. Make the team scouting book a treasured resource available to all your players

throughout the year. They may find it helpful even for summer play when they face opponents in tournament matches.

Sources of information include scouting reports from the previous year's matches, summer tournament play, early-season matches, and finally, the scouting your players do in the warm-up period just before a match begins. Each of these times can provide you with helpful data, and it's up to you to be sure that a report is collected at every opportunity.

Scouting Reports

A scouting report can be helpful to your players only if it is accurate, simple to understand, and easily applied to a game plan (see figure 13.1). Knowledge of what to expect from opponents will help your players relax and focus on the task at hand.

A poor scouting report, on the other hand, can be damaging to your players' confidence and poise once matches are in progress. Game plans crafted on faulty information are doomed to fail, and confidence will fade quickly. Even good information is of little use if it is too complex and detailed for your players to absorb, understand, and include in tactical play.

Scouting Report

Scouted player _____ vs. _____ (circle winner)

School _____ Grade _____ School _____ Grade _____

Date _____ Match score _____ Weather conditions _____

Right or left handed? (circle one)

Style of play: (circle one)

    Counterpuncher   Aggressive baseliner   All-court   Serve-and-volleyer

Best shot _____ Weakest shot _____

Physical characteristics and fitness _____

Movement skills:

    Side to side _____

    Up and back _____

Mental toughness or weakness _____

Stroke characteristics:

    First serve _____

    Second serve _____

    Forehand _____

    Backhand _____

    Midcourt shots _____

    Volley _____

    Overhead _____

    Passing shots _____

    Lobs _____

    Other _____

General comments: _____

Form completed by_____ Date _____

Figure 13.1 Scouting report.

Some players may perform best knowing nothing about their opponent because of the type of game they play and their lack of experience in using scouting information. A serve-and-volley player, for example, knows that he wants to take charge of the net at every opportunity regardless of the style of his opponent. You may want to feed the minimum amount of information to such players early in the season and gradually increase the amount as they gain experience and confidence. By the time you reach championship play, where players often face opponents for the second time of the season, your players may be more ready to apply scouting information.

The simple scouting report form shown in figure 13.1 can be used effectively by you, assistant coaches, or players. Once the form is completed, keep it in the team scouting book and make copies for your players when they are preparing for an opponent.

Some tennis score books include scouting forms along with match result score sheets. You can collect information after every match by asking each of your players to complete the scouting form on his opponent. Your team can then use the information in late-season matches or the next year.

Previous Year's Matches

Scouting reports from the previous year's matches are useful because opposing teams usually have players who compete for several years. The data should be accurate because it was gathered from your players under your supervision. You may find it helpful to assign a JV player to each varsity match to chart the complete match and assist in filing the scouting report after the match. Besides adding another pair of eyes to watch the opponent, this method helps your young players learn to analyze opponents early in their career.

The drawback to information that is a year old is that players may mature physically quite a bit in that time. They may also change their style of play or convert a weak stroke into a weapon. You should also take into account who they played on your team and whether the contrasting styles of play or competitiveness of the match produced a scouting report that may not apply to this year's match.

Summer Tournament Matches

Summer tournament matches are another source of data, especially if they can add to the information your players provided to you during the season the previous year. For this reason, you should strive to see any local tournaments and take thorough notes. Your players will appreciate your support when they compete out of school.

Again, consider the timeliness of data collected during the summer. Information about players from the previous summer may be outdated by the time you see those players the following spring. If your season is in the fall, of course, results from the previous summer will be more up-to-date.

Early-Season Matches

Early-season matches are the key time to scout if you play a team a second time or meet them in championship play. You don't have to worry about your report being out-of-date if the information will be used a few weeks later. You might want to require each player to submit a written scouting report (like the one shown in figure 13.1) as a ticket of admission to the next day's practice after a match. This gives players time to reflect on the match and objectively evaluate the opponent. In the rush of postmatch emotion, schoolwork, and rides home, it is often impossible for players to complete scouting reports. But don't let them slide by—be sure you get their written report before the next practice.

Scouting During the Warm-Up

The warm-up is the final chance for your players to analyze their opponent before play begins. During the ritual 5- to 10-minute warm-up, your players should focus on the key information they want to know about their opponent. Is he a lefty or righty? Which shot is his primary weapon? How is his court movement from side to side and up and back? What kind of spins does he use on various shots? Is there an obvious weakness or tentative shot? What is the likely style of play?

At the conclusion of the warm-up, your players should have a game plan based on all the information collected. If there's time, it's a good idea to check with them briefly, ask one or two probing questions, and give some final reassurances. If you never have this opportunity in matches, you can construct the situation in practice by inviting local adult players, asking them to warm up, and then having a short break to chat with your player about his game plan.

All players should have their game plans about 80 percent completed before the day of the match. Naturally, each player's plan will focus primarily on his own performance and how to best employ his weapons while covering weaknesses. The final 20 percent of the game plan may need to be finalized after the warm-up, especially if the warm-up is the first opportunity to analyze the opponent's weapons firsthand.

If players in your league compete in both singles and doubles, be sure information is shared with the doubles team after singles play. Emphasize information relevant to doubles play.

Team Scouting

When preparing for a match, you should also consider the opposing team's tendencies over the years. Often a coach will insist that her players follow certain strategic principles, especially in doubles play. After your teams have played the same school a few times, you may want to consider these questions:

- Is there a typical style of play?
- Do they attack weak second serves?
- Do they lob well, frequently, or never?
- Do they typically approach to the backhand?
- Do they poach in doubles and use signals?
- Do they serve and volley or play one up and one back?
- Is the net player vulnerable to a lob return of serve?

If you see a pattern of performance and the use of certain strategic principles, share this information with your players so that they will know what to expect and can prepare counterstrategies.

Show Them the Sky

During summer tournament play, one team's players became friendly with some members of one of the school teams they had played several times over the years. In casual conversation, their players mentioned that their coach always insisted that his players try one passing shot and, if it was volleyed back, to lob the next shot. His expression was "show those boys some sky." It was sound strategy against net rushers taught to close in to the net after the first volley, and their lobs often caught our players by surprise.

The next season, the kids knew to watch for this strategy and hold their ground after the first volley. Sure enough, on second shots there were lots of lobs and they were in great position to put away overhead smashes.

PREPARING YOUR TEAM

After weeks of preparation, anticipation builds toward the first match of the season. Goals have been set, skills refined, team positions announced, and game plans made. How you handle the practice the day before a match, and the prematch gathering, can influence your team's performance significantly. Most experienced coaches report that establishing a routine that addresses all players' needs leading up to a match helps to reduce their anxiety and nervousness. Once you've established a prematch routine that works, let your older players take the lead and have them help younger players get ready.

Conduct Prematch Practice

Prematch practices should typically be shorter than normal and high in intensity and quality. This is not the time to introduce new techniques. No player will be able to learn much the day before a match that he can use under pressure the next day. Your primary goals are to focus players on the next day's matches, to allow their bodies to be fresh and rested, to build their confidence, to provide emergency stroke first aid, and to anticipate distractions that might be present the next day.

A word of caution: Never schedule challenge or ladder matches the day before a team match. If you do, your players' energy and emotion will be wasted on competition within your team rather than saved for the opposing team. The day before a match is the time to focus on teamwork, support for teammates, and determination to perform well against another school.

Build Confidence

In practice the day before a match, after the normal warm-up and stretching routine, spend some time building confidence by allowing your players to practice their strengths. Let them hit their favorite shots. As they practice, show enthusiasm for their success and assure them that you think they're ready to compete. Resist the temptation to dwell on weaknesses, because this will only reinforce those limitations. Under pressure the next day, any new technique will break down during the match.

Talk with each player about performance goals for the match. Focus on things under her control such as working her way into the point, playing at a controlled pace, coming in to net on short balls, or improving her percentage of first serves.

Before practice ends, check that each player has a game plan so that there is time for her to think about it overnight. You'll find it helpful to have each player write her plan out on file cards. This will allow her to review the plan that night, the next day, and even during the match when pressure sometimes causes confusion.

Be optimistic and enthusiastic about the upcoming challenge. It's what you've all worked hard for—so enjoy it!

First Aid for Strokes

Over the course of a season, some of your players' strokes will break down in match play. Nothing is more damaging to a player's confidence than a serve that suddenly won't go in or an erratic backhand that hits the back fence.

Your first task as a coach is to help players decide whether the stroke breakdown is the result of faulty mechanics, poor strategy, or simply the pressure of match play. Once an honest evaluation is made, you can both agree on a remedy.

If a stroke breaks down because of poor mechanics, you've got to help the player adjust quickly during match play and then plan some individual work in practice. As a general rule, look first to the preparation for the stroke. Next, check the contact point and hitting area for flaws. Finally, evaluate the finish of the shot, including balance and recovery. Often a quick reminder to "prepare early," "watch the ball at contact," or "stay balanced" will correct a variety of flaws.

Poor strategy is another culprit of stroke breakdown. Players who try to drive the ball too close to the lines are destined for streaks of errors. Trying to pass a net player who has closed in tight is foolish when a lob would work better. Likewise, a hard, flat first serve that rarely lands in the court should be abandoned for a three-quarters-speed serve with good spin and placement.

Pressure and nervousness cause even the best players in the world to choke on shots that are normally routine. While repetition on the practice court will help your players gain confidence in their shots, success under pressure is often a question of improving mental toughness skills (see "Mental Toughness" in chapter 3). Deep breathing, or centering yourself, a ritual before critical serves and between point behavior and relaxation, and early preparation for ground strokes are good antidotes to the natural tightness that comes from pressure. Use your own relaxation rituals both before serving and between points and games.

Help your players know what to do when stroke breakdowns occur. If coaching during a match is not allowed in your league, your players can't rely on your help on match days and will have to be their own coach.

Simulate Match Play

Every prematch practice should include playing points in a competitive situation. You could try 10-point games where one player serves the entire time; when someone earns 10 points, the two players switch roles. Tiebreaker tournaments are also good because they review the tiebreaker order and add the element of pressure. Another good idea is for players to do 10 repetitions of specific shot sequences they favor—for example, serving wide to the deuce court and hitting the second ball deep to the backhand corner.

In general, don't play normal sets and don't emphasize winning and losing during a prematch practice. You want every player to feel success and confidence. Construct situations that ensure success for each player at some point during the play.

Use your scouting information to devise situations players will likely face the next day. You can even use some junior varsity players to imitate the next day's opponent, just as football coaches do. (You might have to give the JV a handicap advantage to make it realistic. For example, if you know one of your players will face a big serve the next day, let the JV player serve from a foot in front of the baseline.)

PREPARING FOR THE EXPECTED OUTCOME

You and your players will have a pretty good idea of the expected outcome of each match based on the past year's experience and competitive scores against other teams. Your wise guidance will be helpful to your players whether they expect to win, lose, or play a close match.

Expecting to Win

Overconfidence is the dreaded nightmare of every coach. You've got to focus players' thoughts on specific performance goals for the match and let them know you expect them to achieve their goals. Low emotional intensity is common in this situation, and your players may struggle to raise their emotional intensity to the optimal level for the match. High positive intensity is often described as feelings of fun, challenge, and positive fight.

Here are some suggestions for preparing your team before a match your players expect to win:

- Begin raising players' intensity in practice the day before through team competition and support.
- Suggest thinking about or watching tapes of role models with high intensity like Leyton Hewitt, Serena Williams, or Andy Roddick.
- Practice on-court activation techniques such as jumping up and down, pumping fists, or slapping a thigh.
- Raise the players' heart rate through other types of physical activity and thinking.

Expecting to Lose

When players expect to lose, they often try to perform at a level beyond their normal capacity, which usually only ensures they will lose quickly. It's natural for players who feel overmatched to hit harder than usual and take greater risks. Their reasoning is that to have a chance to win, they've got to raise their level of play. You've got to convince them that steady, percentage tennis will give them the best chance for success. They should make the favored opponent earn the win and know he was in a battle.

Occasionally, players on your team will "tank" in this situation—that is, they won't really try. By withdrawing emotionally from the embarrassment of an expected loss, they protect their egos. Excuses and rationalization are tools of players who tank for ego protection. Urge these players to discuss their feelings with you. Express your understanding and encourage them to give you 100 percent fighting effort no matter the expected result.

Keep these points in mind when preparing your team for a match against a superior team:

- Talk with your team the day before about giving 100 percent effort, never giving up, and making their opponents earn each point.
- During drills and practice, emphasize consistency in play and percentage tennis.
- Practice playing points deliberately and controlling the pace of the match by taking time between points to breathe deeply, relax, and focus on the next point.
- During practice, work on body posture and attitude.

Help players learn to act confident, poised, and under control regardless of their feelings of inadequacy. Portray the image of a confident fighter determined to put forth a maximum effort.

Expecting a Close Contest

Matches where the outcome could favor either team are the most satisfying to win and most difficult to lose. Pressure, nerves, and choking are normal for players on both teams. Be honest with your kids about the challenge they face and encourage them to talk about their fears, anxiety, and how they plan to combat those feelings.

Fear of failure tends to produce tense muscles, a faster heart rate, and butterflies in the stomach. Thinking becomes hurried and confused. The deep breathing and muscle relaxation skills you introduced in practice weeks before should be rehearsed in simulated pressure drills during practice the day before the match. Point out to your team that all tennis players experience choking, but the best competitors learn how to combat it—and they can, too.

Consider these suggestions when readying your team for a tough match:

- Emphasize playing one point at a time and loving the battle. Tell your players that when they feel pressure, they should smile and enjoy the moment.

Self-confidence, energy, and composure are keys to any winning strategy.

© USTA

After all, poor competitors never reach pressure points in tight matches because they give up early without a fight.

- Review the specific performance goals set for each player and focus attention on achieving those goals. Push thoughts of winning and losing from their mind.

- Spend extra time at practice building confidence by hitting favorite shots.

- Promote and encourage a sense of humor and perspective when your players are preparing for the match of their life.

- Sometimes a little friendly competition in table tennis, miniature golf, or video games can help your players relax and take the edge off their nervousness.

- Take care with your prematch routines and rituals that help reduce player anxiety. Many young people turn to music for relaxation. If you expect them to enjoy it, be sure it is music they choose, not you.

CHAMPIONSHIP MATCHES

Your months of preparation have set the stage, and at last the championship part of the season has arrived. Reassure your players that just like schoolwork, lessons that have been well learned over a period of time will be retained. Trying to teach new strategies or strokes to prepare for season-ending matches is sure to produce confusion, uncertainty, and anxiety.

Players will take comfort in familiar routines and rituals, so you don't want to change their preparation for the final matches. Your challenge is to encourage your players to have the attitude of confident fighters who will give their best effort.

Before the match, reassure your players that, win or lose, they have had a terrific season, and your last expectation for them is that they will give their absolute best effort today. If they do that, you'll be proud of them.

You should also tell them that it is absolutely normal to be nervous for this match and that, in fact, you're a little nervous too. Every athlete, no matter the level, feels nervous before a big event. Even Pete Sampras, Serena Williams, and Andre Agassi admit to feeling nervous before the finals of a Grand Slam. The key is how well a player deals with it.

Suggest that your players get a good, vigorous warm-up, since activity tends to allow muscles to relax. Second, advise them that when they feel nervous they should take some deep breaths and slowly exhale. Third, tell them to concentrate on moving into position early, watching the ball intently, and following through the entire shot. If they do those three things, they'll be just fine.

Upsets Do Happen

The team had lost five conference matches, all by only 1 team point. Approaching the final conference tournament, they were considered a dangerous team, but not a contender. The players talked endlessly about how close they had been in each of those frustrating losses and about things they could have done differently. They realized that for their team to do well in the tournament, every player had to improve his performance just a bit.

In practice that week, the team planned one or two new performance goals with each player and shared them as a team. They all bought into the challenge of the mission, and players helped each other practice specific strategies.

An amazing thing resulted. After the first day of tournament play, the team was in first place by 2 points. A sense of destiny began to build, and each success added to the feeling. The final standings after four days of play showed the team in first place by 10 points! A championship was theirs and a life lesson, too—practice, perseverance, and patience can produce miracles.

By the way, if the match approaches what a player thinks is a pressure point or game, he should stop and take a deep breath and smile! He should be happy to have an important point in a championship match. Only good players ever get to experience such a thrill!

Consider these training suggestions as you prepare your team for championship matches:

- Revise or set new performance goals with each player.

- Review your scouting book and use previous match information to construct game plans with each player.

- Spend some practice time on confidence builders and pressure-reducing strategies and behavior.

- Stick to preparation routines and rituals that have been helpful for the entire season.

SUMMARY

Consider the following points as you prepare your team for matches:

- Develop a simple-to-use scouting form that works for your level of players.

- Collect scouting information from summer play, the previous year's matches, early-season matches, and opposing teams' tendencies over the years.

- Translate the scouting information into individual game plans that are realistic for your players.

- Prepare for each regular season match by taking into account the expected outcome.

- Give your players the best chance for good performance in championship play by sticking with routines and strategies that have worked for them during the year.

CHAPTER 14 HANDLING MATCHES

Sprints have been run, strokes sharpened, and strategy discussed. Finally the day all players and coaches anticipate has arrived—it's time to play a match. Match play is the culmination of all the preparation you and your team have put in, and the degree of thoroughness of this preparation will determine your team's chances for success.

Match play is the time to see where each player stands competitively. No simulated competitive drill or even a ladder match can duplicate the feeling a player experiences during match play. His teammates, friends, family, and spectators are all rooting for him. For an athlete, there is no other moment like it!

CHOOSING A STARTING LINEUP

Tennis is a little easier than some sports when it comes time to deciding on a starting lineup. Using the results of ladder play can make a coach's decision on a singles lineup almost totally objective. However, there are also subjective criteria that a coach applies to every potential starter before naming that player to the starting lineup.

Most seasoned coaches weigh more factors than just ladder results when choosing a lineup. For example, a letter winner's match experience versus a rookie's inexperience must be a consideration. You may find that some players learn how to beat a teammate's game when they play each other repeatedly on the ladder; however, the player who wins on the ladder may not handle interscholastic match pressure as well as the ladder opponent. Results from tournament play in the off-season can also give a coach insight into a player's ability to handle match stress. Level of effort during practice and match play must also be considered. The end result should be a lineup that puts the best match player at number one and continues to rank the players in order of proficiency until all the singles slots are filled.

Compared to ranking your singles starters, choosing a doubles lineup can be much more difficult. In some states, singles players aren't allowed to play doubles. In many states, athletes play both singles and doubles. Regardless of your state's rules, when choosing your doubles teams, you must use a different perspective from the one you use when choosing a singles team.

Compatibility, playing style, temperament, and experience are all factors that go into coming up with good teammates for doubles. Doubles players must constantly communicate if they hope to be an effective team. Verbal communication and encouragement of their partner are key skills for good doubles players. Of course playing skills specific to doubles such as quick, soft hands; a consistent first serve; and a great return of serve are also important. You should try different combinations early in the season, allowing the players to have significant input as to their doubles partner. The final test a doubles team must pass is making the team the top priority, not the individuals. They must believe that it's the team that wins and the team that loses. No finger-pointing at each other after a loss.

Communicate with your squad early in the season about how you will select a starting lineup. By knowing up front what it takes to make the lineup, each player will better understand her place on the team. This communication is essential if you want to keep the nonstarting players involved. Whether they are in the starting lineup or not, all players should feel that they fulfill important roles in the team's success.

Every Player Plays

To maintain interest and continued development of every player on your team, each player needs to experience the challenge of match play during the season. This is essential to bring inexperienced players along who may be needed later in the season if a regular varsity player is forced to miss a match due to illness, injury, or other personal reasons. There are several ways to ensure that each player has that opportunity:

- Substitute players and allow nonstarters to play against weaker opposing teams or after the team match outcome has been decided.
- Arrange to have several "exhibition" matches in singles or doubles to give

substitutes from both teams some match play. (You will need to have an agreement with the opposing coach.) Although these matches do not count in the team match score, the result is still mighty important to the players.

- Schedule junior varsity matches to provide competitive experience (if the depth of your program allows).
- As a last resort, have your substitute players play challenge matches against each other so that they do not fall behind their teammates in competitive matches played.

You can be sure that over the course of a season, you will be forced to play substitute players a number of times. High school players have lots of issues, pressures, health challenges, college visits, and so forth that often force them to miss matches. From the beginning of the season, you need to commit yourself to developing every player on your team and providing some match play for each one so that he is ready to step in at the key moment.

Stacking the Lineup

Although the ladder results typically decide the starting players for your team lineup, many coaches reserve the right to adjust who competes at which slot. As a tennis coach, you are of course thinking that this is tantamount to the sin of "stacking" (the art of lining up your players out of rank order in an effort to create a better chance for success). Many inexperienced coaches complain about players who are seemingly out of position on an opposing team. After playing a team, they think that the number two player on the other team should have played number five. In most cases, their suspicions are unfounded. Different playing styles sometimes make the higher-ranked player in the lineup look inferior to his lower-ranked teammate. In fact, the toughest match players are often not the ones with the prettiest strokes, but the most dogged competitors who simply return every ball. During the course of a season, it will become clearer to you which players on your team are the best match players and may deserve to play higher in the lineup. As for the other team, you need to have confidence that the other coach is acting responsibly and placing his players in their rightful order.

Although most leagues and states have written rules prohibiting it, there is no definitive solution to the ethical question of stacking. Some leagues do not allow you to switch positions once league play has begun. Others may limit the movement of players by position to no more than one spot. For example, the number one and two players may switch positions but not one and three. It's a good idea to protect yourself and your team by following opposing teams' scores through your league or in the newspapers. This will allow you to check the stability of their lineup before you play them. If you are faced with an apparent attempt to "stack," make your protests politely but strongly before the match begins. At the very least, ask for an explanation from the opposing coach.

However, keep in mind that stacking never contributes to team success. It undermines a team and creates a built-in excuse for a player to lose when competing higher in the lineup than he should be. Furthermore, it certainly sets a poor example to young athletes who should be learning how to play by the rules. Over many years of coaching, it is likely you'll be faced with an apparent violation of the stacking rules very few times. Your best plan is to be alert and watchful, deal calmly with the situation, and then move on to play the match.

HOME MATCHES

One of your primary objectives as a tennis coach on match day is to make the experience special for the competing teams. When programs first begin, the match environment is likely to be pretty absent of frills. Through the years you can add to your home match atmosphere in several ways. Each addition and routine should help to make the match experience more pleasant and memorable for the players.

Prematch Routine

Home match preparation for your team should begin at least an hour before the scheduled starting time. During this hour, your players should begin by jogging three laps around three courts and then stretching as a team. This ritual has a calming effect and helps players focus their attention on the upcoming match.

The warm-up progresses with the players pairing off so they can hit all the strokes and find a match rhythm. During this 10- to 15-minute warm-up, you should circulate among the players and mention key focal points each player needs to remember once the match begins. For many players, it is helpful during the warm-up to actually play several simulated points or patterns of play to get them ready for the onset of play and perhaps a fast start.

Warm-up should conclude before the visiting team arrives. During the next 10 or so minutes, each player is allowed to get equipment, water, and other match essentials together. Once the visiting team arrives, you should greet them and show them which courts can be used for warm-up. This is a good time for you and the opposing coach to exchange lineups and discuss any contingencies such as weather conditions that are present or expected.

Ten minutes before the match is scheduled to begin, your team should walk away from the courts to an adjacent area. The purpose of this is to get the players away from girlfriends, boyfriends, parents, and other well-wishers so they can focus on the task at hand. After giving the lineup sheet to a JV team member to write on the scoreboard, you should join the varsity.

During this very important time, performance goals for the day's match should again be emphasized. Prematch preparation can be completed with the team joining hands and chanting your team slogan together. They are now properly focused and ready to play. The team, clad in team uniforms and with all their equipment ready, should return to the court area together.

You should begin the prematch introductions by welcoming the visiting team, pointing out rest rooms and water fountains, and mentioning key rules and instructions to both teams. Good reminders are those covering the scoring system to be used (including tiebreakers), the rules on coaching, and the rule concerning breaks if players split sets. Next, you should introduce yourself to the visiting players and introduce the visiting coach to your players as a group. Following that, you should introduce each member of your team to her opponent on the visiting team. Using the score sheet, read each visiting player's name, followed by her counterpart from your team, and indicate which court they will play their match on.

As your players' names are called, it's a good idea for them to shake hands with the opposing coach and their opponent (with a firm handshake and good eye contact). You should be sure to welcome each visiting player as well, with a handshake and perhaps a wish for a good match. These formalities tend to set a positive tone for the match and should be repeated again at the conclusion of the match.

If your league or state plays doubles after the completion of singles, give the players 5 or 10 minutes to refocus before starting doubles. Never assume that your teams can begin doubles play without your input. After playing a singles match, players need to be reminded about doubles principles before they walk back onto the court. Whether you're using the same or different players for singles and doubles, meet briefly with your doubles players to talk about their game plan. In close team matches, doubles determines the team winner, so your doubles teams can't afford to squander the first few games of their doubles match.

Charting Matches and Supporting the Team

Players who are not competing or aiding scorekeepers should be asked to chart matches. By having these players keep per-

Welcome your opponent with a firm, friendly handshake.

formance goal charts, you can ensure that each member of your team is involved in the match. You should insist that your team members and spectators support all players on the court, which means never belittling an inferior opponent or applauding unforced errors by members of the visiting team.

The entire squad should remain at the match until it is complete except in very unusual circumstances. It's not uncommon for the varsity to be cheering for a JV player whose match was put on court after varsity singles courts became available. Staying until all play is complete is simply part of the match. This emphasizes a most important team concept—no player is more important than another. The entire squad, from the varsity to the scorekeepers, contributes to the team effort.

Enhancing Home Match Atmosphere

One way to enhance the atmosphere on your home courts is to place an umpire's chair on each court. These chairs can perhaps be built by the school's vocational department, and they can be maintained by your team. On match day, the chair is used by a scorekeeper whose only job is to keep score during the match. This person does not settle disputes or overrule line calls. Scorekeepers can be students, junior varsity players, parents, teachers, or team boosters.

Scorecards should be used on every court so that spectators know each match's current score. Many different types of match scorecards are available commercially through tennis equipment catalogs. The typical way to use these scorecards is to have both players change their score as they change sides of the net. An added bonus of these scorecards is that they expose scoring disputes before they get out of hand.

A team scoreboard with the day's matchups should also be in plain view for all to see. As matches are completed, the scorekeepers can record match results on the scoreboard next to the players' names. This allows all specta-

tors to make a quick assessment of the overall match score and keeps them interested in the outcome.

You can also consider posting the season schedule on the scoreboard (along with results) for spectators to observe. If your team is fortunate enough to have achieved team or individual honors in previous years, you might also post them on a portion of the scoreboard. These are all part of your promotional efforts for your team and the players.

One final suggestion for home matches is to have parents volunteer in a rotation system to provide snacks and drinks for the players of both teams during the match. Because of the length of many matches, players can easily become starved for food, and of course they need to replenish fluids after play. Generally, this arrangement provides a useful function for team parents who want to be there anyway to watch their kids compete.

PLAYINGS MATCHES AWAY

Try to keep your prematch routine on the road as similar to your routine for a home match as possible. Plan on arriving at the away site early enough to maintain prematch consistency. During the drive to an away match, some coaches want their players to focus quietly on their opponents. However, most coaches recommend letting players relax during the drive by listening to music, talking, or doing whatever they want. This keeps them loose and relaxed. When you arrive at the courts and begin the prematch routine—that's when it's time to focus.

Once on court for warm-up, it's not always possible to exactly duplicate your home prematch routine. Circumstances such as administrative problems with leaving school early or lack of lighting at the host school's complex can make it impossible to allow enough time to complete normal warm-up. However, the prematch routine may be even more important on the road because it gives players a chance to get used to the speed of the court surface and to adjust to the wind or the sun.

The stretching is always mandatory, but after a car ride it takes on even greater significance. Focusing on the task at hand can be accomplished by a brief prematch talk, during which you should try to focus the players on their performance goals for the day. One addition might be added to this talk for matches on the road: Remind the players to remain poised and handle any adversity they may encounter with dignity. Finally, the ritual of joining hands and saying the team chant unites players before they take the court.

TOURNAMENTS

During the season, you may encounter a situation (such as tournament play or possibly a doubleheader) that requires your team to play more than one match a day. Such a situation calls for careful planning if players are to maintain their competitive edge while waiting to play.

Players should eat two hours before play and only eat enough to maintain their energy level for the match at hand. Overeating or eating too close to their scheduled match time will make them sluggish and ineffective during play. Assistant coaches or parents can help you with feeding your athletes at the proper time. Also remind your players to stay out of the sun while waiting to play. Many a player has stood around at a tournament for hours in the sun only to find herself listless on court when her match is finally played.

Most young players find that listening to music is the best way to pass the time. It is less fatiguing than reading and can help set the emotional tone you want. As the time of the match draws closer, the music chosen should produce energy, enthusiasm, and eagerness for movement.

Electronic games or a deck of cards is also a good choice of entertainment. Players should be encouraged to do things that are relaxing and do not demand too much close attention or concentration. Save that for the match.

Many tournaments, due to facility restrictions, require your players to compete at different sites. This makes assistants and parents even more valuable in coordinating who will stay with which player and how players will be transported to their playing sites. When players are competing at different sites, try to stay with the player who you feel will benefit the most from your presence. Once a match seems to be under control, or your presence can no longer make a difference, move to another site. At the team meeting before play begins, tell the squad your plans for viewing matches so that no one feels slighted. A game plan has been formulated, and each player knows that she can accomplish this plan whether you are watching or not.

ON THE COURT

Monitoring the behavior of your players during match play is critical. Doing so can help you prevent embarrassing situations and ensure that the team competes at a high level of sportsmanship and maturity. During breaks in the action, your league rules may allow you to coach. If so, this gives you the opportunity to help players make tactical adjustments to their opponents or reestablish momentum that has been lost.

Be careful not to offer too much one-way advice. Instead, when players are struggling, ask them for their assessment of what they might change. Always keep in mind that your long-term goal is to develop their independence as competitors and as people.

Coach Conduct

Some coaches feel that their job ends when the players take the court to play. They bring the team to the match site, tell them to have a good match, and then sit and wait to take scores when the matches are completed. However, most involved coaches feel that when players take the court, that's when they go to work! If your players are giving their all on court, the least you can do is visibly support them in every way possible.

If your state doesn't allow coaching during play, you can still applaud outstanding effort by your players. Present yourself to the players in a positive manner at all times, no matter what the circumstances. If audible coaching is allowed in your state, provide your players with technical and emotional support. This is when the players need your presence most, so be there for them.

When a player is having mechanical problems with a stroke, give her one suggestion to correct it. If the problem is with confidence, refocus her attention from negative to positive. Some players just need a little encouragement to let them know that everything is okay as long as they continue to give a good effort.

No matter what the situation is that requires coaching, remember to always project a positive outlook to your players. If things are going poorly, don't be critical—be a problem solver, not a blamer. Constructive suggestions will help your players (and you) achieve success. Be a friend and a helper to your players, not a critic.

In times of match stress, you set the tone. Coaches who react negatively to situations that arise during match play are sending all the wrong messages to their players. Over the years, all successful coaches learn to appear calm, poised, and positive during play. This outward appearance of control sends the right signal to your players during times of stress. It's the most important thing you can do for them during play. That said, it doesn't mean that you are not churning inside with anxiety and nervousness!

Player Conduct

No sport asks more of its competitors than tennis. In most cases, there is no third party (umpire) to officiate school matches. Imagine a football game with no referees: A player could score a touchdown only to return to his teammates and be informed that the opposition had spotted his foot out of bounds, so the score was no good.

Expect your players to exhibit perfect fairness when calling lines on their opponent's shots. Even so, recognize that problems are going to occur when teenagers are put in this type of competitive situation. How you teach your players to react to line calls during play will determine whether they can maintain a proper level of sporting behavior. Teach your players to accept line calls by their opponent. This will allow them to focus on their own play rather than being distracted by arguing or questioning calls. Only if a trend of bad calls by an opponent becomes evident should a player ask for help from a match official.

When a player is out of line on court, discipline her immediately. Your players should know proper conduct and know how you will respond to deviations from it. If you let inappropriate behavior slide even once, it becomes more difficult to correct in the future. If your player's opponent misbehaves, don't try to correct the problem yourself by confronting the player. Instead, inform the player's coach about the infraction and let her handle the problem.

Purchase a copy of the USTA's *A Friend at Court*, where you'll find the rules of tennis and the code of play. (See the resources section on page 193 for ordering information.) This is the tennis umpire's bible. You might even consider having each player carry a copy of the USTA rules and playing code. Some coaches quiz their players on rules at the beginning of the season. This assures the coach that players know the rules well enough not to be taken advantage of or to take advantage of other players. You may know a rule interpretation that a rival coach is unaware of. However, your word is not always good enough in the heat of battle. Armed with the USTA rules (and state or regional rule pamphlets), you can prevent some ugly arguments with your coaching counterpart during a match.

Teach your players to play the calls during a match and to not judge an opponent for just one bad call. Doing so only results in loss of focus and a ready-made excuse for poor play. If a pattern of close calls becomes apparent, and your player asks for help, request that a competent adult officiate. If no one is available, use a player from each team stationed on opposite sides of the court. Only when there is no other choice should coaches go on court to umpire a match. Although having someone on court to verify calls usually has a calming effect on both players, help with line calls should only be provided as a last resort. Players have to learn to handle adverse situations.

Most states either have a policy on how to handle disputes over line calls or they resort to the USTA rules. If your state or conference doesn't have a policy to follow in these circumstances, you may want to suggest addressing the issue and creating one. With a standard operating policy in place, the disagreements can be handled uniformly to minimize controversy.

Opposing Coach Conduct

Most coaches are competent and capable of handling match situations. Always assume that your coaching counterparts will handle their players reasonably. They may not handle a situation in the same way that you would, but as long as your players are not put at a disadvantage, mind your own business.

Game Plan Adjustments

To make adjustments in a player's game plan, you need to have a plan before play begins. Discuss performance goals and match strategy with each player the day before a match. These same goals and strategy should be served up as reminders during warm-up and again at the team gathering just before play begins. Some coaches have found it very helpful to ask players to carry the game plan on court by using index cards with a few key notes. Players can refer to these notes during changeovers to help focus on the things you've discussed.

Tips On Court

Here are a few examples of helpful reminders that your players may want to include on their index cards:

- Play your way into every point by getting your first serve in and getting returns back in play. Give your opponent a chance to make the first mistake.

- Vary your shots from the baseline by changing the height, spin, and speed of the ball.

- If you get a short ball, attack! Play the ball down the line and be ready for a passing shot or a lob.

- If you find an opponent's weakness, keep pounding away at it until he changes his game.

- Slow down play if you lose a string of points. Rethink your tactics and increase your consistency. Most opponents will hit a bad patch too.

- If a couple of close calls go against you, or you miss a few close shots, aim farther inside the lines for a greater margin of error.

- Once you've fallen behind and you are sure your tactics will not work against your opponent, consider switching your tactics.

- If you are making too many unforced errors, focus on getting into position early, watching the ball intently, and swinging smoothly through the shot.

Losing Momentum

Many factors require your attention during match play. At times it will appear that your player is cruising along, in total control. Tennis, however, is not a timed sport, which means that momentum will swing from player to player at various times in a match. Subtle changes at crucial times in a match are often missed by teenage players. Watch for the following possible developments and point them out to your player before momentum is lost:

- **Changes in tactics by an opponent.** These may be very apparent to you but not to a player who is in control of a match.

- **Motivation lapse after success.** After your player has gained momentum (e.g., by breaking serve), remind her not to let up but to intensify her focus in order to get off the court as quickly as possible.

• A letdown in concentration. Concentration lapses are common at the end of a hard fought first set. Remind your players about momentum before they start the new set. If they lost the first set, they need to regain momentum by digging in at the beginning of the new set. If they won the first set, they need to stay focused on keeping the momentum at the beginning of the new set.

Helping Players Think for Themselves

One way you can foster independent thinking is by having your players develop their own personal coaching notebook. This notebook, which can be developed during practices, lists each detail of every stroke in the player's repertoire. At practice sessions and individual lessons, the player makes entries into the notebook after discussing technique with you. Before a match, it may be helpful for each player to make a few key notations on the game plan index card; these notations can be reminders of what to do when a shot is giving him problems (and can be taken from information in his notebook). Of course, on the other side of the card are the match play tactics he wants to remember.

The real key to helping athletes adjust during the heat of the battle is to keep the directions simple, concise, and in language they can easily understand. Giving a player too many choices under pressure is a sure formula for producing a confused and frustrated athlete.

Stay Upbeat

Never get down on players during a match, either verbally or with your body language. They want the same thing you do. Sometimes when a player repeats a mistake several times, it's hard not to vent your frustrations, but coaching successfully means doing what's best for your athletes in the heat of battle. Screaming at them or communicating your disgust by gesturing is never in your athletes'

best interest. Strive to remain positive at all times. You can teach them best how to deal with what their opponent is throwing at them by remaining undaunted against any odds. Remember—you set the tone. Be positive!

COACHING DURING THE MATCH

If coaching is permitted during crossover games or between points, you can verbally assist your player in making changes to get back on track. Changes in a game plan can be classified under three headings—technical, tactical, and emotional.

Whichever area your player needs help with during a match, keep this key coaching tip in mind: Don't give her too much information at once. It is impossible to keep a player's attention very long during the stress of match play. Whether you are telling her to get her racket back early, approach down the middle, or fight harder, don't give her too much information. Instead, pick one thing that you feel can help your player immediately. Overloading a player results only in confusing her or turning her off completely to your suggestions.

When coaching is necessary, remember to treat each player as an individual. A player's personality determines how you should coach her during a match. Some players will eagerly await your instruction, whereas others will only be distracted by your presence. You must know each player's personality well enough to help rather than hinder her during match play.

During the heat of the battle, many coaches get caught up in the moment. Remember to remain composed and think about what you are going to say to your player before opening your mouth. The following are examples of what you can tell players in various situations.

When players are beating themselves, here are some suggestions you can give them:

• Change poor shot selection.
• Increase the margin of error over the net and keep shots away from the lines.

- Maintain better court position.
- Be conscious of balance when setting up for shots.
- Stop the negative talk and gestures.

When players are very nervous, you can tell them the following:

- Everything will be okay no matter what happens.
- Slow down between points and breathe deeply.
- Bounce on toes between strokes (if players are sluggish).
- Think positive.
- Play their way into the match—don't panic early.
- Focus on fundamentals (react, bounce, hit).

When players are overconfident, you can give them this advice:

- Refocus on concentration and discipline.
- Respect their opponent's effort no matter what the player's skill level.
- Work on weaker shots in their own game.
- Concentrate on getting off court as quickly as possible.

When players have stroke mechanics problems, here are some suggestions to give them:

- Reread the information about the problem shot in their personal stroke production notebook.
- Make one adjustment (balance, grip, swing, contact point, follow-through).
- Concentrate on strokes that are working well rather than dwelling on negative strokes.
- Find a weakness in the opponent's strokes and play to it.

When players are acting inappropriately, you can suggest the following:

- Refocus on their game plan.
- Maintain their dignity by displaying some good sporting behavior.
- Don't use their opponent as an excuse— find a solution to the challenge presented.

You, the coach, should discipline the player but don't blame or assess punishment.

POSTMATCH PROCEDURES

Always conduct a team meeting after the match is completed. This is a good time to make sure you have all the accurate scores of each match. It is appropriate for you to point out some positive things that your team as a whole achieved during the match and perhaps emphasize a few highlights by individual players. This is *not* the time to mention or highlight poor performances.

Different players handle wins and losses differently. The one constant you can give them at the end of every match is praise for effort. Reestablish the personal worth you feel for each player regardless of the outcome of his match. After a victory, allow your players to celebrate their accomplishment, but with a sense of humility. You should always give the players credit for a victory. At a home match, make a point of mingling with the opposition and congratulating them on their effort. After all, it is this effort that makes the victory worth celebrating. After the opposition departs, hold your meeting, congratulate each other, clasp hands, and chant the team slogan once more. On the road, you and your team can mingle with the opposition and then move away from the courts to hold your team meeting.

Young people in today's society have a hard time accepting a loss. Thus, some of the greatest coaching lessons you can expose your players to come after a defeat. If you teach your players to be humble in victory, you should also teach them to be gracious after a loss. Begin as you would after a win by congratulating the opponent's effort. Then check with each player to see whether he thinks he met his performance goals for the match. Remain objective without assigning blame as you talk to your team. If they worked to meet their performance goals, and they don't blame factors beyond their control (such as line calls or wind) for the loss, they are winners regardless of the match outcome.

Save your stroke breakdown analysis for later. Some players will want feedback from you as soon as they finish their match, but usually this is the worst time to critique a match. Instead, give them some positive reassurance and allow them some time, at least overnight, before you analyze the match in detail. During this time, they can settle down and think clearly about what occurred during play. They will have the time to detach themselves emotionally from the match and think about it clearly. A time lapse before your critique of the match also develops some independent thinking in your players.

In the next day or two, go over the highs and lows of the match with your players. Review both the positive and negative highlights of the match using objective criteria from shot charting or videotaping whenever possible. Report facts in a nonemotional way. Once an evaluation has been completed, it is time to begin laying plans to capitalize on success or restore lost confidence. Structure practice goals together and affirm your belief in each player's ability to overcome weaknesses. If overconfidence creeps in after an impressive performance by a player, encourage that player to rededicate his efforts toward higher goals.

Put yourself in the hot seat by asking players if your coaching was effective or if there are changes you can make before the next match to increase your effectiveness. This will show your players that you are not above criticism, even if you are the head coach. Together, formulate a plan to minimize stroke breakdown in future matches.

SUMMARY

For match play, follow these coaching principles:

- Determine a fair lineup for match play by using results of ladder play and by considering players' effort, experience, mental toughness, and style of play.

- Form doubles teams by pairing players that possess doubles-specific skills, are compatible, communicate well, and win or lose as a team.

- Develop a consistent prematch routine for your team.

- Give all the players, not just the varsity, a role to play during a match.

- Remain positive at all times during a match. Be there for your players during match play.

- Teach your players to display an air of confidence on court without being combative with their opponent.

- Discipline poor sporting behavior from your players immediately but allow your coaching counterpart to handle his own players' problems.

- Use index cards for players to carry their game plan on court.

- If the game plan needs to be adjusted during play, keep changes as simple as possible.

- Focus doubles teams before they take the court.

- Always conduct a team meeting after a match, and try to say something positive to each player.

- Wait to talk about breakdowns during match play until the day after the match.

- Be objective when critiquing the previous day's match play.

- Be humble in victory and gracious in defeat.

CHAPTER 15 EVALUATING PERFORMANCE

When the match season is completed, a coach's job doesn't end—it just changes. Every successful coach evaluates and plans in the off-season. Coaching is a year-round endeavor if you hope to be successful. You must review each season, whether it was a good one or bad. A straightforward and thorough annual evaluation of each player and your program as a whole is key to continued success.

EVALUATING PLAYERS

Information needed to measure a player's progress should come from your own observations as well as those of the player's teaching pro (if he has one) and your assistant coaches. Players, especially seniors, can also help you evaluate the progress of other players. Decisions on who must be cut and what position in singles and doubles a player should play are much easier to make with input from everyone associated with your program. If everyone can give and receive constructive criticism, your tennis program will flourish.

Preseason Evaluation

As the tennis season approaches, you should spend time with each returning player to review the progress made on off-season goals. Ask the player how much she thinks she has progressed. Contribute your own thoughts based on off-season observations you made at tournaments or team matches.

Have each player complete a form similar to the one presented in figure 15.1. Ask the players to bring their presummer goal cards with them when you evaluate their off-season progress. These goal cards are the ones you and your players discussed at the end of the previous season.

Once a review of the off-season is completed with each player, it is time to make plans for the upcoming season. Team goals should be discussed at the preseason meeting of returning letter winners. At this time, you can evaluate where you are as an overall team, where you want to go, and how to get there by the end of the season. The preseason evaluation ends with each player filling out an information card like the one shown in figure 15.2.

Name_____

1. What progress did you make this summer toward your off-season goals?

2. What tournaments did you enter?

3. What summer tennis camp did you attend?

4. Develop some new Now goals for the fall tennis clinics or restate summer goals you haven't achieved yet.

5. What do you see yourself contributing to this year's team?

6. What did you do this summer to strengthen your relationships with your family members?

7. What are your academic goals for this school year?

8. What can I do to help you achieve your family, school, and tennis goals this year?

Figure 15.1 Off-season progress self-evaluation form.

Name_____

Parent's name_____

Address_____

Phone #_____

Year in school_____

1st period class_____

Birthdate_____

Where do you usually play tennis?

_____

Put your complete class schedule on the back and include all teachers' names.

Figure 15.2 Player information card.

Team Tryouts and Selection

You should follow the guidelines for selecting your team that were outlined earlier in chapter 4. If you are in the position of having more players try out than you can accommodate, it is important that you establish a plan for those underclassmen who may want to compete for a spot in future years. They may become important team members for you in the future, and you want to set them on the right path of development.

Handling Player Cuts

Before making the final decision about which players to cut, accumulate information from assistant coaches and teaching pros who work with the players. Use as much data as possible to make a good decision about which athletes should make your squad. This is the toughest decision you will have to make as a coach. Deciding who will play singles and doubles pales in comparison to telling a player that she didn't make the squad.

Talk personally to each player that will be cut. Don't use a posted list of players who made the team as a means of notifying athletes they were cut. Try to make your conversation with the cut players as positive as possible. During this discussion, remind each player that there are other avenues available for her to pursue tennis during the year.

Refer the players to local teaching pros who can work with them to improve their game. Distribute a list of tennis programs, clinics, and USA Team Tennis programs that are available in your area.

Invite all cut players back to try out again the following year (unless they're seniors). Remind them that this experience, although disappointing, can be used to better themselves if they keep it in proper perspective. Failure to make the squad should be treated as a learning experience. The player can use it as motivation to improve as a tennis player in the next 12 months or to channel her energies into another endeavor she is better suited for.

Evaluating Practice

Being organized at every practice makes evaluating player progress much easier. Use a master plan broken down into monthly activities such as the one that was presented in chapter 6. Draw daily practice plans from your monthly guide. Set general goals for the team as they progress through the day's practice plan. These goals allow you to evaluate your players' progress on a daily basis.

Keep written records of all practices, and at the end of the season, review them to see what changes should be made in the year ahead. Ask players for their suggestions since they will have a good sense of how effective their time was spent during team practices.

Learn from your mistakes so that you will be able to prevent them from reoccurring later in your career. Practice time can be used more wisely when you don't repeat the same coaching mistakes you made the year before. Keep what works, but don't be afraid to try new techniques. Change is the essence of good coaching, and you should expect change each year since the group of players will be new, their goals may be different, and certainly the team personality will vary from year to year.

The one common denominator all successful teams have is a great work ethic. Don't base your daily evaluation of players during practice solely on the number of errors they make. Take the time to watch the amount of *effort* your players give as they try to master proper technique. Usually a team's success during match play is directly related to the amount of effort and concentration they produce during practice. The old coaching adage "they'll play at the same level as they practice" holds true almost all the time.

Athletes always report that they enjoy sports when team practices are *fun*! It's your job to make sure practices include time for fun along with hard work. If you model your coaching after coaches of professional sports who take on a businesslike attitude, chances are you'll lose a lot of young, talented players.

Make sure each practice is well planned, has a good variety of drills and activities, includes some competition, and presents opportunities for your players to see that they are actually improving as players. These elements help make the time fun for most players.

Measuring Improvement

Your players will increase their motivation and self-confidence as they see improvement in their play. Here are some ideas to help them gauge their progress:

- Establish standard tests of skill that all team members perform. Record each player's score and compare the results. A test can be simply feeding 10 balls and counting the number of balls a player can hit deep crosscourt on both forehand and backhand. Another test is a rally test of consecutive hits that land behind the service area without an error. Keep a team record and award prizes for best performance.

- Position all players on the court for doubles play and play four games. Winning teams then move toward the number 1 court while losing teams stay for the next match. The team that stays the longest on the top court is the winner. Refer to the king- or queen-of-the-hill doubles drill in chapter 12 for more details.

- Videotape players and analyze their technique with them. After a period of intense work on a specific shot, show them the improvement.

- Set up certain agility, endurance, and movement tests. Using a stopwatch, time each player. As the season progresses, they should start to see some improvement in their times.

- Use shot charts during match play to keep track of winners, unforced errors, double faults, first serves in, aces, and so forth. Compare matches over time and point out improvement.

Use the veterans on your team as a barometer of the team's effort level during different segments of practice. Veterans have been through at least a year of your practices and know what it takes to succeed. Be sure that these veterans are close to giving 100 percent effort at all times. Younger players on your squad will follow the veterans' lead. This will create a practice atmosphere conducive to learning.

Without these types of measuring indexes, players often become confused or frustrated about their rate of improvement. They will tend to rely more on how they feel, which is often a poor indicator. Be creative in the types of measures you use and tailor them to the skill level of your players. As their scores and performances improve throughout the season, you can point out their progress, award gold stars for good work, and reinforce outstanding effort.

Evaluating Matches

To evaluate players during match play, you can rely on input from assistants, data from match charts, and personal observations. Once you have compiled the information from match play, you need to put it in a form you can use for evaluation. Accomplish this by giving everyone who evaluates play during matches a specific job.

Assistant Coach

It is impossible for one person to watch each match on court during play, although your players will expect you to do so. If you have assistant coaches, use them as extra sets of eyes. Your assistants can report to you during play if a problem arises that requires your coaching attention. After the match is over and the players have gone home, meet with your assistants to debrief each other about how each player performed. During this meeting, discuss player evaluations and form a practice plan to correct flaws in players' games that came to light during match play.

Head Coach

Presenting a positive image and acknowledging good play are your first priorities. Imparting coaching suggestions warranted during play is easier when players realize you're working together toward the same goals.

Which matches you choose to watch carefully will depend on the opponent, the challenge each player faces, and the point in the season. Your job is to watch as much as you can to get a sense of the flow of the match, general trends, tactical plans, and technical errors that crop up.

Some coaches like to make short written notes as the match progresses. Others prefer to carry a small tape recorder with them to record comments. In either case, it is important to remain as unobtrusive as possible so that you don't upset your player. After his third double fault, if he sees you make a note, he knows he'll be held accountable. Your actions may just increase the pressure and frustration he is feeling.

Some players will raise their game when you stand behind their court, while others will fall apart. You need to talk with your players collectively and individually to let them know what role you plan to take during a match and why. Your presence should be incidental to them if they have learned to focus their attention on the court.

Charting Matches

Since the head coach cannot watch all matches at once, you should set up alternative methods of recording what happens. One method is to use shot charts that are completed by alternates or junior varsity players. Along with providing you and your players with essential data, this method ensures that younger players will also watch carefully and learn.

The fundamental theme of your coaching should be a player's attention on performance goals rather than simply winning or losing. The person completing the chart may need to

```
┌────────────────────────────────────────────────────────────────────────────┐
│                   General code for charting errors and winners               │
│                                                                              │
│  F    = Forehand          V     = Volley          P    = Passing shot        │
│                                                                              │
│  B    = Backhand          OH    = Overhead        Win  = Winner              │
│                                                                              │
│  1/2  = Half-volley        SR    = Service return  W    = Wide                │
│                                                                              │
│  D    = Deep              N     = Net             X    = Point won due to ace │
│                                                                              │
│  SW   = Service winner    APP   = Approach        U    = Unforced error       │
│                                                                              │
│                                                   DF   = Double fault         │
└────────────────────────────────────────────────────────────────────────────┘
```

Figure 15.3 Codes for charting errors and winners.

know what the performance goals are so that those are added to the basic chart. A sample of an effective charting system is shown in figure 15.3. Over time, you will probably develop your own system that works for you and your program.

When JV players chart, give them two or three aspects of match play to watch for that correspond to the game plan on the player's match index card. An example might be charting the number of successful first serves during play. The second performance goal charted could be unforced errors committed from the baseline. The last performance goal might involve the number of times the player took midcourt short balls and came to the net using a slice approach shot.

The speed of doubles play makes it difficult for one person to chart both members of a team. Instead, chart doubles play by making one charter responsible for each member of a doubles team. This allows each person charting the match to focus on a single player.

Once the match is completed, the charter calculates numbers for the performance goals and presents the tally sheet to the coach. The performance summaries are discussed by the coaching staff after play (see figure 15.4), and a strategy to improve weak areas is constructed for future practice sessions.

The evaluation sheets are discussed individually with the players the next day at practice. Nothing can be gained by rehashing match play until the player is receptive to suggestions. Most coaches will tell you that it's best to wait until the next day to discuss specific evaluations of match play. However, you may want to let the player check the charting sheets immediately after play if he wants to get an idea of how he performed in relation to his match cards.

The same chart can be used by a more experienced assistant coach to chart every aspect of match play. Referenced comments, such as "player stood flat-footed between shots," can be noted in the margins of the chart to provide extra information related to prematch performance goals. Another use of this tool is evaluating future opponents by charting statistics of one of their matches during tournament play. Find a performance chart that you feel comfortable with to evaluate play during singles and doubles. Once you have decided which chart you want to use, devise a coding system to follow play, or use the one in figure 15.5.

Figure 15.5 charts a single game in a match. As you see, the serve is charted in the first row. When charting serves, place a 1 in the box if the first serve is in and a 2 in the box if the second serve is in. DF signifies double fault, and A signifies ace. The server occupies the second row and the receiver the third row. Each column signifies one point played.

Directions: Use this chart to tally unforced ground stroke errors and ground stroke winners. Log unforced error totals for each stroke in the second row and winner totals in the third row. If the number of unforced errors is higher or equal to winners, then the player should focus on that particular stroke for improvement in practice.

	Forehand	Backhand	Approach	Lob	Half-volley
Unforced errors	20	15	6-F/8-B	4	9
Winners	14	6	5-F/3-B	1	0

Directions: Use this chart to tally unforced volley errors and volley winners. Log unforced error totals for each stroke in the second row and winner totals in the third row. Set a number of errors that appears reasonable as a goal for players. If the number exceeds the targeted goal, then work needs to be done on that stroke.

	Forehand volley	Backhand volley	Overhead
Unforced errors	5	3	1
Winners	14	11	4

Directions: Use this chart to tally serves.

Total serves	First serves	% in	DF	Aces	Service win
110	60	54.5	3	5	11

A good percentage of first serves would be in the 60% range. As a rule, double faults should be less than aces and service winners combined.

Code
Total = Total number of serves hit
First serves = First serves that were good
% in = Percentage of first serves in (divide first serves by total serves)
DF = Double faults committed
Aces = Clean aces hit
Service win = Serves that couldn't be put in play by opponent

Figure 15.4   Performance summary.

1. Figure 15.5 charts your player, Jim, who is serving. His opponent is Bob.

2. Jim hits in his first serve (signified by the 1 in the first box of the top row), but loses the point by hitting an unforced backhand into the net (signified by UB-N). Note that the error committed is listed in the receiver's box, indicating the reason why Jim's opponent, Bob, won the point. Score: Love-15.

3. Point two begins with Jim getting a second serve into play (signified by the 2 in the second box of the top row). The point was finished when Jim hit a forehand winner (signified by the F-Win). Score: 15-15.

4. Jim double-faults the third point away (signified by the DF). Bob won the point due to the double fault. Score: 15-30.

5. Jim serves an ace on the fourth point of the game (signified by the A in the service box and the X in Jim's row). Score: 30-30.

6. In the fifth point, Jim hits in a second serve and eventually wins the point by hitting a forehand volley winner (FV-Win). Score: 40-30.

1	2	DF	A	2	1	1	2
	F-Win		X	FV-Win		OH-Win	B-P
UB-N					FAPP-D		

Figure 15.5 Sample game chart.

7. Jim makes his first serve on the sixth point, which he eventually loses by hitting a forehand approach shot deep (signified by FAPP-D). Score: Deuce.

8. The seventh point is won by Jim, who hits an overhead winner (signified by OH-Win). Score: Jim's advantage.

9. The game ends on the eighth point when Jim's second serve is chipped by Bob, who approaches the net and is passed by a backhand (signified by B-P).

Use figure 15.6 to chart an entire match.

Postseason Evaluation

It is critical that you spend some quality time at the end of the season with each individual player who will be returning the next year. You and the player should both bring a written analysis of her overall tennis game to this meeting, including a list of the key items that should be targeted for improvement. Once you compare your list with the player's list, and you both have agreed on the key items, you can work out a plan for action together.

If your high school season has been the culmination of a long year of tennis, the best course of action is to suggest that your players take some time off to do other things. A break from tennis sometime during the year is essential to keep players at all levels enthusiastic and eager for play. It is a good idea, however, to encourage them to continue with some form of regular physical activity to maintain their fitness level and build strength during the off-season.

Next, you need to figure out when players should attempt to make technical changes to their game—for example, a player who needs to change her grip in order to learn a dependable spin serve to replace the soft, flat one that opponents feast on. Players should make technical changes at a time when it will not interfere with their competitive play. A series of lessons with a certified teaching professional may be the answer, provided the player does not plan to play competitively during that time. Nothing is more frustrating for players than to be thrust into competition with "new shots" that they have little confidence in. They'll soon revert to their old habits, and the opportunity for improvement will be lost.

If your competitive season is in the spring, it might make sense for your players to spend the summer participating in competitive play because it may be more available and affordable in the summer months. Technical changes can be put off until the fall or winter months. In some parts of the country, varsity tennis is in the fall. This changes your approach to the year and your planning for the off-season. The months immediately following the season are cold winter months that are ideal for rest, other sports, and time off from tennis. If indoor tennis is possible, encourage your players to use it to work on off-season goals. Wait until the spring and

Game # 1 (1-0) Bob

1	2	A	2	1	1					
UF		X		SW	FW					
	FV win		B win							

Server: Jim
Receiver: Bob

Game # 2 ◯

Game # 3 ◯ Server: _____
Receiver: _____

Server: _____
Receiver: _____

Game # 4 ◯

Game # 5 ◯ Server: _____
Receiver: _____

Server: _____
Receiver: _____

Game # 6 ◯

Game # 7 ◯ Server: _____
Receiver: _____

Server: _____
Receiver: _____

Game # 8 ◯

Game # 9 ◯ Server: _____
Receiver: _____

Server: _____
Receiver: _____

Game # 10 ◯

Game # 11 ◯ Server: _____
Receiver: _____

Server: _____
Receiver: _____

Game # 12 ◯

Server: _____
Receiver: _____

Figure 15.6 Sample match chart.

warmer weather to concentrate on improving overall play through competitive events.

SUMMERTIME PLAY

Summer offers many opportunities for tennis players to sharpen their skills and develop their games, including summer leagues, tournaments, individual tennis lessons, and summer camps. If players remain active during the summer, and their plan to improve has been well designed, you can expect significant improvement by most of your players.

You need to carefully check the rules in your league and state concerning a coach's direct involvement with his players out of season. Some states forbid any contact whatsoever on the court. Others have no rules, and some have limited restrictions. You may be able to be involved in coaching players as part of a team or in a recreational program, but not be allowed to work with them individually. It may be a good idea anyway to limit the one-on-one contact since it puts you in some awkward positions relative to compensation and favoritism.

If your players can't afford to play competitive tournaments or USA Team Tennis all summer without working, help them find jobs teaching younger players in your town recreational programs or perhaps at a tennis camp. By being immersed in tennis for the summer (and around other players), they will be more likely to play, learn, and improve their skills even without serious competition.

Summer Leagues

USA Team Tennis is recognized nationally through the USTA, and most towns and cities sponsor teams in this program. The program includes divisions of play that allow kids ranging in age from 6 through 18 to participate. The appeal of team tennis is that it is similar to high school tennis and provides the fun and friends that come with being part of a team while competing. One other benefit is that USA

Team Tennis is a coed sport, which holds an attraction all its own. If your town doesn't have a USA Team Tennis league, contact your USTA sectional office for the information necessary to form a league in your area.

You should also consider helping or encouraging your community to establish USA Team Tennis leagues for younger players in the middle school range so that your prospective players can develop. If no one is willing to take charge, consider taking on the organization of the league yourself, and perhaps have a few of your varsity players assist with the team coaching. This can be the basis of a great feeder system.

Tournaments

Summer is an excellent time for players to test their skills in tournaments and for you to evaluate their tennis progress. The better players in your program should enter as many USTA sanctioned tournaments as possible. Unranked novice players can find smaller local tournaments to begin testing themselves in matches.

Depending on the location of your town, USTA tournaments may require quite a bit of travel and expense. For players who must work during the summer months, and those who come from households with modest income, tournaments may be out of reach. You can help them get the experience of a few events by arranging car pools, shared lodging, and the splitting of costs among several families. The expense may be well worth it if your players need to compete at a higher level of play than they can find locally.

In the best of all worlds, it would be good for your players to experience some tournaments *and* team play. Typically, the highest skilled players on your team will want to test themselves in tournament play against other good players from surrounding areas. On the other hand, team play can be more fun, less expensive, and closer to home. Each player has to make these decisions based on her own situation and some guidance from you.

Summer Camps

There are many fine summer tennis camps to be found throughout the country. At these camps, players can get a perspective on their game from coaches they don't work with every day. You should keep a listing of summer camps for players to consider and be prepared to give some advice on the quality of the camp, the cost, and the optimal length of stay.

Many tennis camps are listed in the major tennis publications (such as *Tennis* magazine) each spring. Some will offer discounts if more than one player from a team attends. Other possibilities include the tennis academies, which are run by well-known coaches and are typically found in warm weather climates. A one- or two-week stay at a good academy may give your players a whole new outlook and provide the incentive to work hard to reach the next level.

Another alternative is for your high school players to apply for jobs as staff members at summer tennis camps. Most camps have some younger staff who are essentially instructors in training. At a good camp, your players will learn a lot about tennis from teaching younger kids, and often they will have time to play every day with other staff members. Don't expect much in the way of compensation however. Once the camp owner has absorbed the cost of room and board, there is little left for salary.

EVALUATING YOUR PROGRAM

Develop a system of evaluation that you can use at the end of every year. Reevaluate the goals you set, what you did to try to accomplish them, and where you stood at the end of the year. If the end result was not what you anticipated, then change is warranted. Don't become a coach who coaches 20 years using the same lesson plan each year.

Review your season practice plans thoroughly and then evaluate them against the performance of your team during the season. You may find that you left no stone unturned in preparing your players, but more likely there will be a few specific areas that were overlooked. Perhaps not enough time was given to your doubles teams, resulting in disappointing losses at crucial points in a match. Consider whether enough emphasis was placed on physical conditioning to get your team through long, exhausting matches. Did your players handle pressure well or did they fold when things got tough? Did players look forward to practices and exert 100 percent effort every day throughout the season? These are the types of general questions that form the basis for your self-evaluation of your coaching job.

Getting Feedback

One of the most essential components of the postseason evaluation process is obtaining feedback from your coaching staff, peers, and players.

- **Coaching staff.** If you are fortunate enough to have assistant coaches, ask them to make a separate independent evaluation of the season. Outline the types of questions you are asking yourself and solicit their honest opinion. They have seen the season unfold from a different perspective than yours and can often point out areas that need to be shored up.

- **Players.** Meet with your players to get their feedback. If you can, squeeze in one-on-one meetings with each player, because they are more likely to be open without the fear of peer reaction. This should be a friendly meeting. Prepare some specific questions to guide the conversation with each player.

A neutral starting point is to review the player's preseason goals and evaluate together her success in reaching them. Give her a chance to react first and restrict yourself to helpful questions and clarifying statements. Ask her how she might adjust her goals now that the season is behind her—this will naturally lead to a discussion of the off-season and the next year.

Once you've agreed generally on the season result for that player, you should spend time advising her on options to improve her play during the next year. Follow the advice outlined earlier in this chapter when selecting the methods you recommend for each player, and then let her decide which ones to use.

Don't let the meeting end without some candid discussion of your performance as a coach. You can allay your players' fears of criticizing you by holding a conversation something like this:

Coach: I was wondering if you have any suggestions for me on how I can improve my coaching before next season?

Player: Uh . . . not really.

Coach: What one thing did you think I did really well this year?

Player: Well, you sure are organized . . . down to the last detail.

Coach: Yeah, I'm a bit compulsive sometimes. Well, what about one thing I could do better next year?

Player: Maybe you could stay a little calmer during matches. It makes me nervous when you get upset.

Coach: Hmmm . . . I see what you mean. I'll think about some ways I can do that. Thanks.

An additional evaluative tool to consider is a postseason form that your players can complete. Figure 15.7 is a sample that you can modify to suit your needs. The anonymity that a written evaluation form offers your players may elicit comments more candid than those you get in one-on-one meetings.

Your conversation with senior players will be special because they will not be returning for another year. They have also had the opportunity to be part of the program for several years, and with their increasing maturity, they can provide a more objective viewpoint than that of underclassmen. Some coaches prefer to receive a written evaluation from the outgoing seniors, although getting their attention may be quite difficult because of graduation celebrations and activities.

Let the seniors know that their feedback is important in helping you improve the program and your performance as coach. Since seniors have little to lose from criticism, they can provide the tough comments that you may not like to hear but may find invaluable. Here are some possible questions for seniors:

1. What were your best experiences in our tennis program during your career?
2. How could we improve practice?
3. What part of practice did you dread?
4. How confident did you feel during team matches and what could we do to ensure that each player puts forth a terrific effort?
5. How can we improve leadership from within the players' ranks?
6. How did you manage your time during the tennis season so that your schoolwork didn't suffer?

If you've been able to assist your seniors in choosing a college with a tennis program appropriate for their level of play, you might want to use this opportunity to suggest some areas of their game to focus on before they try out in the fall. This is also a special time to send seniors off with good memories of their high school career. With the help of parents, friends, or a booster club, you can collect pictures, video, slides, and other memorabilia to present to your seniors at a farewell dinner that will last them a lifetime.

Personal Evaluation

Your next task is to begin the process of self-evaluation, which should take several months to complete. The advantage of starting shortly after the season's end is that ideas and feelings are fresh in your mind. As you gather input from other sources, add it to your initial impressions.

Start your self-evaluation with a review of your own goals set before the season began. It's helpful to reflect on both the performance goals you had as a coach and the outcome goals you set for the team. Next, you should consider your own performance in terms of your communication skills, teaching skills, and organizational and administrative skills.

Program Evaluation Form for Players

Please complete each of the following questions, being as honest and constructive as possible. Your input into this tennis program is essential for its future success.

1. In terms of tennis skills and strategies, I learned . . .

1	2	3	4	5	6	7
Nothing						A lot

2. My performance of tennis skills and strategies improved . . .

1	2	3	4	5	6	7
Not at all						A lot

3. I enjoyed playing tennis this season.

1	2	3	4	5	6	7
Not at all						A lot

4. The coaching staff helped me develop as a player.

1	2	3	4	5	6	7
Not at all						A lot

5. The coaching staff helped me develop as a person.

1	2	3	4	5	6	7
Not at all						A lot

6. Players are treated fairly on the team.

1	2	3	4	5	6	7
Not at all						A lot

7. Players on the team respected team rules.

1	2	3	4	5	6	7
Not at all						Very true

8. Practices were well organized, challenging, and fun.

1	2	3	4	5	6	7
Not at all						Very true

9. The role I played in matches was the best for the program.

1	2	3	4	5	6	7
Not at all						Very true

10. I feel more positively about the program now than I did at the beginning of the season.

1	2	3	4	5	6	7
Not at all						Very true

The best thing about being a player in this tennis program:

_____

The worst thing about being a player in this tennis program:

_____

Name specific changes you would make to improve or eliminate the worst things about the program:

_____

_____

What can the coaching staff do to make the program better than it was this past season?

_____

_____

Additional comments (use reverse side):

Figure 15.7 Postseason player evaluation.

Communication Skills

When evaluating your communication skills, refer to the checklist of topics covered earlier in chapter 2. Consider your success in communicating with players, parents, media, and other team supporters. Rely on your conversations with each player at season's end for enlightening comments and suggestions for improvement.

Here's what one coach learned from his players:

At the end of the season, my players gave me a plaque that read, "To the Greatest Coach Who Ever Yelled." It was an expression of my coaching style as well as their feeling about it. And it was with pride that I hung the plaque on my wall.

As I continued through my coaching career, I discovered that yelling did not always bring success and admiration from the team. I had a player who was yelled at all the time, and in a derogatory way. She survived by tuning out everyone who raised his voice to her. She tuned me out, too.

Although that style of coaching worked with some players, I realized it didn't work for everyone. Needless to say, I had to change if I wanted her to be receptive to my advice and criticism. I discovered a more mellow approach to coaching that actually became more pleasurable and successful for me.

Another coach shared what she learned:

After my third year of coaching, my senior co-captains met with me after the season and rocked my world when I asked them for feedback on the coaching job I had done. This was their comment: "Coach, you're a terrific teacher, and we learned so much from you in three years about tennis technique but . . . maybe you could help future players more by helping them learn to win really tough matches. Our team always seemed to fall apart when the match was on the line."

At first I was taken aback, but as I reflected on their comment it became clear to me that I needed to learn more about developing "mental toughness" in young players. I had often thought that players were either tough under pressure or not.

Now I realized that part of my coaching responsibility was to teach and develop those skills, and I did. A few books read over the summer and a memorable coaching conference sponsored by the USTA got me started, and the next couple of years "mental toughness" was part of our practices from the first day of the season.

Teaching Skills

There are many ways to assess your teaching performance. Figure 15.8 charts teaching performance based on tennis technique, physical training, strategy and tactics, mental toughness, and match play. The following section provides questions you can use to evaluate use of resources, organization, and administration. Take the time to write out your answers to each question so that you will have a clear plan for improving your coaching skills in the months ahead.

Organization and Administration

The tasks of organization and administration that confront a high school coach can be daunting. Experience is likely the best teacher, but here are a few things to consider when evaluating your program's progress in these areas:

Coach Evaluation

Date _____

Name _____ Position _____

Each of the following sections should be filled out based on your own evaluation of your teaching skills in regards to technique, physical training, strategy, tactics, mental preparation, and match play. Be specific and include examples of unique teaching strategies where you excelled or failed, for future reference.

1. Tennis technique

   In what areas of teaching technique did you excel? What areas need improvement? Were athletes responsive to your methods? Did every player receive equal attention and practice time?

2. Physical training and preparedness

   Were your athletes physically prepared for each game? What drills were most successful for practicing physical endurance and stamina? How can more physical training be incorporated into your program?

3. Strategy and tactics

   What strategies and tactics worked most frequently for your team? Were athletes able to devise their own strategies during match play successfully or did they often require guidance? What can you do to improve self-reliance in younger, less experienced players?

4. Mental toughness

   Were athletes mentally prepared for every practice and match? What tactics did you employ to prepare them for tough matches, for wins, for losses? What can you do to improve team cohesiveness?

5. Match play

   What improvements need to be made for you and your athletes at home matches? Away matches? Court? Is additional community support necessary?

Coach's signature_____

Figure 15.8 Coach evaluation.

1.   Did you make effective use of resources at hand such as assistant coaches, team captains, team managers, scorekeepers, volunteers, booster clubs, and the media?

2.   Were you able to delegate tasks effectively, make efficient use of your time, and give attention to the details of organization?

3.   What improvements were made to the tennis facilities and equipment this year (e.g., courts, nets, water coolers, scorekeepers, spectator seating, ball machines, teaching carts, and targets)?

4.   Was the current budget adequate? What changes in priorities or additions should be made for next year? Do you or your team need to devote some time in the off-season to fundraising in order to provide better equipment or group experiences for the team next year?

5.   How appropriate was the schedule of matches in terms of frequency, spacing, and level of difficulty?

6.   Generally evaluate the organization of team practices and variations in quality, intensity, and duration of practices throughout the season.

7.   Were your team policies and rules effective and infractions handled properly?

CONTINUING EDUCATION

Your personal assessment should conclude with a plan for continuing education and improvement as a coach. Consider becoming certified as a tennis professional through the United States Professional Tennis Association (USPTA) or the Professional Tennis Registry (PTR). Typically, certification requires that you pass a written test on tennis strategy, rules of the game, and coaching strategies along with an on-court practical test of teaching ability and tennis skill.

The USPTA has added a membership category specifically for high school coaches. It does not require testing and does not result in certification. You can take advantage of opportunities to increase your coaching

knowledge by using their resources such as web site, conventions, books, magazines, and so on. You can contact the USPTA at 713-97-USPTA and the PTR at 803-785-7244.

Other advice to improve your coaching skills includes rereading this book over the winter, attending conferences or workshops in your area, and ordering instructional books or videos from the USTA. (See the resources section on page 193 for ordering information.) You might also consider volunteering to work as an assistant coach for a local teaching professional or at a tennis camp. Much can be learned by working closely with other coaches.

Many areas offer high school coaching clinics or workshops during the off-season. These may be conducted by the United States Tennis Association, one of the teaching organizations (PTR or USPTA), or by other experienced coaches. In addition to professional presentations on court and in the classroom, these workshops provide terrific opportunities to exchange ideas with coaches from other schools in your state. Most coaches enjoy expressing their opinions and are readily willing to share their experiences. Don't let a

Tennis in a Can

The well-known tennis coach of champions, Nick Bollettieri, has put together a terrific resource called "Tennis in a Can." Along with the book of the same title, Nick and his staff have written several additional books on tennis coaching that are included in the package. Most valuable though is a complete series of outstanding videotapes that demonstrate each stroke, doubles and singles play, feeding technique, and much more. You and your team can take advantage of the knowledge Nick has accumulated in his 40-plus years of coaching the best players in the world. The videotapes are ideal for preseason and off-season viewing for your kids. And one more thing, if you can't afford to purchase the complete package, Nick has worked out some donation programs particularly for schools where money is an issue.

year go by without attending at least one of these events. If you don't take advantage of these opportunities, you'll be falling behind other coaches in your league who do spend the time and money. (Ask your athletic director for support if there is a registration fee or travel and lodging are required.)

SUMMARY

Here are points to consider as you evaluate your program:

- Develop a system of evaluating your program and your coaching performance.
- Gather information from players, parents, and assistant coaches.
- Write out your personal evaluation using the questions presented in this chapter.
- Set specific goals for the off-season to begin your preparation for the next year.
- At the end of the season, you and your players need to carefully evaluate the season, compare notes, and agree on a plan for the off-season.
- For most players, summer is the key time of the year to raise their level of play. You need to suggest summer activities that will help them improve, such as tournament play, team tennis, tennis camps, or employment in a tennis program.
- Investigate the role you can play in off-season development of your players according to your league and state rules.

- As the next season approaches, have your players evaluate their progress during the off-season and establish their goals for the upcoming season.
- Handle team selection very carefully. Take the time to help those who don't make the team map out their plan for development in the year ahead. These players may become important team members in the future.
- Team practices should be continually evaluated and modified to fit the goals and needs of each squad of players. Written plans and observations are essential for smooth organization and implementation.
- Establish various ways to measure player improvement and allow practice time for these tests. Nothing builds player confidence like seeing objective improvement in their skills or play.
- Because several matches will be played at the same time, match play evaluation requires that you enlist the help of other coaches or of team members who are not playing. You may wish to use written notes or a tape recorder to register your thoughts during a match.
- Match charting provides an objective measure of each match and is essential to collect information. Junior varsity players can be very helpful here and will learn much from the experience. The match statistics should be shared with players immediately if they wish, but the discussion should be postponed until the next day.

OFF-SEASON TRAINING FOR TOURNAMENT PLAY

Stretch before and after each workout.

Day 1   Drill with partner or on ball machine (2 hours)

Basics: ground strokes, crosscourt, midcourt put-aways, down-the-line approach shots

Strength training

Day 2   Drill with partner or on ball machine (2 hours)

Basics (same as day 1)

Distance run (2 miles)

Day 3   Drill with partner (1 hour)

Basics (same as day 1)

Play minimum of three sets

Distance run (1 mile)

Strength training

Day 4   Private lesson with coach (1 hour)

Ground stroke mechanics: crosscourt from baseline; defensive lob; approach shot; hit out or chip; volley; offensive-defensive

Work on serve

1/2 hour of hitting

Two to five games to 21 points

Distance run (2 miles)

Day 5   Play match

Distance run after match (1 mile)

Strength training

Day 6   Drill with partner (1 hour)

Basics (same as day 1)

Play two different opponents a pro set each

Distance run (2 miles)

Sit-ups, push-ups—four sets each (25-15)

Day 7   Private lesson with coach (1 hour)

Same content as day 4 lesson

Directional hitting, crosscourt and down the line (1/2 hour)

Play match

Light run (1 mile)

Day 8   Play three sets

Circuit train (index card)

Strength training

Day 9   Private lesson with coach (1 hour)

Review basics, work on individual weakness, work on strengths, service return

25 serves to each court

Return serve from partner (25 each court)

Play match

Light run (1 mile)

Day 10 Play match

Jump rope (10 to 15 minutes)

Strength training

Day 11 Play two different opponents a match

Circuit train (index card)

Day 12 Private lesson with coach (1 hour); emphasis on maintaining a positive attitude during play

Work on strengths, approach, split-step, volley (offensive-crosscourt, defensive-down the line), overhead

Hitting with partner (1/2 hour)

Play match

No running

Day 13 Play match

Circuit train (index card)

Strength training

Day 14 Hit with partner (2 hours)

Deep Court game; Crosscourt/Down-the-Line game; Approach If Short Ball game; One Up, One Back game (play to 10 points)

Distance run (2 miles)

Day 15 Play match

Four 1/4-mile repeats (30 seconds between)

Strength training

Day 16 Private lesson with coach (1 hour)

Review "situation shots," serve, service return

Play match

Circuit train (index card)

Day 17 Play matches with two different opponents

Four 50-yard sprints (25 seconds between)

Strength training

Day 18 Drill with partner

Basics (same as day 1)

Play match

Circuit train (index card)

Day 19 Private lesson with coach (1 hour)

Review, fine-tune strokes, stress player's strengths

Tell the player to control the ball on the strings and not overhit

Directional hitting with partner, crosscourt and down the line (1 hour)

Jump rope (two 10-minute periods, 3 minutes between)

Strength training

Day 20 Directional hitting with partner, crosscourt and down the line (1 hour)

Serve and service return (served from short court by partner)

Circuit training (index card)

Day 21 (Light day)

Play match

No running

Day 22 2 hours hitting (games from day 14)

Circuit training (index card)

Begin eating for tournament

Day 23 Play match

Five 30-yard sprints (20 seconds between)

Day 24 Directional hitting (1/2 hour)

Private lesson with coach

Look at all strokes, be positive, drill strengths

Play match

Five 30-yard sprints (20 seconds between)

Day 25 Play match

Five 20-yard sprints (15 seconds between)

Day 26   Play match

Six 10-yard sprints (10 seconds between)

Continue eating for tournament and drink more fluids

Day 27   Light workout with partner and coach

Two out of three tiebreakers

Jump rope (10 minutes)

Day 28   Travel to tournament, work out on match courts

APPENDIX B WELLNESS REGIMEN FOR IN- AND OFF-SEASON TRAINING

The key to movement strength, power, speed, and flexibility is maintaining your fitness level in and out of season. Remember these seven tips as you begin your training regimen.

Strength—power—speed—flexibility

1. Eat properly
2. Get enough rest
3. Lift with a partner
4. Do the full range of motion with all lifts
5. Stress repetition, not amount of weight
6. Stretch before and after workout
7. Stop lifting one week before a tournament

Off-season program

Three days per week (one day rest minimum between lifting sessions)

1. **Bent-knee sit-up.** Hook feet under sit-up board strap or have partner hold feet down. Keep knees bent 45 degrees. Fold arms on chest. Lie back until lower back touches. Pull up concentrating on abdominal muscles. Inhale down, exhale up. (1 to 2 sets, 25 to 50 per set)

2. **Seated barbell twist.** Place light barbell on shoulders. Sit at end of bench with feet firmly on floor. Twist torso to right, then left, twisting at waist only. Do not move head from side to side. Keep back straight and head up. Inhale to right, exhale to left. Can also be done standing. (1 set, 25 to 50 per side)

3. **Dumbbell press.** Lie on bench with feet flat on floor. Hold dumbbells at arm's length with palms facing each other. Lower dumbbells straight down to sides of chest, arms close to sides. Push back to starting position using same path. Arms must be in close at all times. Inhale down, exhale up. (3 sets of 12-10-10)

4. **Dumbbell pullover.** Lie on bench, head at end, feet flat on floor. Start with hands flat against inside plate of dumbbell at arm's length above chest. Lower dumbbell in semicircular motion behind head as far as you can without pain. Return dumbbell to starting position, elbows locked. Inhale down, exhale up. Breathe heavily, keep head down, chest high, hips on bench. Can also be done with barbell. (2 sets of 12-10)

5. **Standing military press.** Raise barbell to chest, hands shoulder-width apart.

Lock legs and hips solidly. Keep elbows in slightly under bar. Press bar to arm's length overhead. Lower to upper chest. Be sure bar rests on chest and is not supported by arms between reps. Hold chest high. Inhale up, exhale down. (3 sets of 12-10-10)

6. **Dumbbell rowing.** Place dumbbell on floor in front of bench (between you and bench). Stand with left leg back (knee locked) and right knee bent slightly. Bend over and hold dumbbell with left hand, palm in, about 6 inches off floor. Put right hand on bench with elbow locked. Pull dumbbell straight up to side. Return to starting position using same path. Inhale up, exhale down. Reverse position and repeat movement on right side. (3 sets of 12-10-10)

7. **Dips.** Hold yourself erect on bars. Keep elbows in to sides and lower body by bending shoulders and elbows. Continue down as far as you can. Pause, then press back to arm's length. Do not let body swing back and forth. Inhale down, exhale up. (2 to 3 sets, 15 per set—add weight later)

8. **Seated dumbbell curl.** Hold dumbbells. Sit at end of bench with feet firmly on floor. Keep back straight and head up. Start with dumbbells lowered at arm's length, palms in. Begin curl with palms in until past thighs, then turn palms up for remainder of curl to shoulder height. Keep palms up while lowering until past thighs, then turn palms in. Keep upper arms close to sides. Concentrate on biceps while raising and lowering weights. Inhale up, exhale down. (1 to 2 sets, 10 per set)

9. **Seated palms-down barbell wrist curl.** Hold barbell with both hands, palms down, hands 16 inches apart. Sit at end of bench with feet on floor about 20 inches apart. Lean forward and place forearms on upper thighs. Place wrists over knees. Lower bar as far as you can, keeping a tight grip. Curl bar as high as you can. Do not let forearms raise up. Inhale up, exhale down. (2 sets, 15 to 20 per set)

10. **Seated palms-up barbell wrist curl.** Hold barbell with both hands, palms up, hands 16 inches apart. Sit at end of bench with feet on floor about 20 inches apart. Lean forward and place forearms on upper thighs. Place backs of wrists over knees. Lower bar as far as you can, keeping a tight grip. Curl bar as high as you can. Do not let forearms raise up. Inhale up, exhale down. (1 to 2 sets, 15 per set)

11. **Jump squat.** Stand erect with arms crossed over chest. Keep head up, back straight, feet about 16 inches apart. Squat until upper thighs are parallel to floor (or lower). Keep head up, back straight, knees slightly out. Jump straight up in the air as high as possible, using thighs like springs. Immediately squat and jump again. Inhale up, exhale down. Can also be done with barbell held on upper back or with dumbbells hanging at sides. (3 sets, 15 to 20 per set)

12. **Barbell front lunge.** Place barbell on upper back. Use comfortable hand grip. Keep head up, back straight, feet about 6 inches apart. Step forward as far as possible with left leg until upper left thigh is almost parallel to floor. Keep right leg as straight as possible. Step back to starting position. Inhale out, exhale back. Repeat with right leg. (2 sets, 15 to 20 per set each leg)

In-season program

Two days per week (one to two days' rest minimum between lifting sessions). Stop two days before matches.

1. **Incline bench.** Lie on incline bench. Hold dumbbells together at arm's length above shoulders with palms forward. Slowly lower dumbbells to chest until 10 inches from each side of chest. Keep elbows in line with ears and forearms slightly out of vertical position. Return to starting position using

same path. Inhale down, exhale up. (2 sets of 12-10)

2. **Dumbbell pullover.** Lie on bench, head at end, feet flat on floor. Start with hands flat against inside plate of dumbbell at arm's length above chest. Lower dumbbell in semicircular motion behind head as far as possible without pain. Return dumbbell to starting position, elbows locked. Inhale down, exhale up. Breathe heavily, keep head down, chest high, hips on bench. Can also be done with barbell or standing medicine ball throw. (1 set of 12)

3. **Seated side lateral raise**. Sit at end of bench with feet firmly on floor. Hold dumbbells with palms in and arms straight down at sides. Raise dumbbells in semicircular motion a little above shoulder height. Pause, then lower to starting position using same path. Keep arms straight. Inhale up, exhale down. Can also be done standing. (2 sets of 12-10)

4. **Medium grip front chin-up.** Use chinning bar about 6 inches higher than you can reach with arms extended overhead. Hold bar with hands 18 to 20 inches apart. Pull up, trying to touch chin to bar. Return to starting position. Try to keep back slightly hyperextended. Do not swing back and forth. Inhale up, exhale down. (Do as many as possible.)

5. **Seated dumbbell triceps curl.** Hold dumbbell with both hands and raise overhead to arm's length. Rotate hands while raising dumbbell so top plates of dumbbell rest in palms, thumbs around handle. Sit at end of bench with feet firmly on floor, back straight, and head up. Keep upper arms close to head. Lower dumbbell in semicircular motion behind head until forearms touch biceps. Inhale down, exhale up. (2 sets of 12-10)

6. **Wrist roll curl.** Place light weight on end of rope of wrist roller. Stand erect with back straight and head up. Hold wrist roller with both hands, palms down. Extend arms straight out. Roll weight up by curling right hand over and down, then left hand over and down. Keep arms parallel to floor. Continue curling right to left hand until weight touches bar. Lower weight to starting position by reversing movement. (1 set)

RESOURCES

BOOKS AND PRINTED MATERIALS

Bollettieri, N. *Tennis in a Can*. The following resource is available from Nick Bollettieri. This resource package includes several books and instructional videos. Contact him at 800-872-6425 or at Bollettieri Tennis Academy, 5500 34th St. West, Bradenton, FL 34210.

International Tennis Federation. *Rules of Tennis*. Published yearly by the United States Tennis Association.

Loehr, J. 1986. *Mental Toughness Training for Sports: Achieving Athletic Excellence*. New York, NY: Viking Penguin.

The following print resources are available from the USTA publications department and are published yearly. To order materials, call 800-832-8291, or for more information, call the USTA publications department at 914-696-7000.

United States Tennis Association. *A Friend at Court*.

United States Tennis Association. *Basic 10 Flexibility Exercises*.

United States Tennis Association. *Strength Training for Tennis*.

The following print resources are available from Human Kinetics. Contact them at 800-747-4457 or on the Web at www.HumanKinetics.com for more information.

Clark, N. 1990. *Sports Nutrition Guidebook: Eating to Fuel Your Active Lifestyle*. Champaign, IL: Human Kinetics.

Martens, R. 1987. *Coaches Guide to Sport Psychology*. Champaign, IL: Human Kinetics.

Orlick, T. 1986. *Psyching for Sport*. Champaign, IL: Human Kinetics.

Thompson, R., and R. Trattner Sherman. 1993. *Helping Athletes with Eating Disorders*. Champaign, IL: Human Kinetics.

United States Tennis Association. 2002. *Coaching Youth Tennis*, 3rd Ed. Champaign, IL: Human Kinetics.

United States Tennis Association. 1996. *Tennis Tactics: Winning Patterns of Play*. Champaign, IL: Human Kinetics.

VIDEOS

The following video resources are available from Human Kinetics. Contact them at 800-747-4457 or on the Web at www.HumanKinetics.com for more information.

United States Tennis Association. 1993. *Advanced Footskills for Tennis*. Champaign, IL: Human Kinetics.

United States Tennis Association. 1990. *Movement Training for Tennis*. Champaign, IL: Human Kinetics.

ADDITIONAL RESOURCES

Coaching Youth Tennis Online Course

Designed for Team Tennis coaches
Course Length: 6-8 hours
Resources included: *Coaching Youth Tennis* book, *Games Approach to Coaching* video
Special Discounted Price: $30.00
Save $15.00 over list price
Register at http://hstennis.usta.com

This course is developed, supported, and delivered through a partnership between USTA and the American Sport Education Program (ASEP).

High School Coaches Web Site

Visit the USTA web site designed specifically for coaches of high school varsity tennis teams. Look for the latest in coaching information, trade ideas with other coaches, and send your queries to the Coaches Mailbag.

Log onto: http://hstennis.usta.com

INDEX

Note: The italicized *f* and *t* following page numbers refer to figures and numbers, respectively.

ABOUT THE AUTHOR

The United States Tennis Association (USTA) is the governing body for tennis in the United States. The USTA's membership consists of more than 670,000 individuals and thousands of organizations, including schools, park and recreation departments, community tennis associations, and tennis clubs.

Encompassing all 50 states, Puerto Rico, the U.S. Virgin Islands, American Samoa, and Guam, the USTA is composed of 17 geographical sections, each of which maintains its own staff to administer USTA programs, establishes its own tournament schedule, and issues its own rankings. Thousands of volunteers and full-time personnel implement the varied USTA programs on the sectional, district, and local levels.

The USTA is known as the owner and operator of the U.S. Open Championships, one of the four Grand Slam professional tournaments in worldwide tennis competition. The U.S. Open is the highest annually attended sporting event in the world. In addition, it owns 96 pro circuit events throughout the United States and selects the U.S. teams for the Davis Cup, Fed Cup, Olympic Games, and Paralympic Games.

National coordination and administration of the USTA's efforts are facilitated by the full-time staff at the national headquarters in White Plains, New York, the USTA National Tennis Center in Flushing Meadows, New York, and the USA Tennis High Performance headquarters in Key Biscayne, Florida. The USTA works closely with the two major coaching certifying organizations—the U.S. Professional Tennis Association (USPTA) and the Professional Tennis Registry (PTR). These alliances emphasize coaching education and development through an ambitious offering of coaching seminars, workshops, and conferences.

Ron Woods coordinated the development, and wrote selected chapters, of this new edition of *Coaching Tennis Successfully*. Ron has served the USTA for almost 20 years as director of player development as well as the director of the USTA's Community Tennis Programs. He was a college tennis coach for 17 years and has been a member of the United States Olympic Coaching Committee and the International Tennis Federation Coaching Commission. Woods has written or contributed to many coaching books and videos over the past 15 years. He and his wife, Kathy, live in Westport, Connecticut.

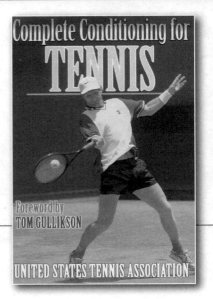
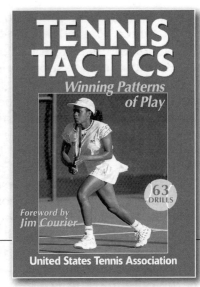